STAR TREK

VOLUME 9

Written by
MIKE JOHNSON

Art by
TONY SHASTEEN

Colors by
**TONY SHASTEEN (Ch. 1–4) and
DAVIDE MASTROLONARDO (Ch. 5–6)**

Letters by
NEIL UYETAKE

Series Edits by
SARAH GAYDOS

CHAPTER 1

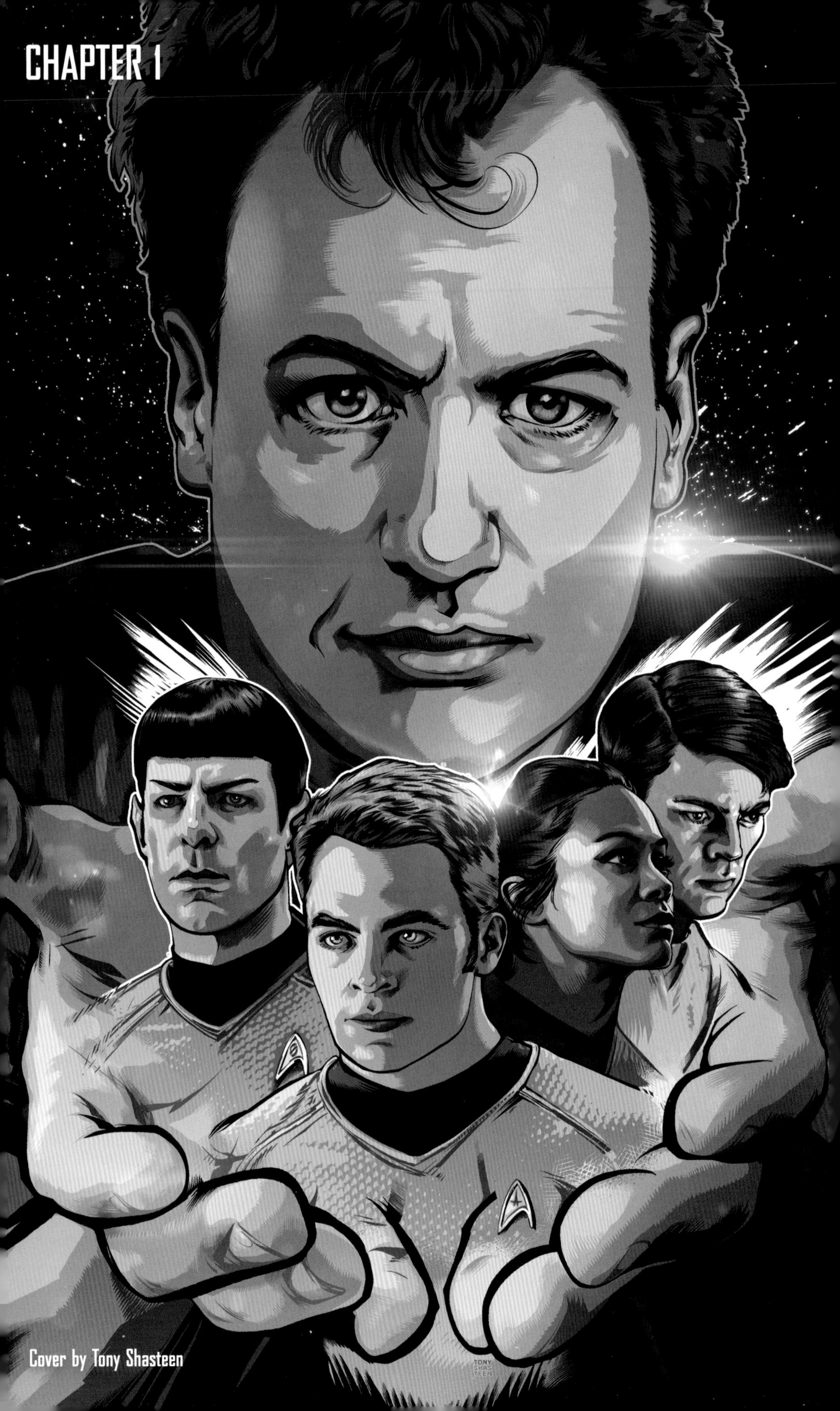
TONY SHAS TEEN

Cover by Tony Shasteen

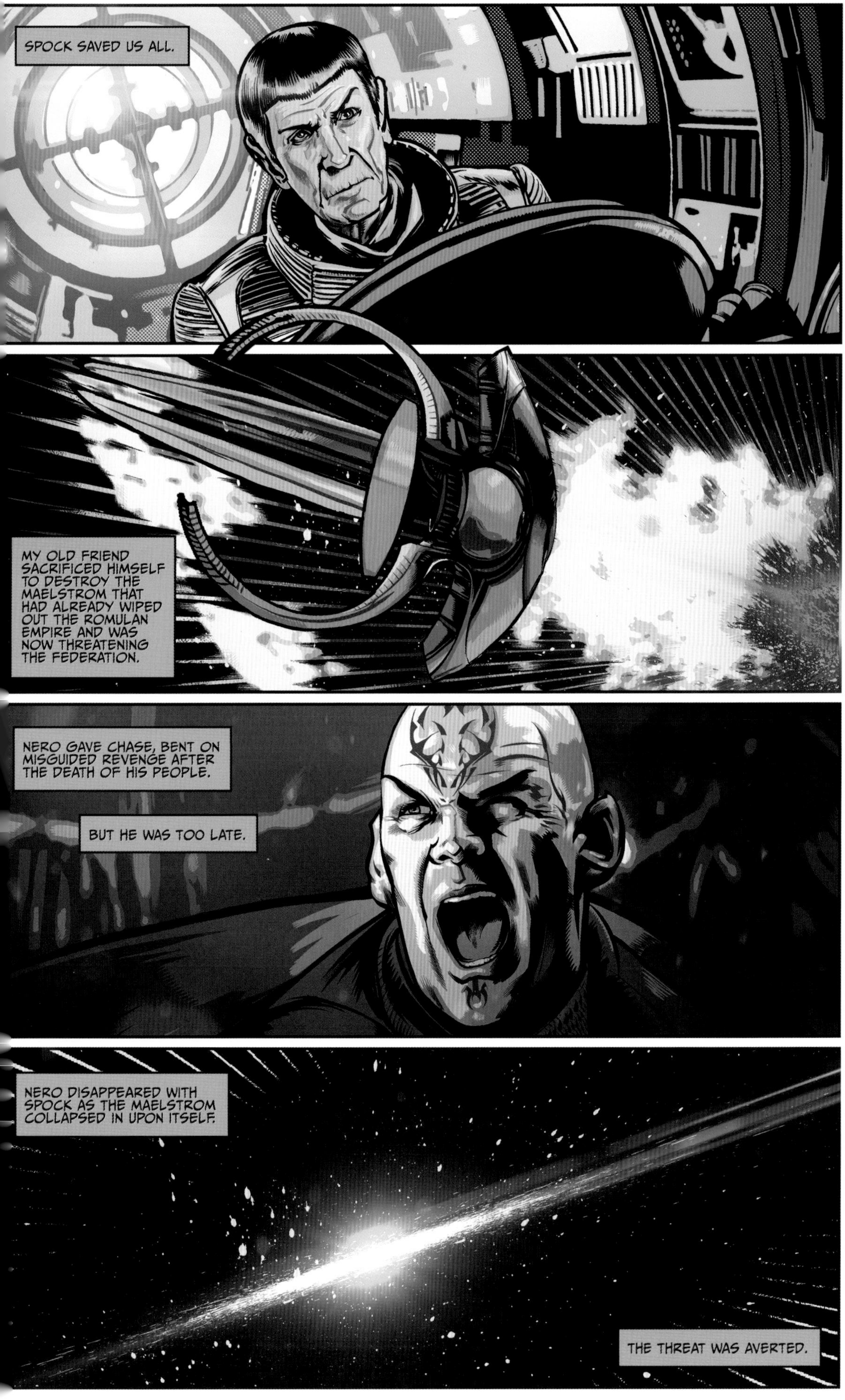
SPOCK SAVED US ALL.
MY OLD FRIEND SACRIFICED HIMSELF TO DESTROY THE MAELSTROM THAT HAD ALREADY WIPED OUT THE ROMULAN EMPIRE AND WAS NOW THREATENING THE FEDERATION.
NERO GAVE CHASE, BENT ON MISGUIDED REVENGE AFTER THE DEATH OF HIS PEOPLE.
BUT HE WAS TOO LATE.
NERO DISAPPEARED WITH SPOCK AS THE MAELSTROM COLLAPSED IN UPON ITSELF.
THE THREAT WAS AVERTED.

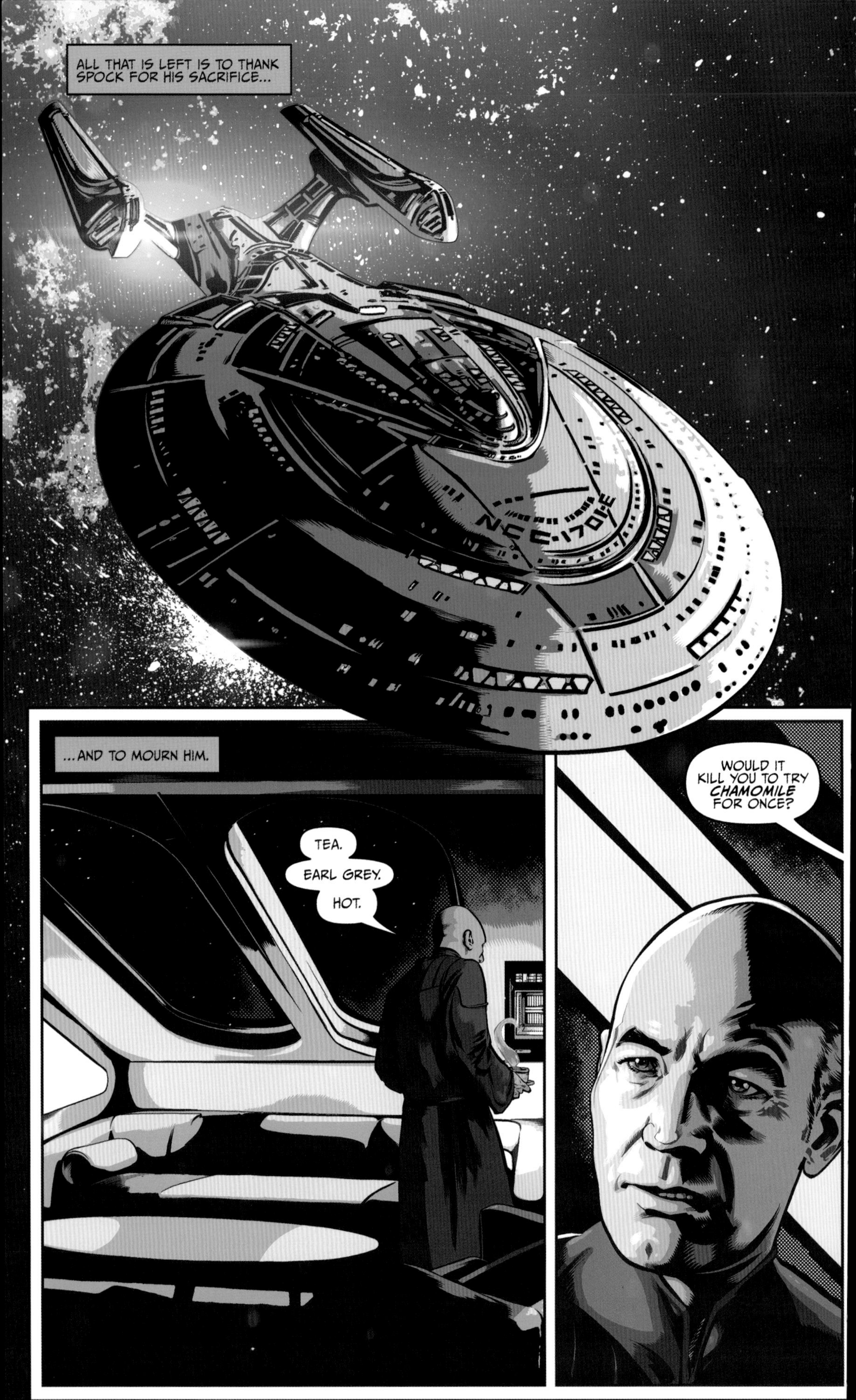

ALL THAT IS LEFT IS TO THANK SPOCK FOR HIS SACRIFICE...
NCC-1701-E
...AND TO MOURN HIM.
TEA.
EARL GREY.
HOT.
WOULD IT KILL YOU TO TRY *CHAMOMILE* FOR ONCE?

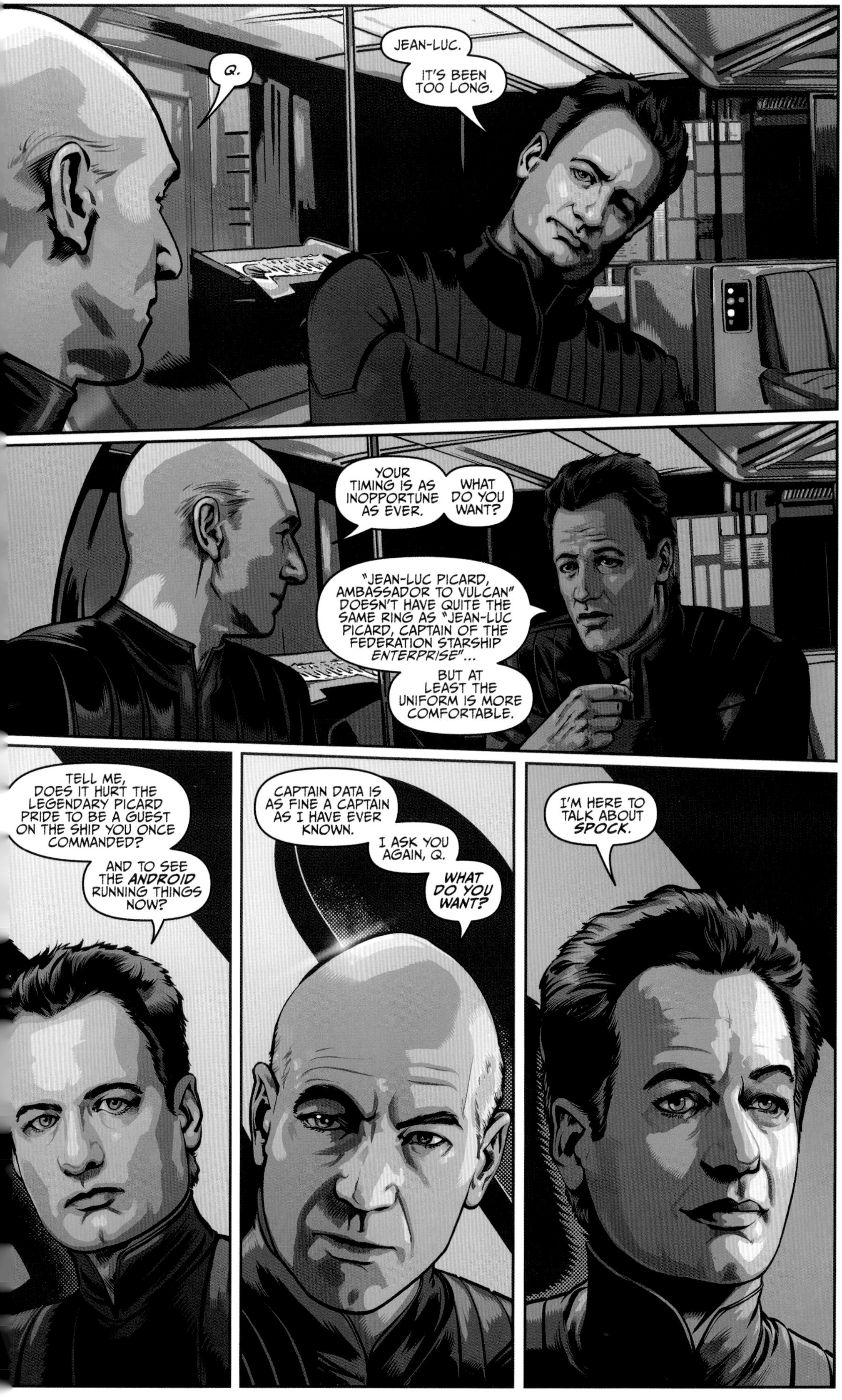
Q.
JEAN-LUC.
IT'S BEEN TOO LONG.
YOUR TIMING IS AS INOPPORTUNE AS EVER.
WHAT DO YOU WANT?
"JEAN-LUC PICARD, AMBASSADOR TO VULCAN" DOESN'T HAVE QUITE THE SAME RING AS "JEAN-LUC PICARD, CAPTAIN OF THE FEDERATION STARSHIP *ENTERPRISE*"...
BUT AT LEAST THE UNIFORM IS MORE COMFORTABLE.
TELL ME, DOES IT HURT THE LEGENDARY PICARD PRIDE TO BE A GUEST ON THE SHIP YOU ONCE COMMANDED?
AND TO SEE THE ***ANDROID*** RUNNING THINGS NOW?
CAPTAIN DATA IS AS FINE A CAPTAIN AS I HAVE EVER KNOWN.
I ASK YOU AGAIN, Q.
WHAT DO YOU WANT?
I'M HERE TO TALK ABOUT ***SPOCK***.

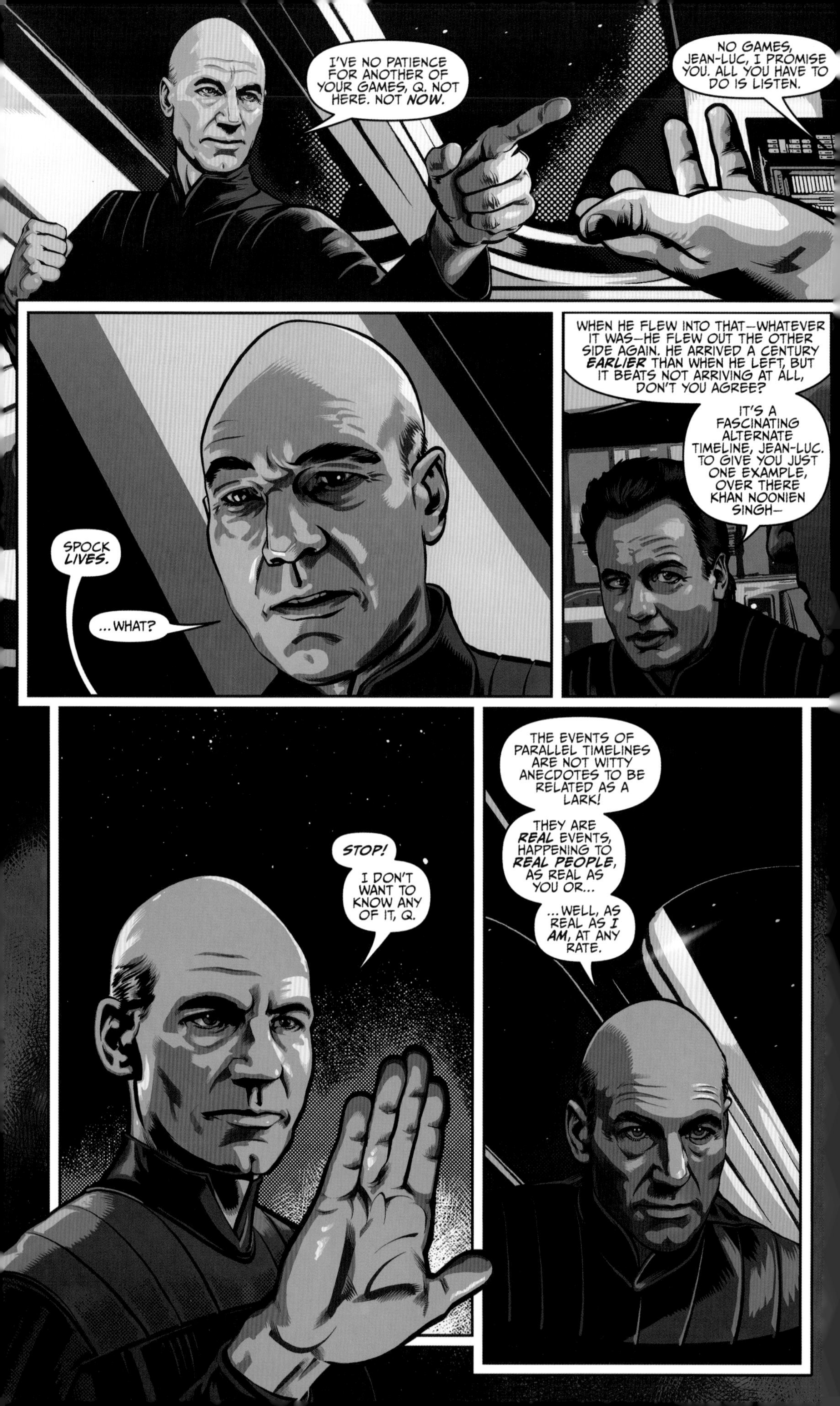
I'VE NO PATIENCE FOR ANOTHER OF YOUR GAMES, Q. NOT HERE. NOT *NOW*.
NO GAMES, JEAN-LUC, I PROMISE YOU. ALL YOU HAVE TO DO IS LISTEN.
SPOCK *LIVES.*
...WHAT?
WHEN HE FLEW INTO THAT—WHATEVER IT WAS—HE FLEW OUT THE OTHER SIDE AGAIN. HE ARRIVED A CENTURY *EARLIER* THAN WHEN HE LEFT, BUT IT BEATS NOT ARRIVING AT ALL, DON'T YOU AGREE?
IT'S A FASCINATING ALTERNATE TIMELINE, JEAN-LUC. TO GIVE YOU JUST ONE EXAMPLE, OVER THERE KHAN NOONIEN SINGH—
STOP!
I DON'T WANT TO KNOW ANY OF IT, Q.
THE EVENTS OF PARALLEL TIMELINES ARE NOT WITTY ANECDOTES TO BE RELATED AS A LARK!
THEY ARE *REAL* EVENTS, HAPPENING TO *REAL PEOPLE*, AS REAL AS YOU OR...
...WELL, AS REAL AS *I AM*, AT ANY RATE.

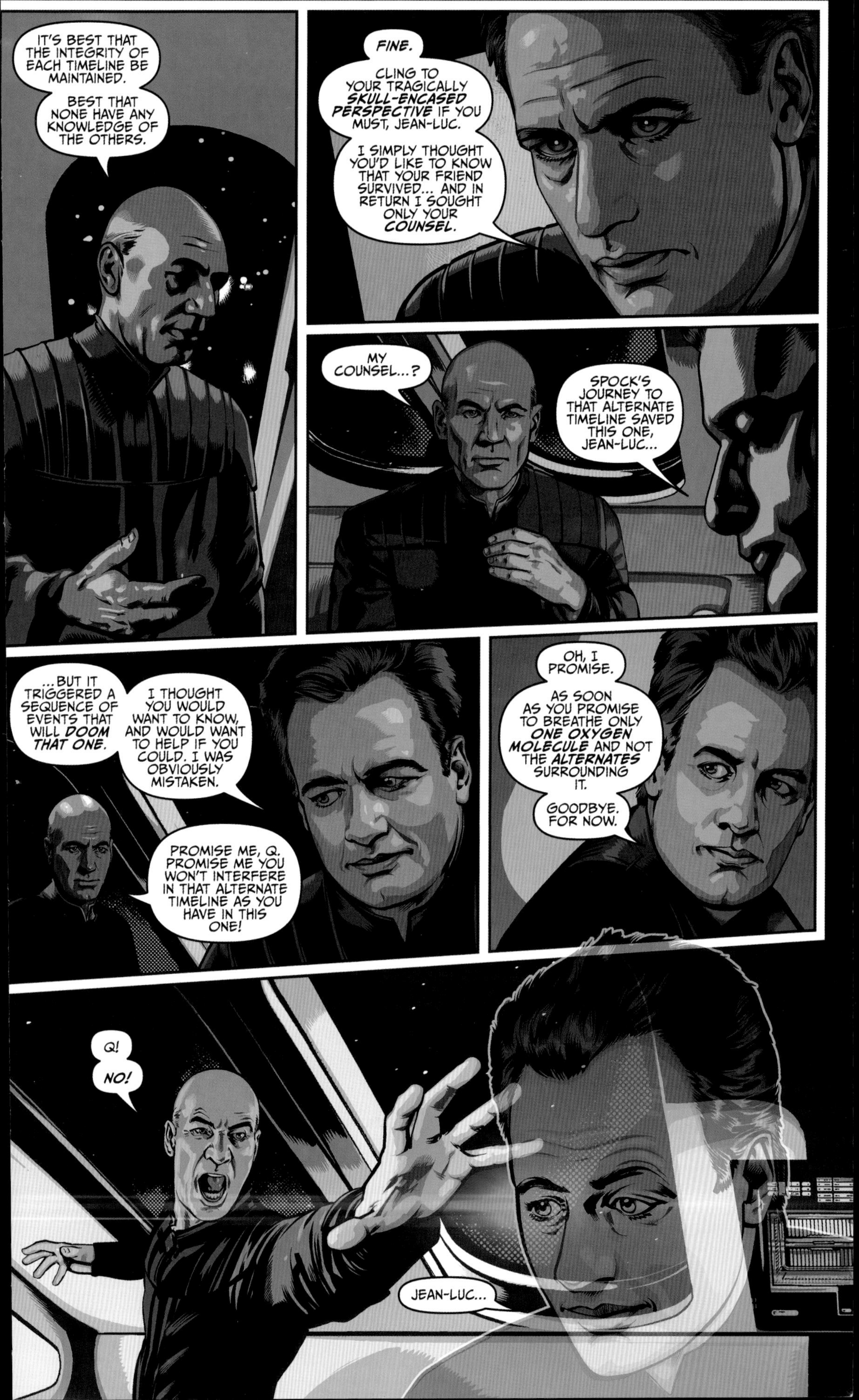

IT'S BEST THAT THE INTEGRITY OF EACH TIMELINE BE MAINTAINED.
BEST THAT NONE HAVE ANY KNOWLEDGE OF THE OTHERS.
FINE.
CLING TO YOUR TRAGICALLY SKULL-ENCASED PERSPECTIVE IF YOU MUST, JEAN-LUC.
I SIMPLY THOUGHT YOU'D LIKE TO KNOW THAT YOUR FRIEND SURVIVED... AND IN RETURN I SOUGHT ONLY YOUR COUNSEL.
MY COUNSEL...?
SPOCK'S JOURNEY TO THAT ALTERNATE TIMELINE SAVED THIS ONE, JEAN-LUC...
...BUT IT TRIGGERED A SEQUENCE OF EVENTS THAT WILL DOOM THAT ONE.
I THOUGHT YOU WOULD WANT TO KNOW, AND WOULD WANT TO HELP IF YOU COULD. I WAS OBVIOUSLY MISTAKEN.
PROMISE ME, Q. PROMISE ME YOU WON'T INTERFERE IN THAT ALTERNATE TIMELINE AS YOU HAVE IN THIS ONE!
OH, I PROMISE.
AS SOON AS YOU PROMISE TO BREATHE ONLY ONE OXYGEN MOLECULE AND NOT THE ALTERNATES SURROUNDING IT.
GOODBYE. FOR NOW.
Q!
NO!
JEAN-LUC...

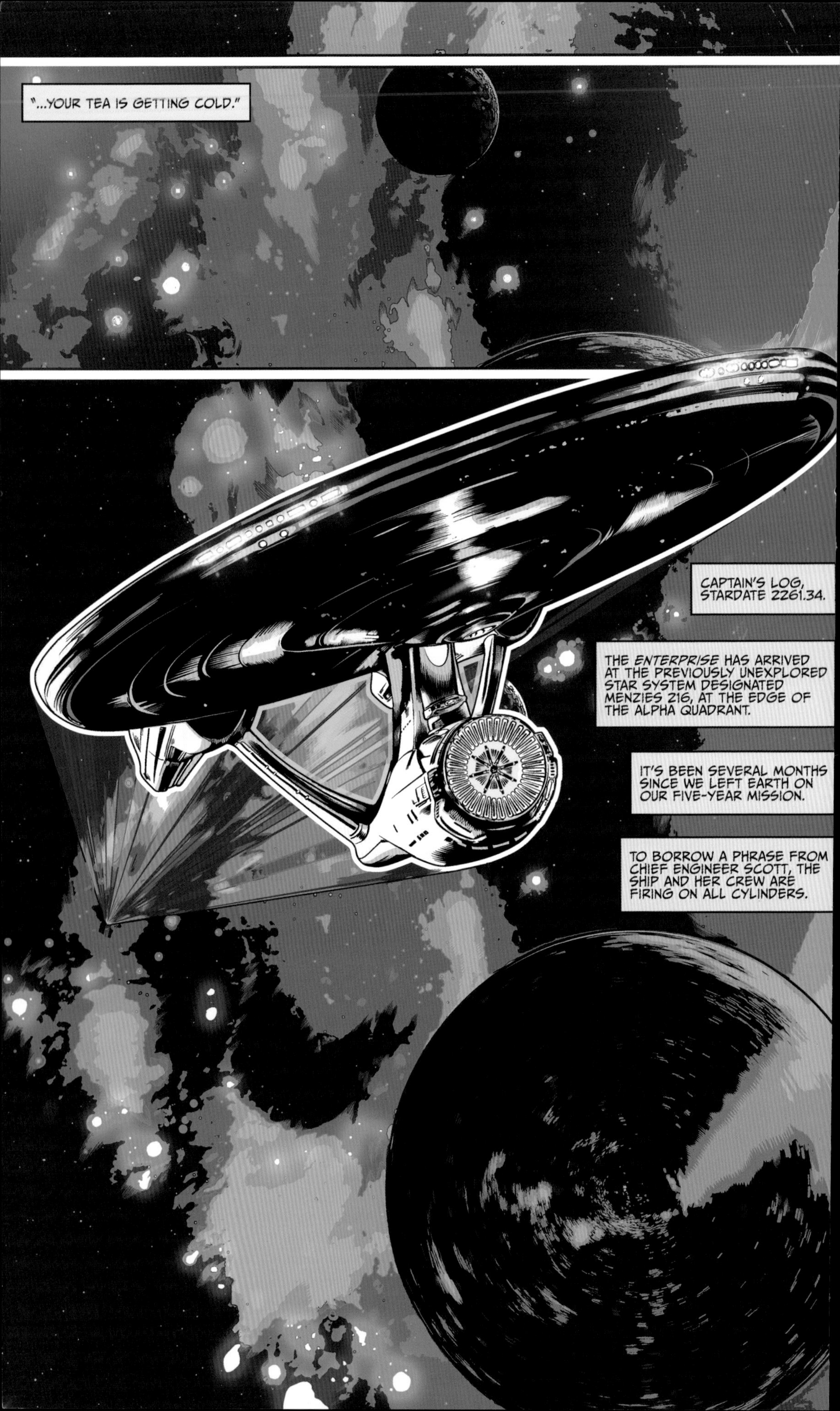
"...YOUR TEA IS GETTING COLD."
CAPTAIN'S LOG, STARDATE 2261.34.
THE *ENTERPRISE* HAS ARRIVED AT THE PREVIOUSLY UNEXPLORED STAR SYSTEM DESIGNATED MENZIES 216, AT THE EDGE OF THE ALPHA QUADRANT.
IT'S BEEN SEVERAL MONTHS SINCE WE LEFT EARTH ON OUR FIVE-YEAR MISSION.
TO BORROW A PHRASE FROM CHIEF ENGINEER SCOTT, THE SHIP AND HER CREW ARE FIRING ON ALL CYLINDERS.

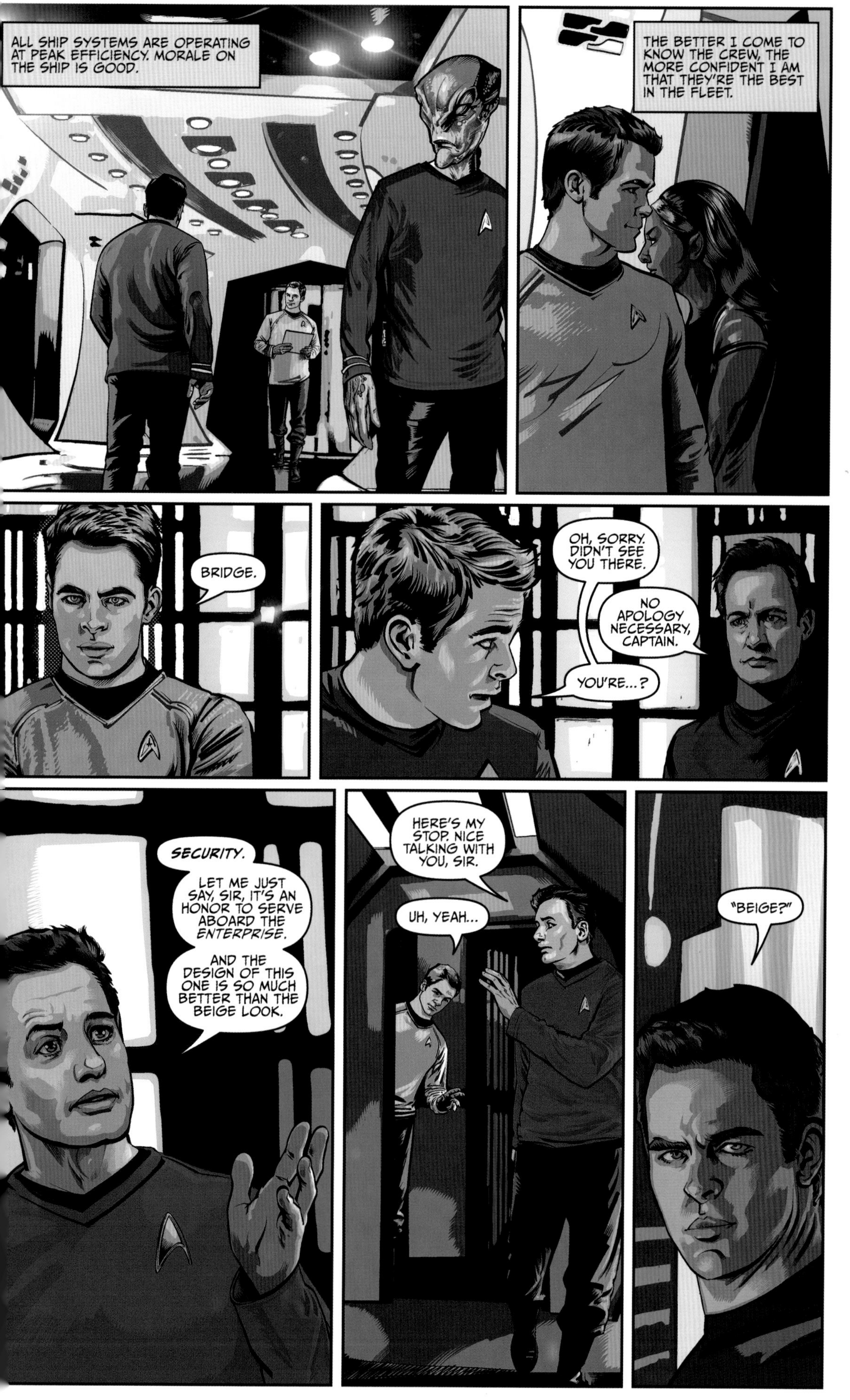
ALL SHIP SYSTEMS ARE OPERATING AT PEAK EFFICIENCY. MORALE ON THE SHIP IS GOOD.
THE BETTER I COME TO KNOW THE CREW, THE MORE CONFIDENT I AM THAT THEY'RE THE BEST IN THE FLEET.
BRIDGE.
OH, SORRY. DIDN'T SEE YOU THERE.
NO APOLOGY NECESSARY, CAPTAIN.
YOU'RE...?
SECURITY.
LET ME JUST SAY, SIR, IT'S AN HONOR TO SERVE ABOARD THE ENTERPRISE.
AND THE DESIGN OF THIS ONE IS SO MUCH BETTER THAN THE BEIGE LOOK.
HERE'S MY STOP. NICE TALKING WITH YOU, SIR.
UH, YEAH...
"BEIGE?"

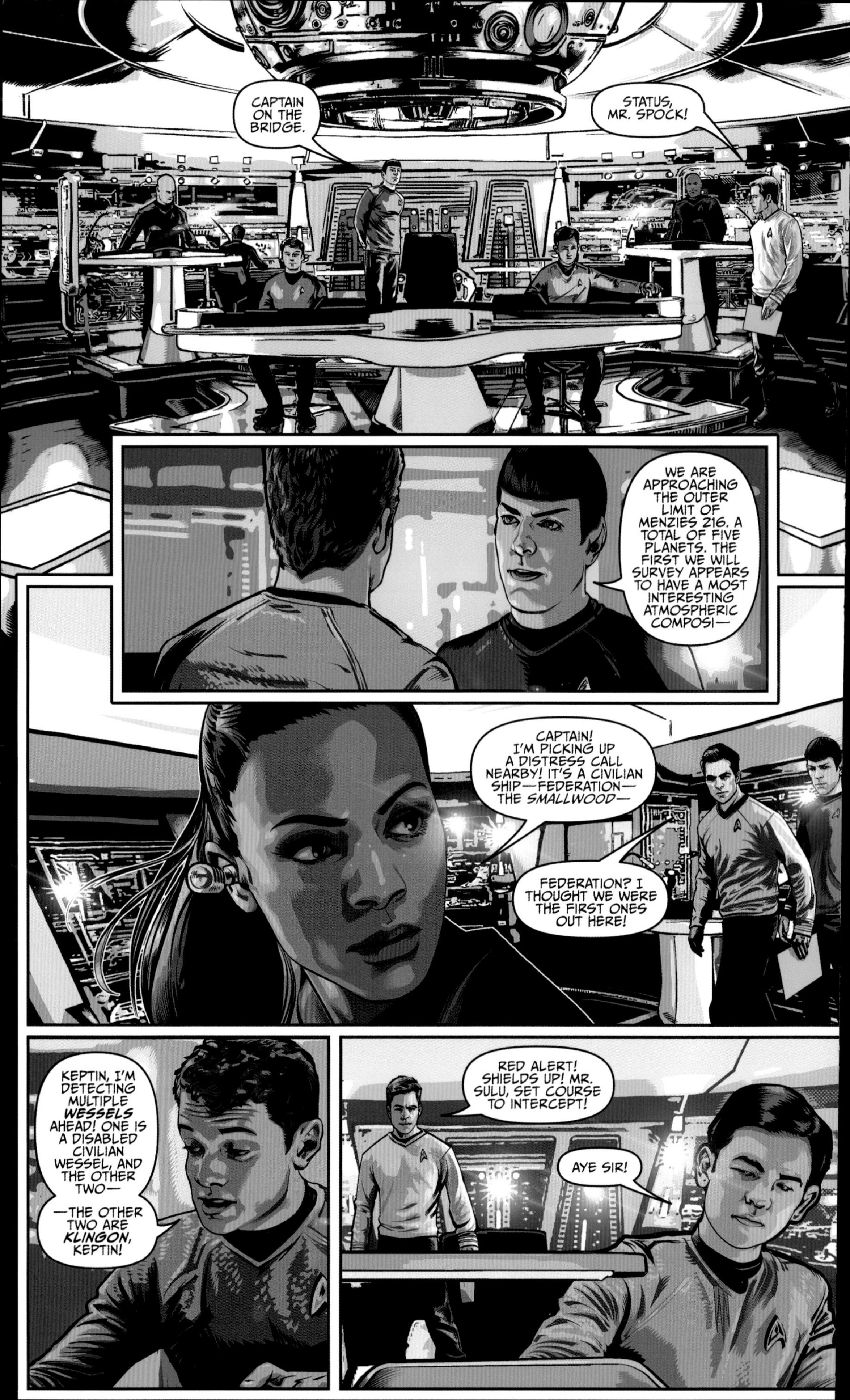
CAPTAIN ON THE BRIDGE.
STATUS, MR. SPOCK!
WE ARE APPROACHING THE OUTER LIMIT OF MENZIES 216. A TOTAL OF FIVE PLANETS. THE FIRST WE WILL SURVEY APPEARS TO HAVE A MOST INTERESTING ATMOSPHERIC COMPOSI—
CAPTAIN! I'M PICKING UP A DISTRESS CALL NEARBY! IT'S A CIVILIAN SHIP—FEDERATION—THE *SMALLWOOD*—
FEDERATION? I THOUGHT WE WERE THE FIRST ONES OUT HERE!
KEPTIN, I'M DETECTING MULTIPLE ***WESSELS*** AHEAD! ONE IS A DISABLED CIVILIAN WESSEL, AND THE OTHER TWO—
—THE OTHER TWO ARE ***KLINGON,*** KEPTIN!
RED ALERT! SHIELDS UP! MR. SULU, SET COURSE TO INTERCEPT!
AYE SIR!

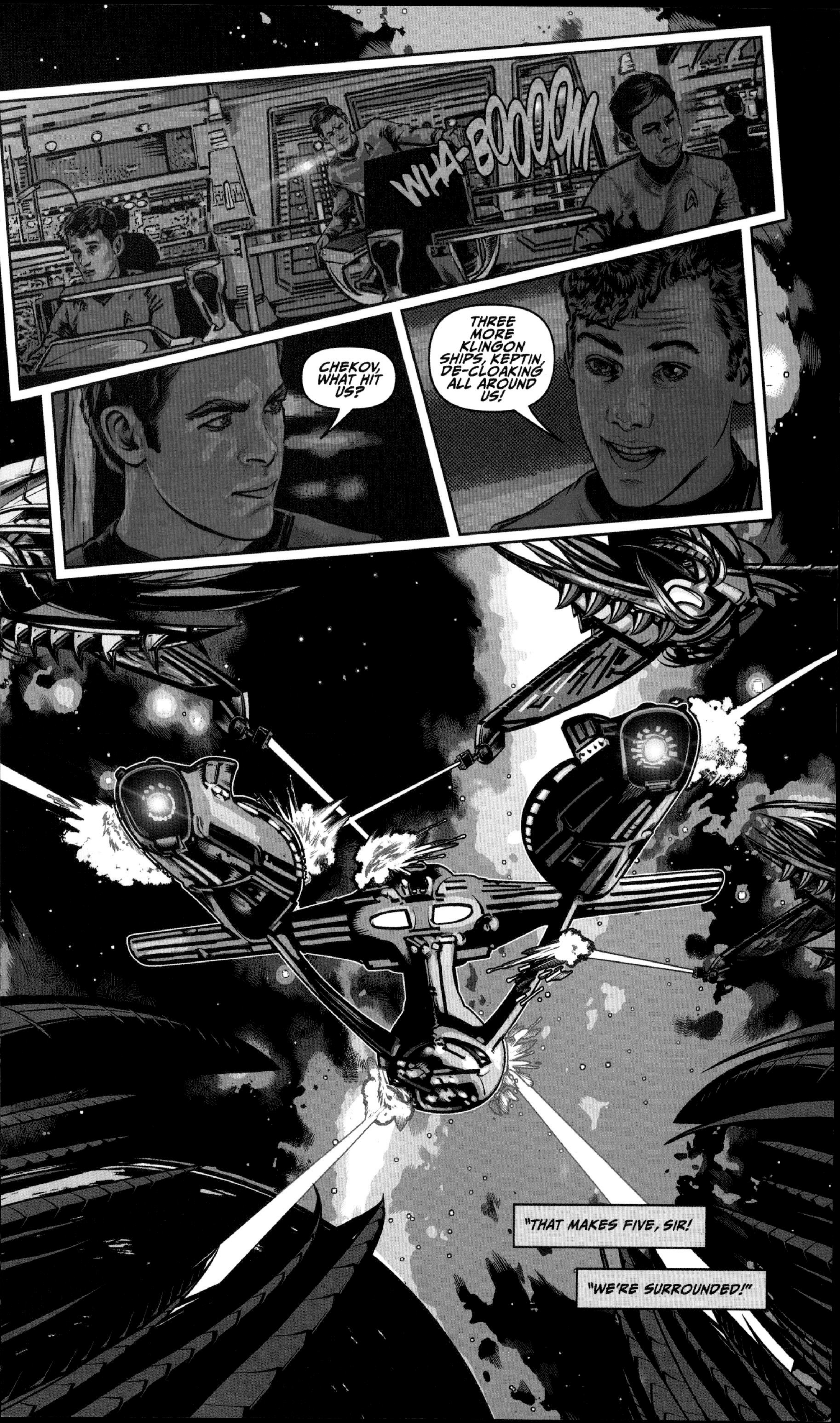
WHA-BOOOOM
CHEKOV, WHAT HIT US?
THREE MORE KLINGON SHIPS, KEPTIN, DE-CLOAKING ALL AROUND US!
"THAT MAKES FIVE, SIR!
"WE'RE SURROUNDED!"

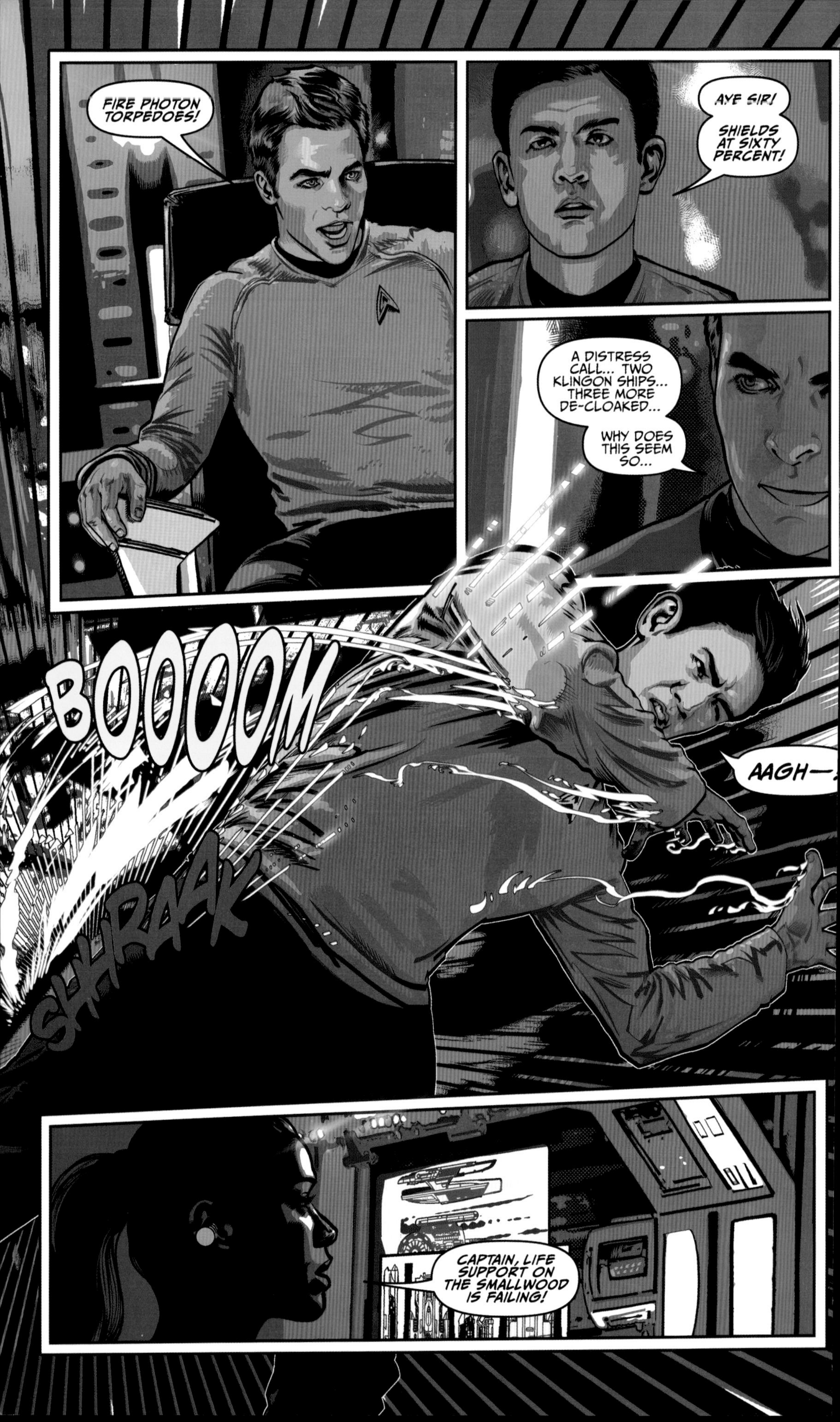
FIRE PHOTON TORPEDOES!
AYE SIR!
SHIELDS AT SIXTY PERCENT!
A DISTRESS CALL... TWO KLINGON SHIPS... THREE MORE DE-CLOAKED...
WHY DOES THIS SEEM SO...
BOOOOM
SHRAAK
AAGH—!
CAPTAIN, LIFE SUPPORT ON THE SMALLWOOD IS FAILING!

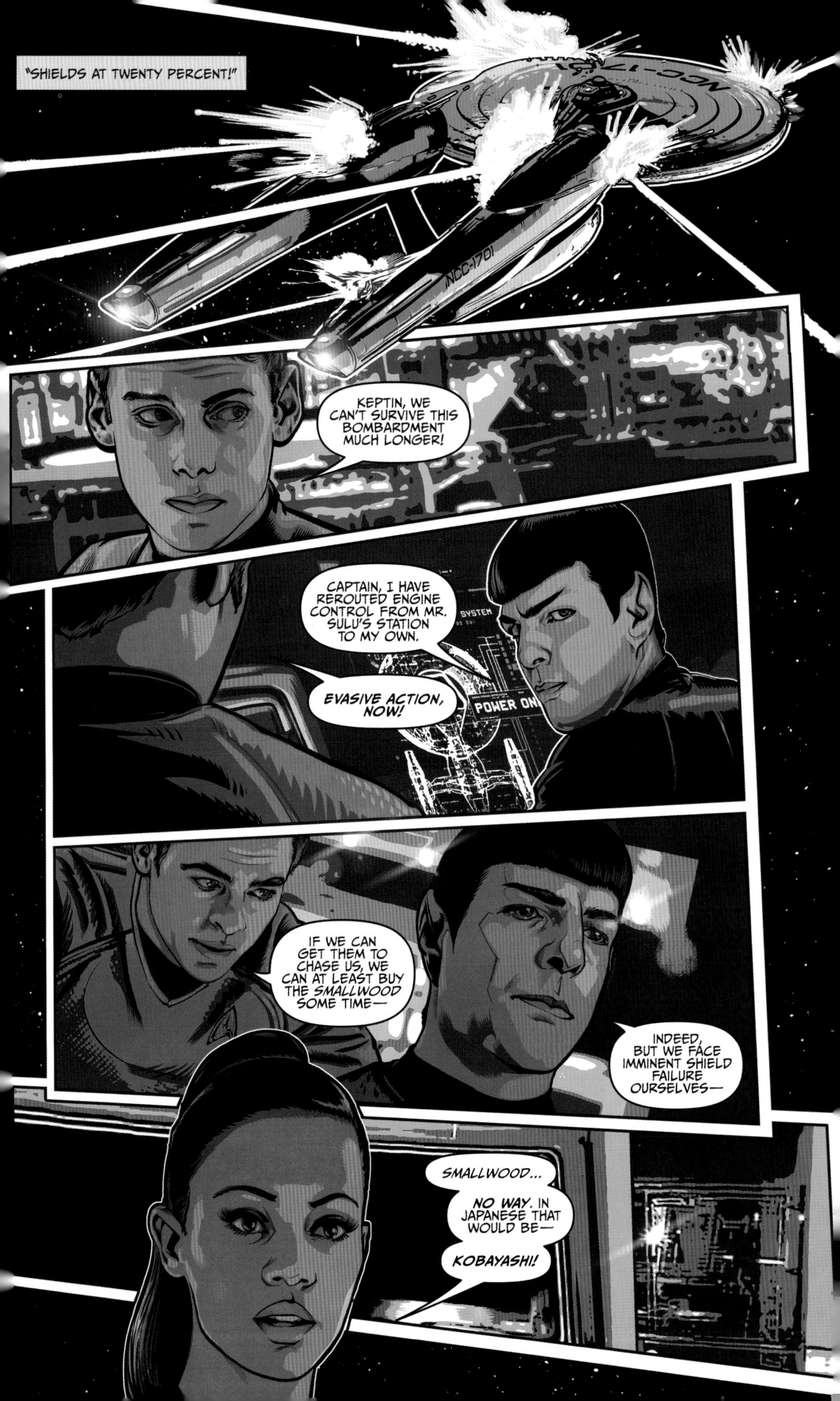
"SHIELDS AT TWENTY PERCENT!"
NCC-1701
KEPTIN, WE CAN'T SURVIVE THIS BOMBARDMENT MUCH LONGER!
CAPTAIN, I HAVE REROUTED ENGINE CONTROL FROM MR. SULU'S STATION TO MY OWN.
SYSTEM
POWER ON
EVASIVE ACTION, NOW!
IF WE CAN GET THEM TO CHASE US, WE CAN AT LEAST BUY THE SMALLWOOD SOME TIME—
INDEED, BUT WE FACE IMMINENT SHIELD FAILURE OURSELVES—
SMALLWOOD...
NO WAY. IN JAPANESE THAT WOULD BE—
KOBAYASHI!

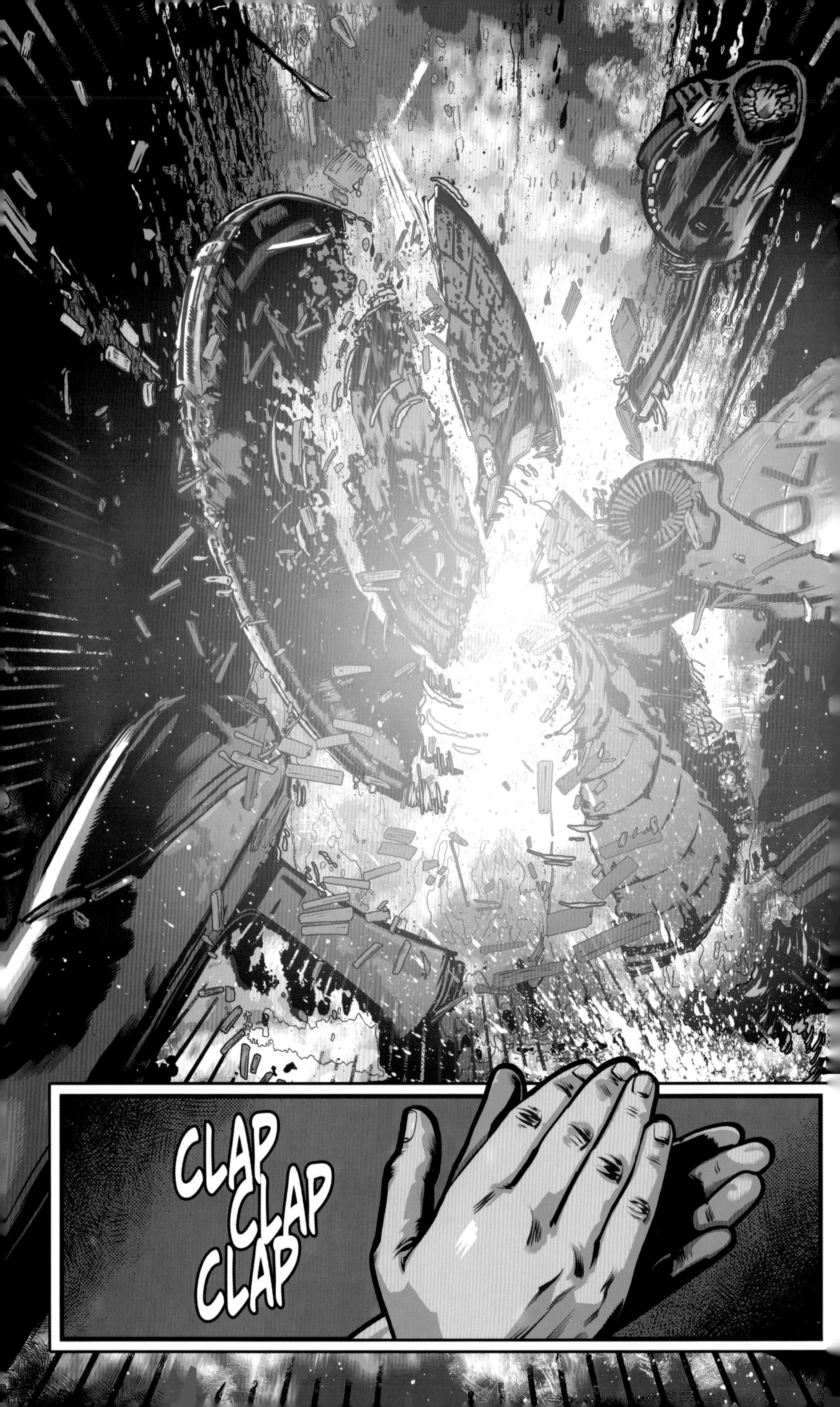
CLAP
CLAP
CLAP

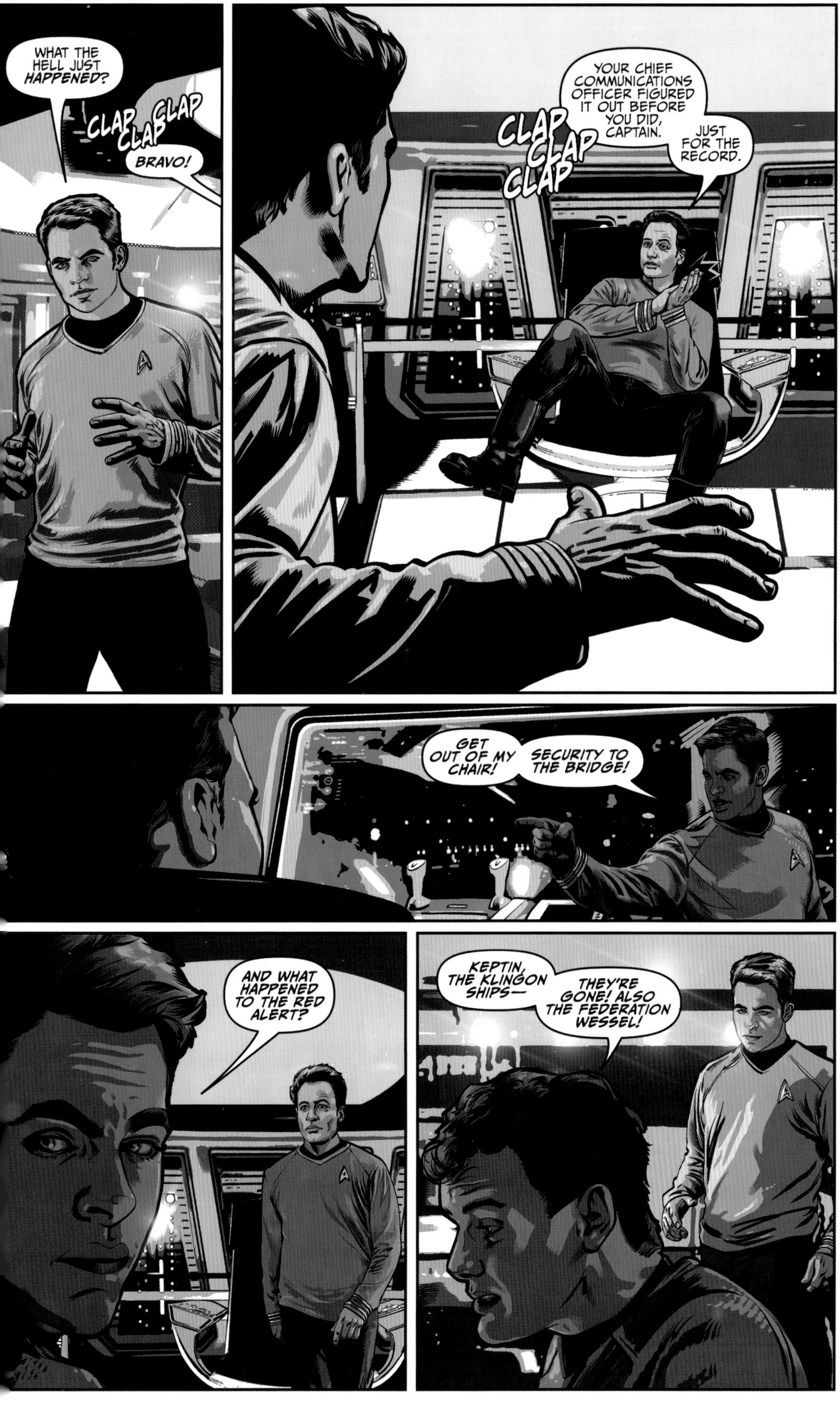
WHAT THE HELL JUST *HAPPENED?*
CLAP CLAP CLAP
BRAVO!
YOUR CHIEF COMMUNICATIONS OFFICER FIGURED IT OUT BEFORE YOU DID, CAPTAIN.
JUST FOR THE RECORD.
CLAP CLAP CLAP
GET OUT OF MY CHAIR!
SECURITY TO THE BRIDGE!
AND WHAT HAPPENED TO THE RED ALERT?
KEPTIN, THE KLINGON SHIPS—
THEY'RE GONE! ALSO THE FEDERATION WESSEL!

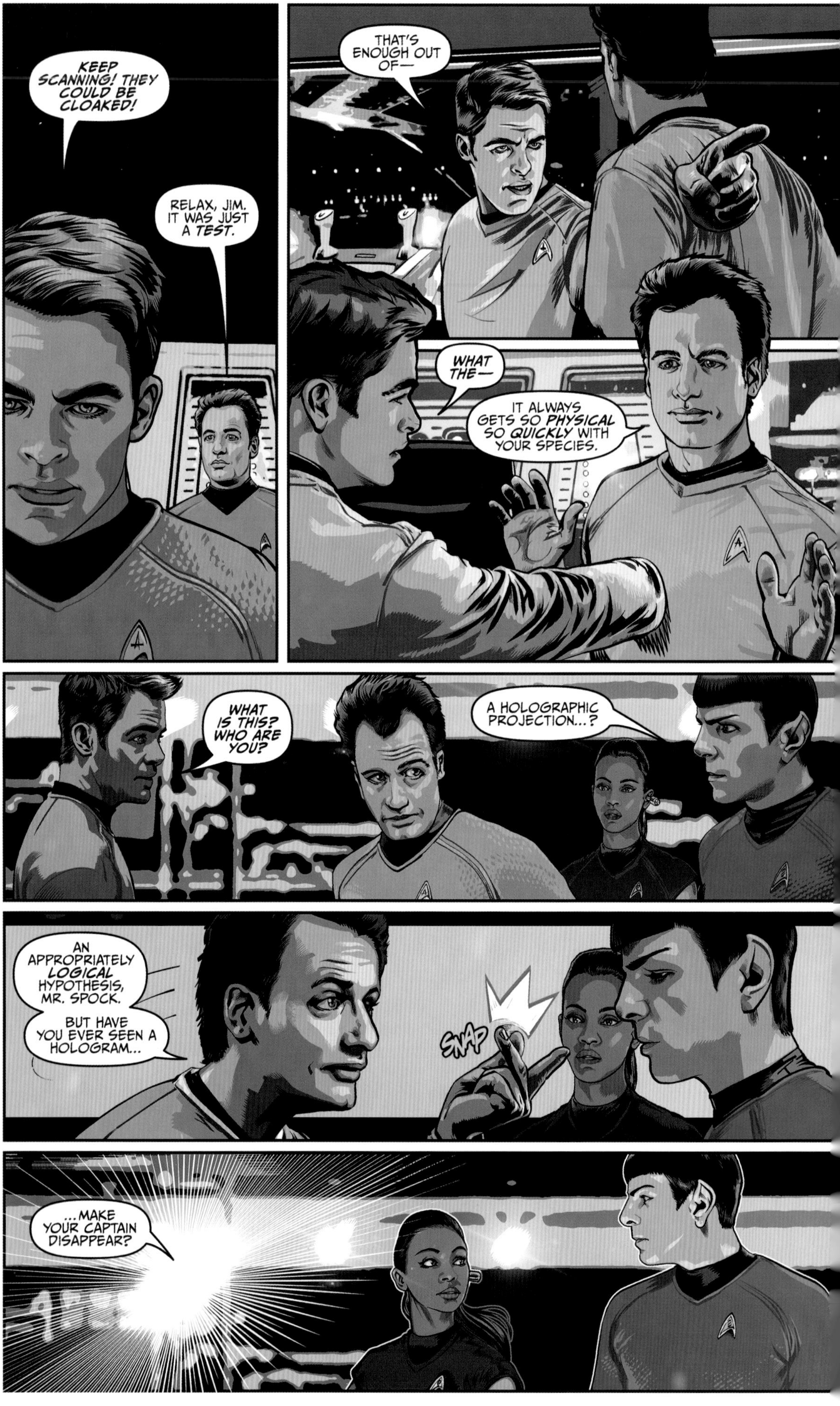
KEEP SCANNING! THEY COULD BE CLOAKED!
RELAX, JIM. IT WAS JUST A TEST.
THAT'S ENOUGH OUT OF—
WHAT THE—
IT ALWAYS GETS SO PHYSICAL SO QUICKLY WITH YOUR SPECIES.
WHAT IS THIS? WHO ARE YOU?
A HOLOGRAPHIC PROJECTION...?
AN APPROPRIATELY LOGICAL HYPOTHESIS, MR. SPOCK.
BUT HAVE YOU EVER SEEN A HOLOGRAM...
SNAP
...MAKE YOUR CAPTAIN DISAPPEAR?

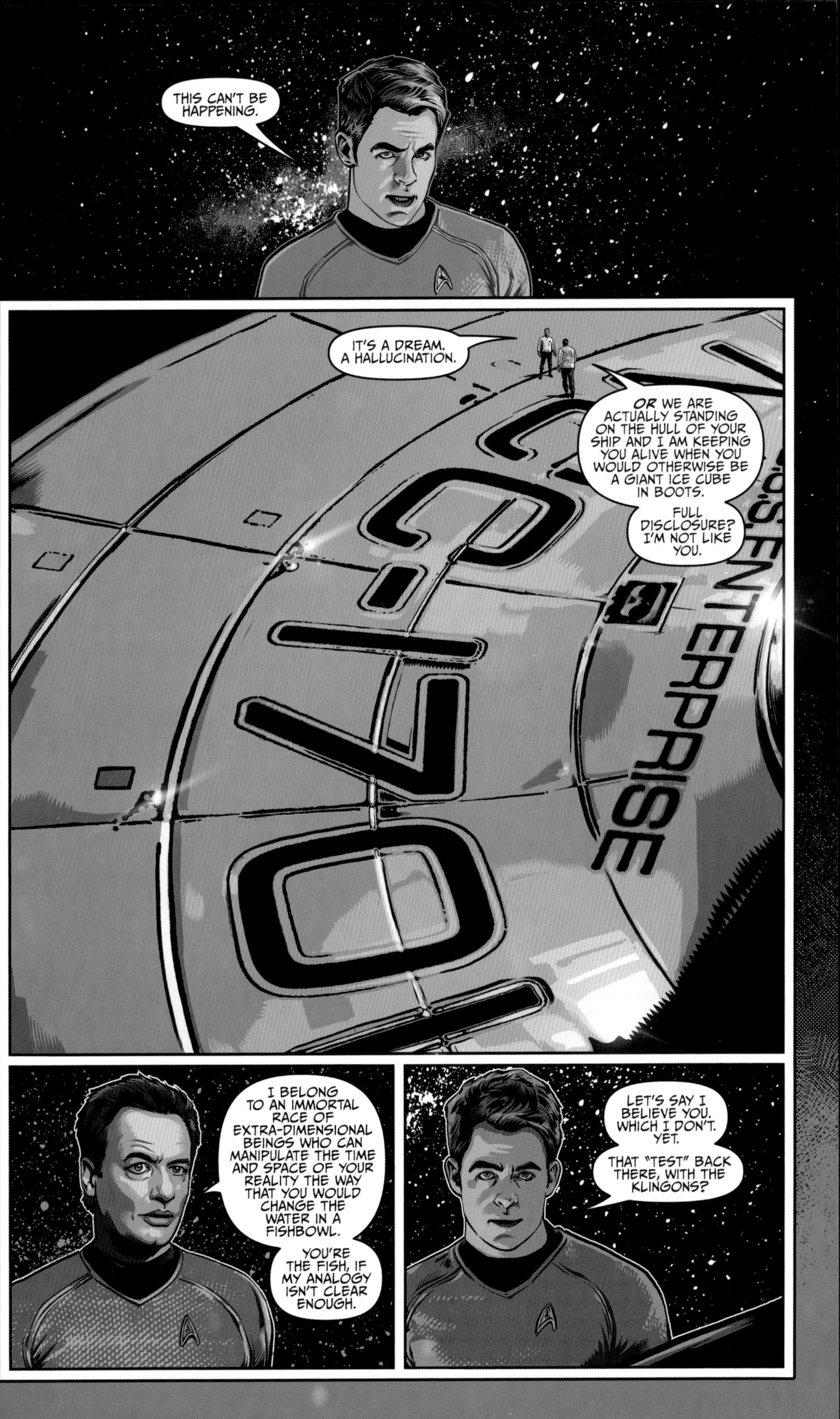
THIS CAN'T BE HAPPENING.
IT'S A DREAM. A HALLUCINATION.
OR WE ARE ACTUALLY STANDING ON THE HULL OF YOUR SHIP AND I AM KEEPING YOU ALIVE WHEN YOU WOULD OTHERWISE BE A GIANT ICE CUBE IN BOOTS.
FULL DISCLOSURE? I'M NOT LIKE YOU.
U.S.S. ENTERPRISE
NCC-1701
I BELONG TO AN IMMORTAL RACE OF EXTRA-DIMENSIONAL BEINGS WHO CAN MANIPULATE THE TIME AND SPACE OF YOUR REALITY THE WAY THAT YOU WOULD CHANGE THE WATER IN A FISHBOWL.
YOU'RE THE FISH, IF MY ANALOGY ISN'T CLEAR ENOUGH.
LET'S SAY I BELIEVE YOU. WHICH I DON'T. YET.
THAT "TEST" BACK THERE, WITH THE KLINGONS?

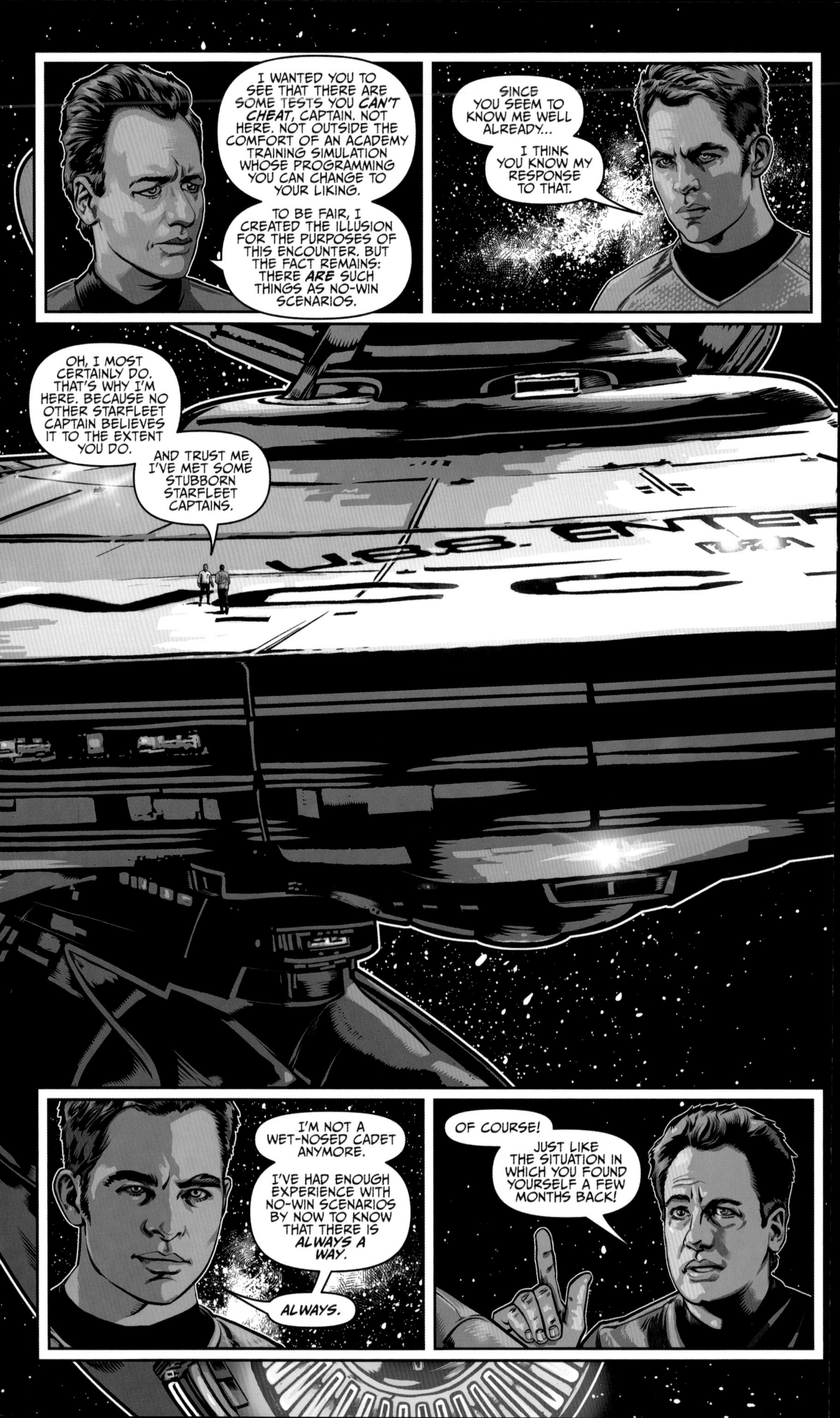
I WANTED YOU TO SEE THAT THERE ARE SOME TESTS YOU CAN'T CHEAT, CAPTAIN. NOT HERE. NOT OUTSIDE THE COMFORT OF AN ACADEMY TRAINING SIMULATION WHOSE PROGRAMMING YOU CAN CHANGE TO YOUR LIKING.
TO BE FAIR, I CREATED THE ILLUSION FOR THE PURPOSES OF THIS ENCOUNTER. BUT THE FACT REMAINS: THERE ARE SUCH THINGS AS NO-WIN SCENARIOS.
SINCE YOU SEEM TO KNOW ME WELL ALREADY...
I THINK YOU KNOW MY RESPONSE TO THAT.
OH, I MOST CERTAINLY DO. THAT'S WHY I'M HERE. BECAUSE NO OTHER STARFLEET CAPTAIN BELIEVES IT TO THE EXTENT YOU DO.
AND TRUST ME, I'VE MET SOME STUBBORN STARFLEET CAPTAINS.
I'M NOT A WET-NOSED CADET ANYMORE.
I'VE HAD ENOUGH EXPERIENCE WITH NO-WIN SCENARIOS BY NOW TO KNOW THAT THERE IS ALWAYS A WAY.
ALWAYS.
OF COURSE!
JUST LIKE THE SITUATION IN WHICH YOU FOUND YOURSELF A FEW MONTHS BACK!

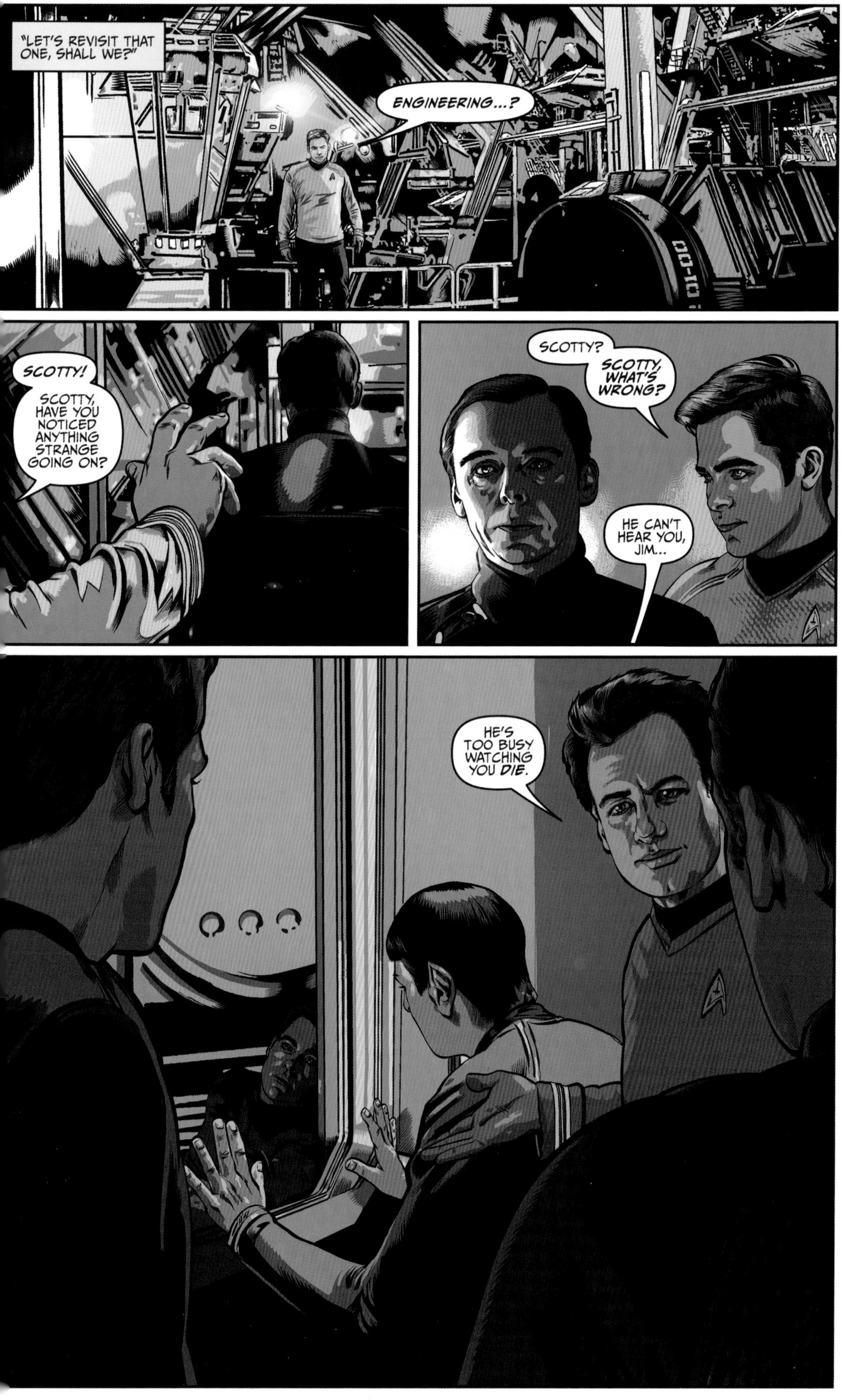
"LET'S REVISIT THAT ONE, SHALL WE?"
ENGINEERING...?
DD-10
SCOTTY!
SCOTTY, HAVE YOU NOTICED ANYTHING STRANGE GOING ON?
SCOTTY?
SCOTTY, WHAT'S WRONG?
HE CAN'T HEAR YOU, JIM...
HE'S TOO BUSY WATCHING YOU DIE.

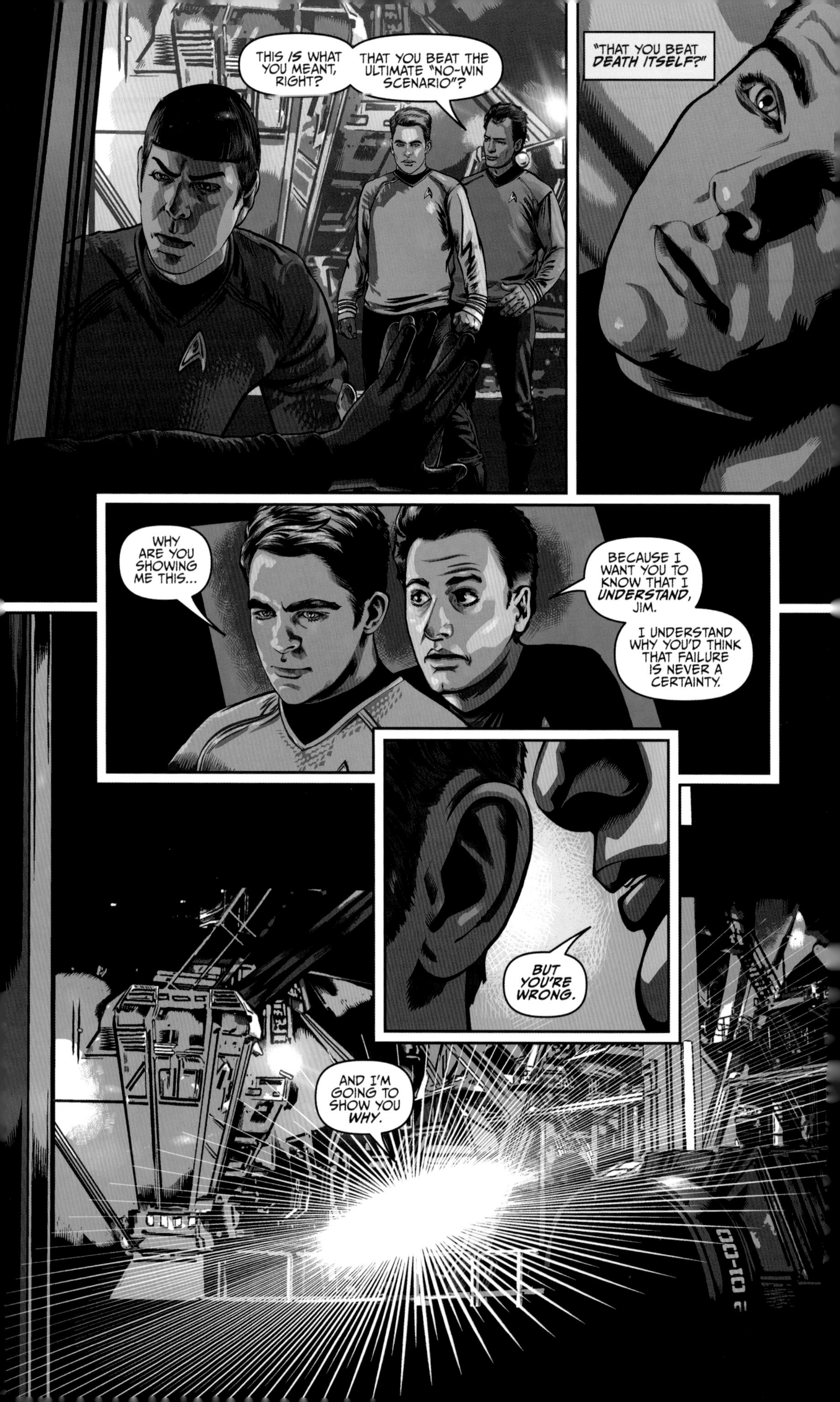
THIS *IS* WHAT YOU MEANT, RIGHT?
THAT YOU BEAT THE ULTIMATE "NO-WIN SCENARIO"?
"THAT YOU BEAT *DEATH ITSELF*?"
WHY ARE YOU SHOWING ME THIS...
BECAUSE I WANT YOU TO KNOW THAT I *UNDERSTAND*, JIM.
I UNDERSTAND WHY YOU'D THINK THAT FAILURE IS NEVER A CERTAINTY.
BUT YOU'RE WRONG.
AND I'M GOING TO SHOW YOU *WHY*.

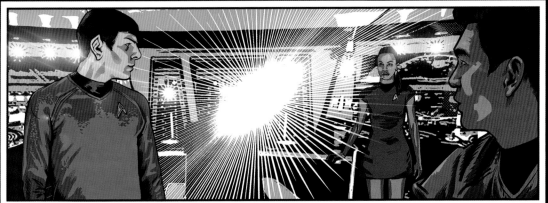

CAPTAIN? ARE YOU ALL RIGHT?

FINE, SPOCK. WHERE'S OUR INTRUDER?

HE'S GONE, SIR!

KEPTIN! NAVIGATIONAL SENSORS ARE DETECTING SOMETHING... IMPOSSIBLE!

SPECIFICS, MR. CHEKOV!

WELL, SIR, IF THESE READINGS ARE CORRECT—

"WE ARE SUDDENLY ON THE OPPOSITE SIDE OF THE ALPHA QUADRANT!"

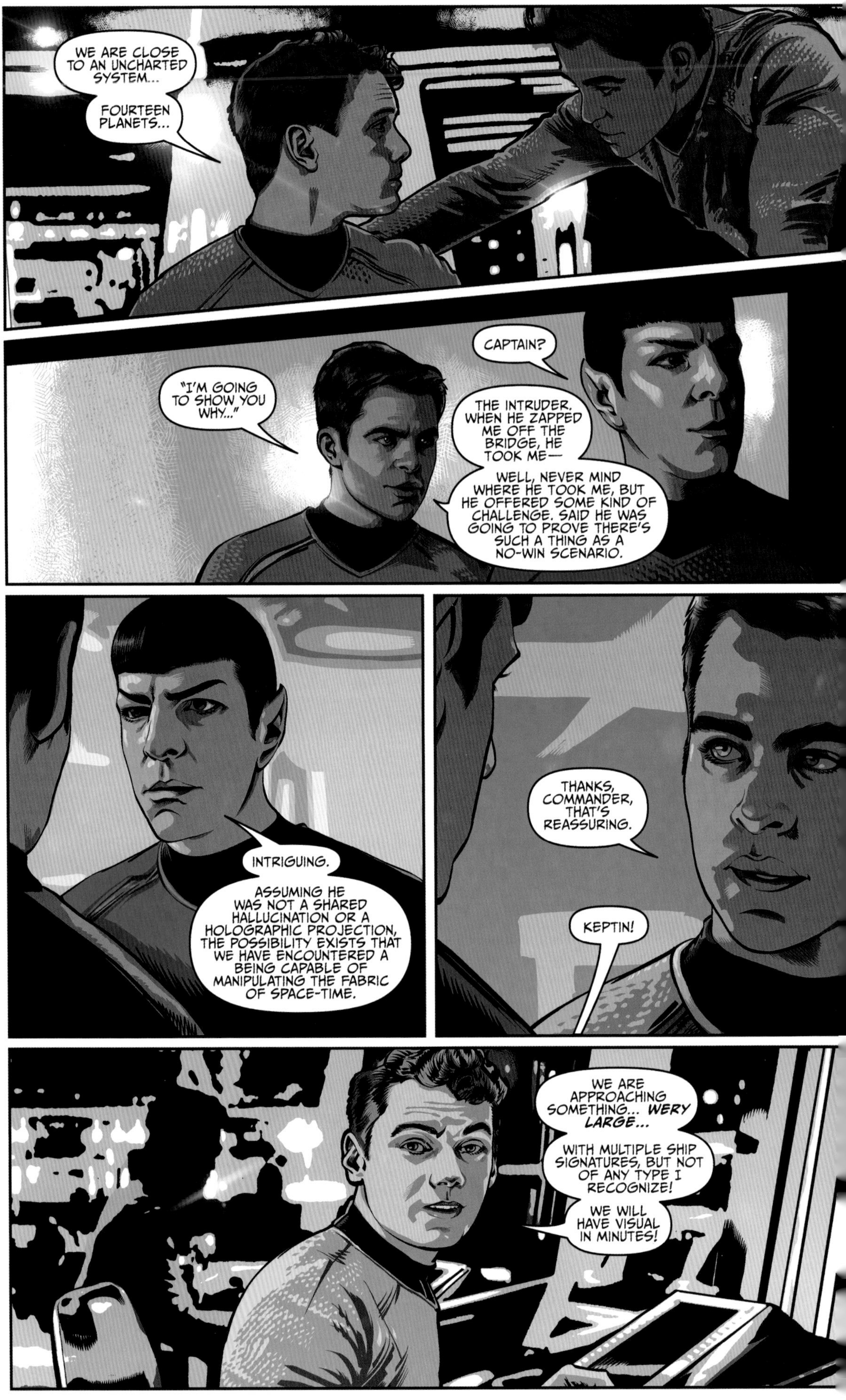

WE ARE CLOSE TO AN UNCHARTED SYSTEM...
FOURTEEN PLANETS...
CAPTAIN?
"I'M GOING TO SHOW YOU WHY..."
THE INTRUDER. WHEN HE ZAPPED ME OFF THE BRIDGE, HE TOOK ME—
WELL, NEVER MIND WHERE HE TOOK ME, BUT HE OFFERED SOME KIND OF CHALLENGE. SAID HE WAS GOING TO PROVE THERE'S SUCH A THING AS A NO-WIN SCENARIO.
INTRIGUING.
ASSUMING HE WAS NOT A SHARED HALLUCINATION OR A HOLOGRAPHIC PROJECTION, THE POSSIBILITY EXISTS THAT WE HAVE ENCOUNTERED A BEING CAPABLE OF MANIPULATING THE FABRIC OF SPACE-TIME.
THANKS, COMMANDER, THAT'S REASSURING.
KEPTIN!
WE ARE APPROACHING SOMETHING... *WERY LARGE...*
WITH MULTIPLE SHIP SIGNATURES, BUT NOT OF ANY TYPE I RECOGNIZE!
WE WILL HAVE VISUAL IN MINUTES!

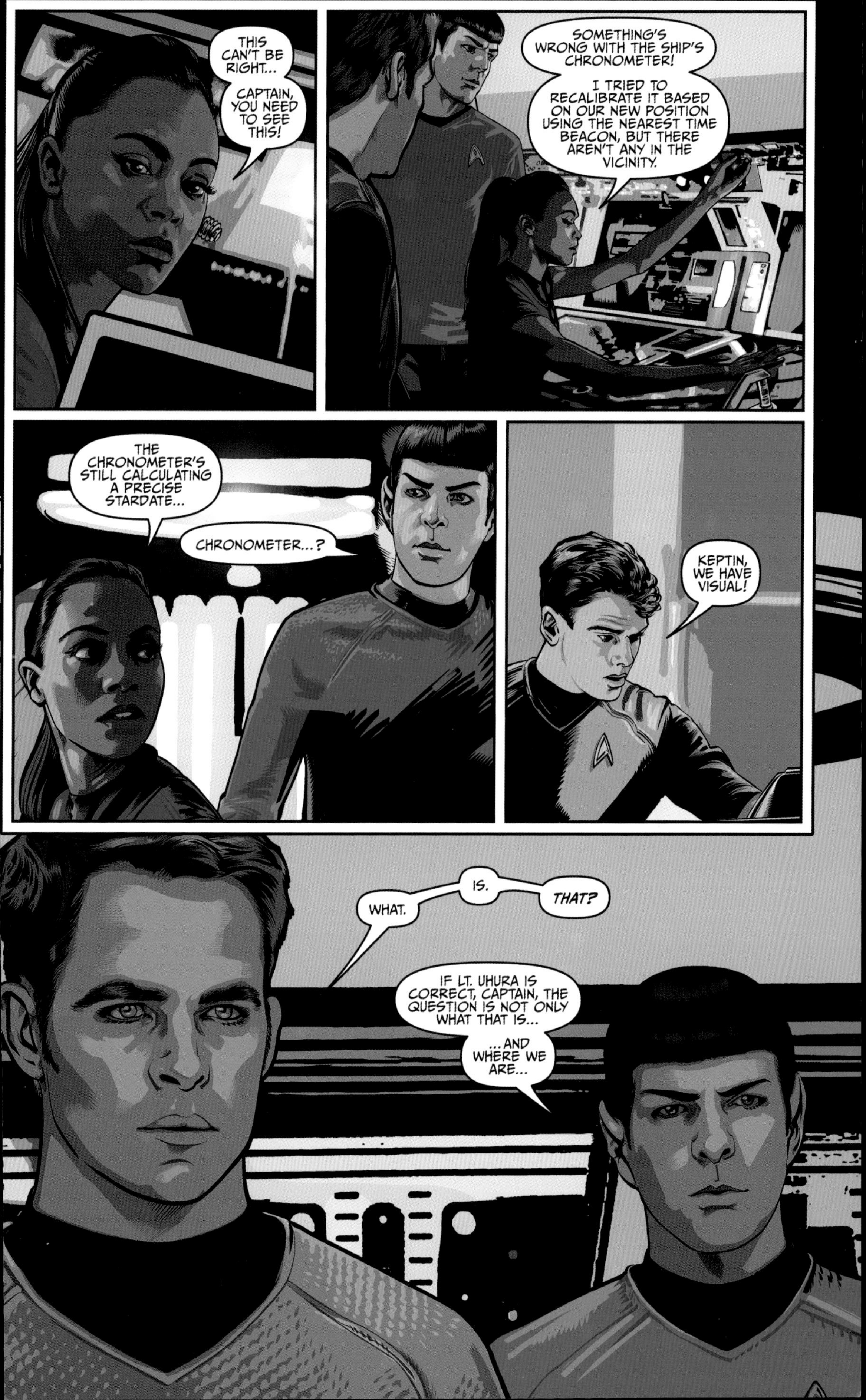
THIS CAN'T BE RIGHT...
CAPTAIN, YOU NEED TO SEE THIS!
SOMETHING'S WRONG WITH THE SHIP'S CHRONOMETER!
I TRIED TO RECALIBRATE IT BASED ON OUR NEW POSITION USING THE NEAREST TIME BEACON, BUT THERE AREN'T ANY IN THE VICINITY.
THE CHRONOMETER'S STILL CALCULATING A PRECISE STARDATE...
CHRONOMETER...?
KEPTIN, WE HAVE VISUAL!
WHAT.
IS.
THAT?
IF LT. UHURA IS CORRECT, CAPTAIN, THE QUESTION IS NOT ONLY WHAT THAT IS...
...AND WHERE WE ARE...

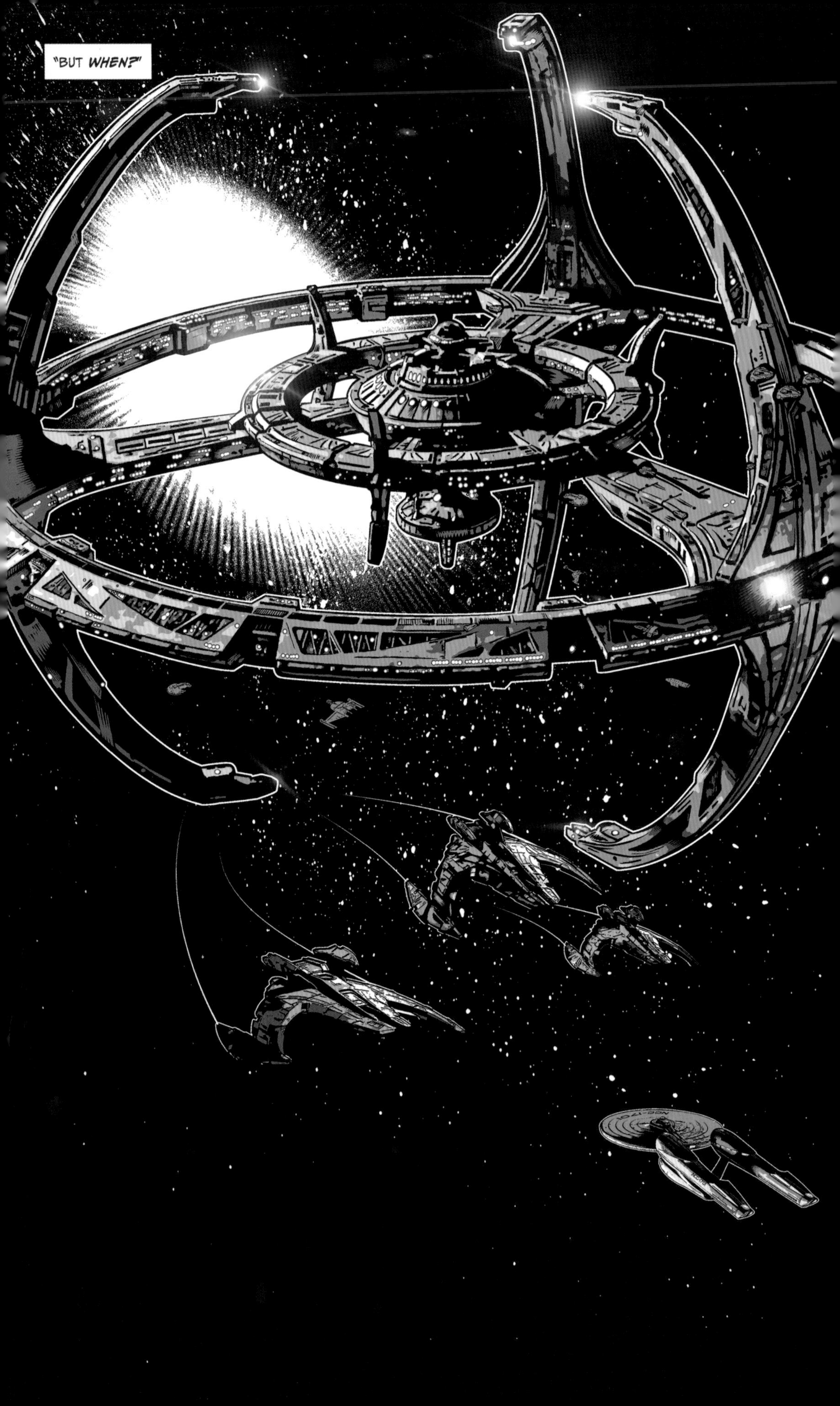
"BUT WHEN?"

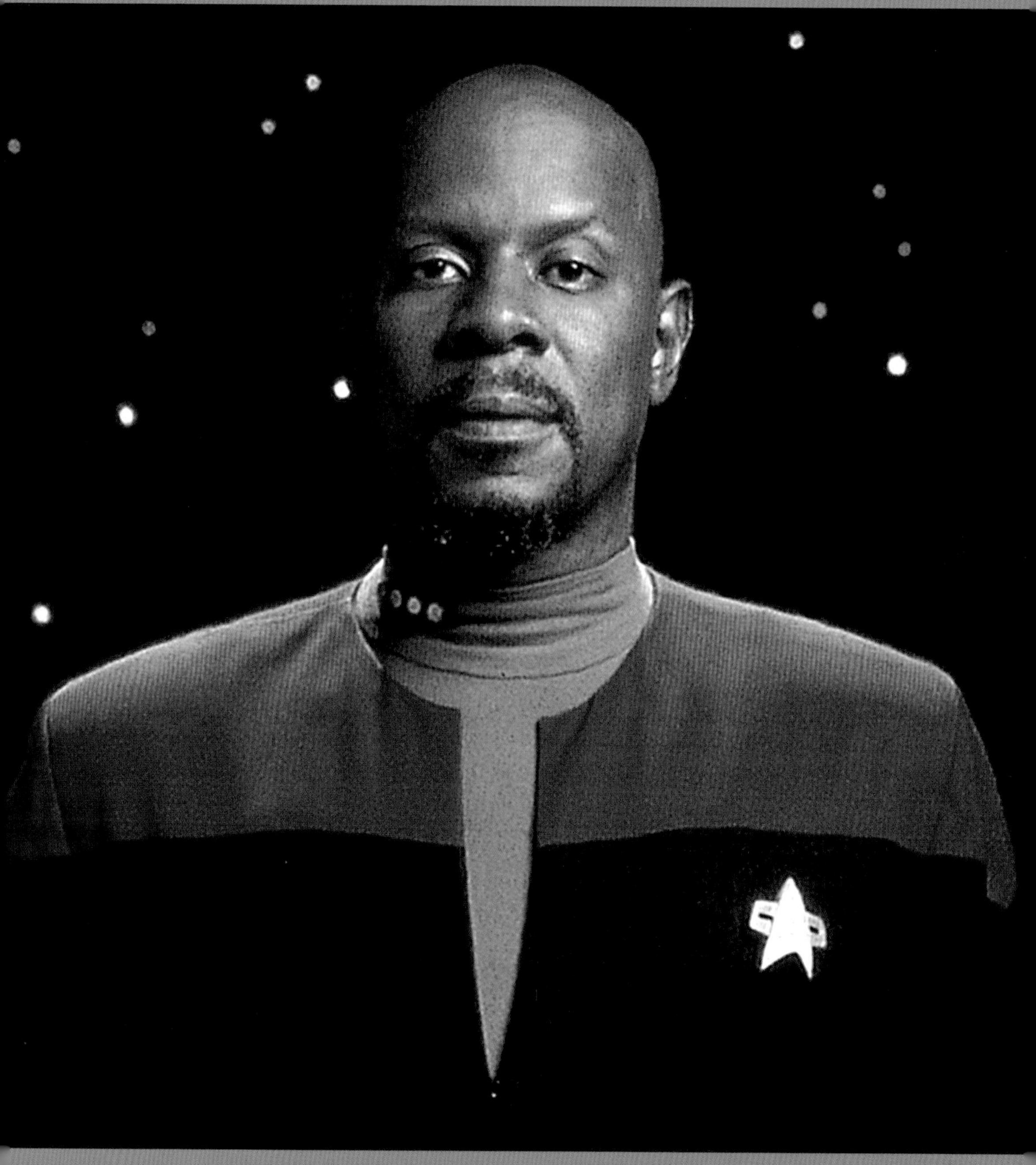

CHAPTER 2

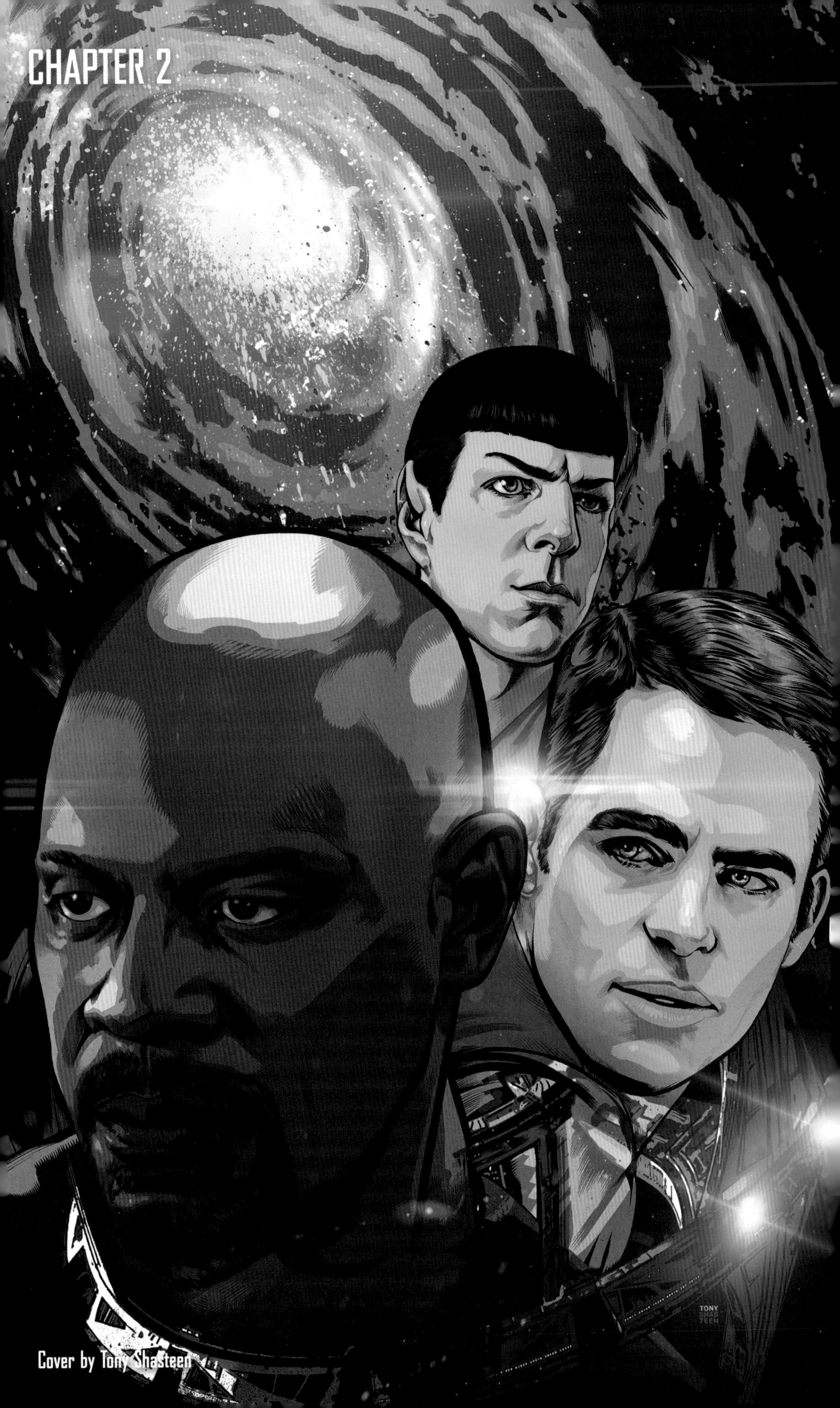
TONY
SHAS
TEEN

Cover by Tony Shasteen

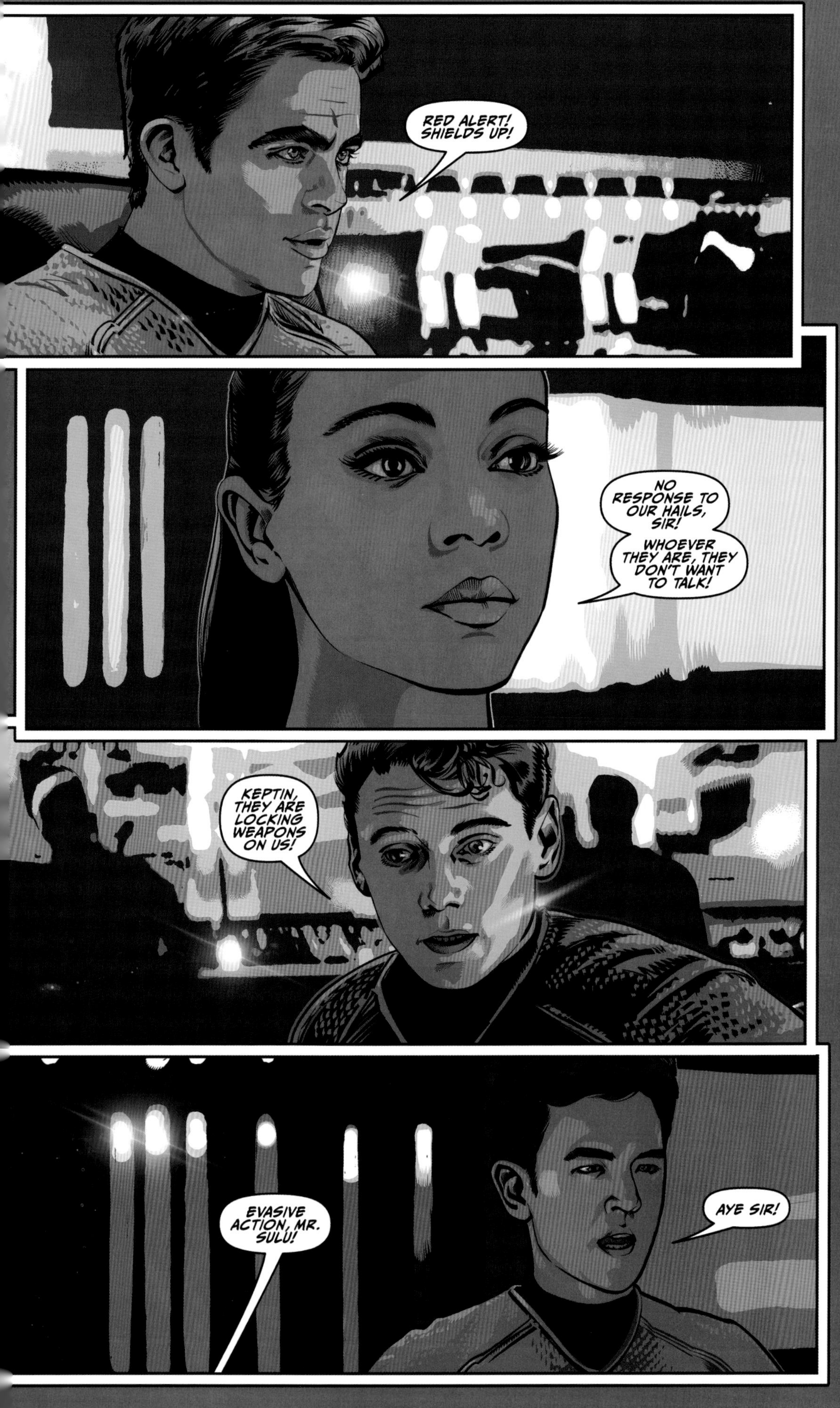
RED ALERT! SHIELDS UP!
NO RESPONSE TO OUR HAILS, SIR!
WHOEVER THEY ARE, THEY DON'T WANT TO TALK!
KEPTIN, THEY ARE LOCKING WEAPONS ON US!
EVASIVE ACTION, MR. SULU!
AYE SIR!

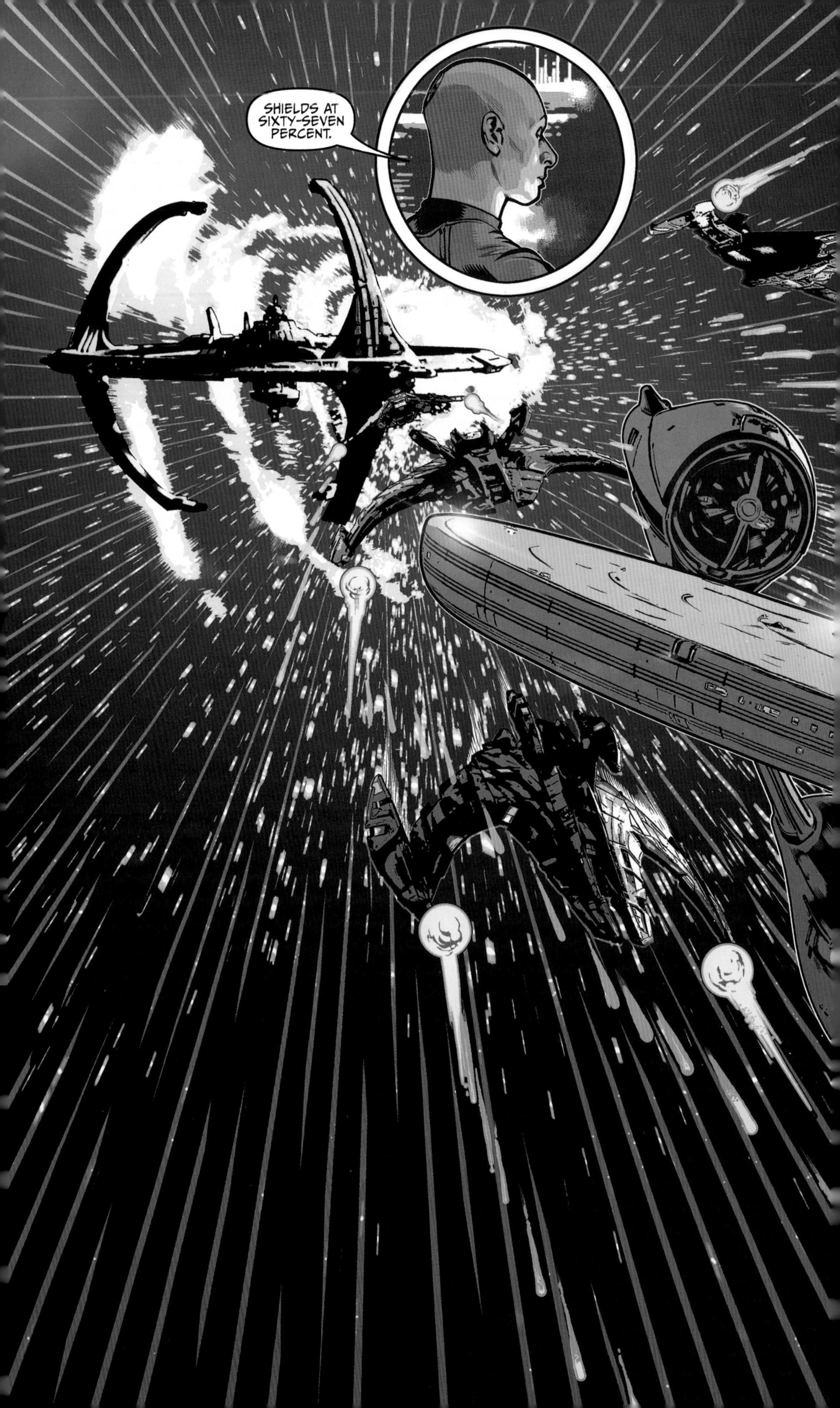
SHIELDS AT SIXTY-SEVEN PERCENT.

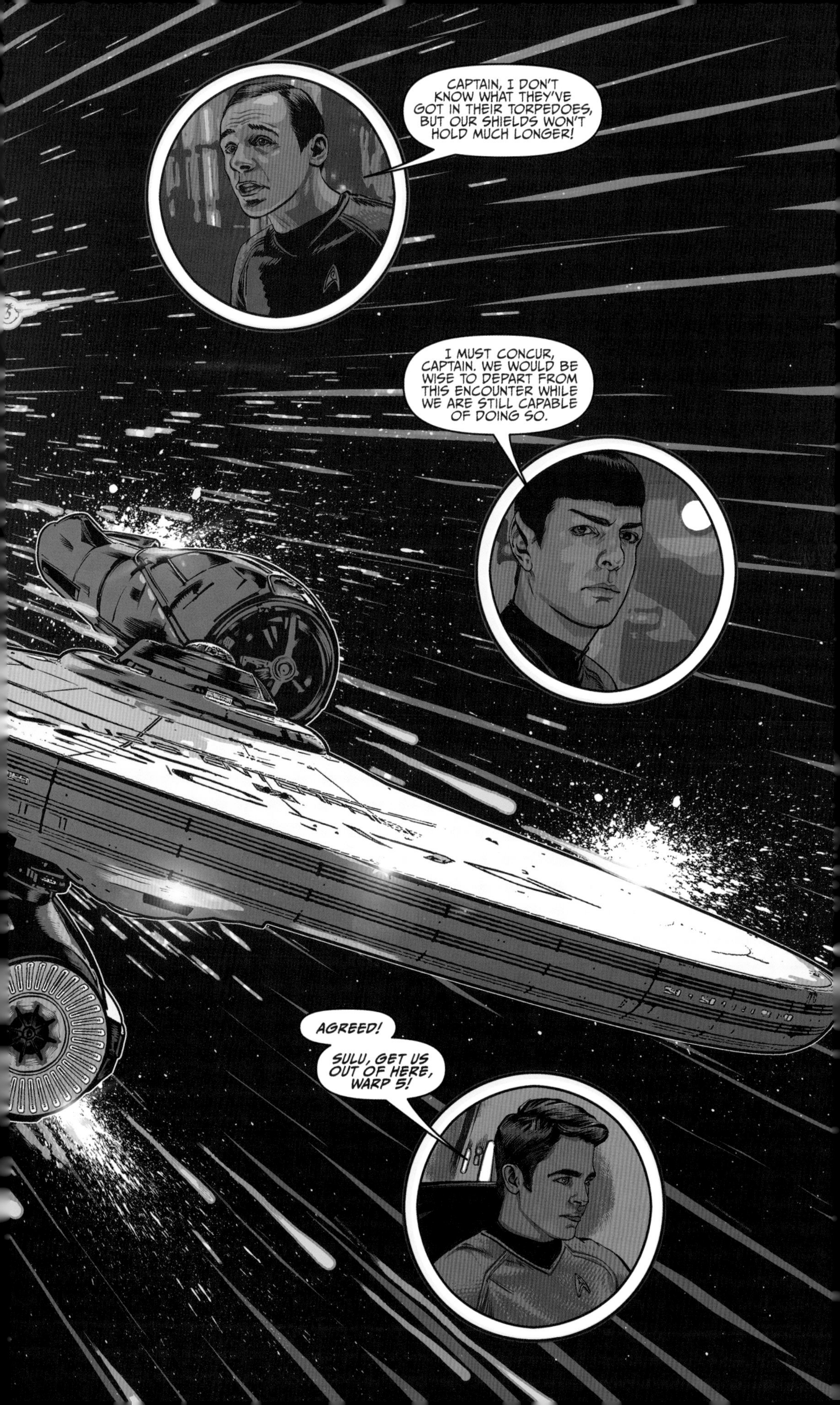
CAPTAIN, I DON'T KNOW WHAT THEY'VE GOT IN THEIR TORPEDOES, BUT OUR SHIELDS WON'T HOLD MUCH LONGER!
I MUST CONCUR, CAPTAIN. WE WOULD BE WISE TO DEPART FROM THIS ENCOUNTER WHILE WE ARE STILL CAPABLE OF DOING SO.
AGREED!
SULU, GET US OUT OF HERE, WARP 5!

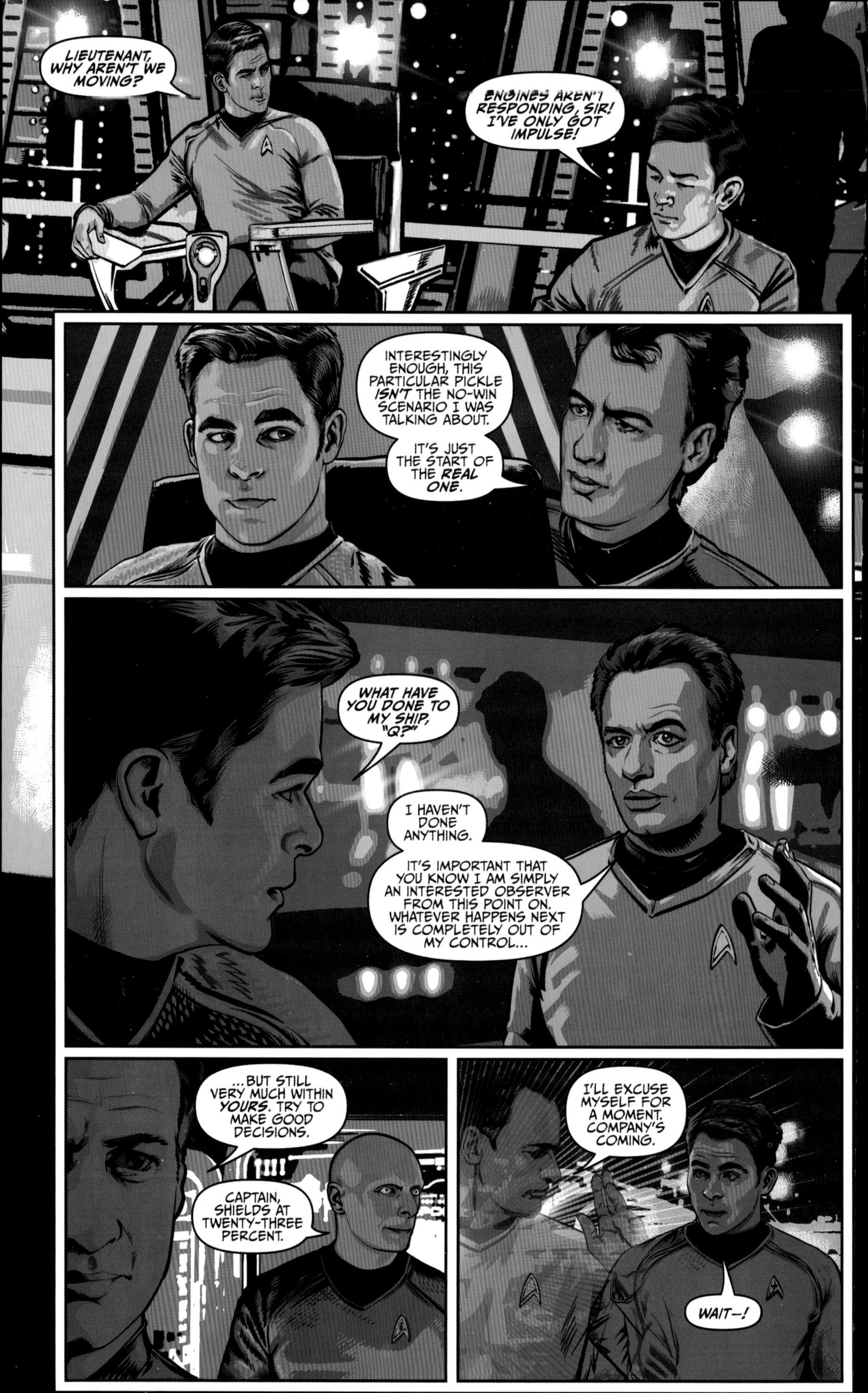
LIEUTENANT, WHY AREN'T WE MOVING?
ENGINES AREN'T RESPONDING, SIR! I'VE ONLY GOT IMPULSE!
INTERESTINGLY ENOUGH, THIS PARTICULAR PICKLE ISN'T THE NO-WIN SCENARIO I WAS TALKING ABOUT.
IT'S JUST THE START OF THE REAL ONE.
WHAT HAVE YOU DONE TO MY SHIP, "Q?"
I HAVEN'T DONE ANYTHING.
IT'S IMPORTANT THAT YOU KNOW I AM SIMPLY AN INTERESTED OBSERVER FROM THIS POINT ON. WHATEVER HAPPENS NEXT IS COMPLETELY OUT OF MY CONTROL...
...BUT STILL VERY MUCH WITHIN YOURS. TRY TO MAKE GOOD DECISIONS.
CAPTAIN, SHIELDS AT TWENTY-THREE PERCENT.
I'LL EXCUSE MYSELF FOR A MOMENT. COMPANY'S COMING.
WAIT--!

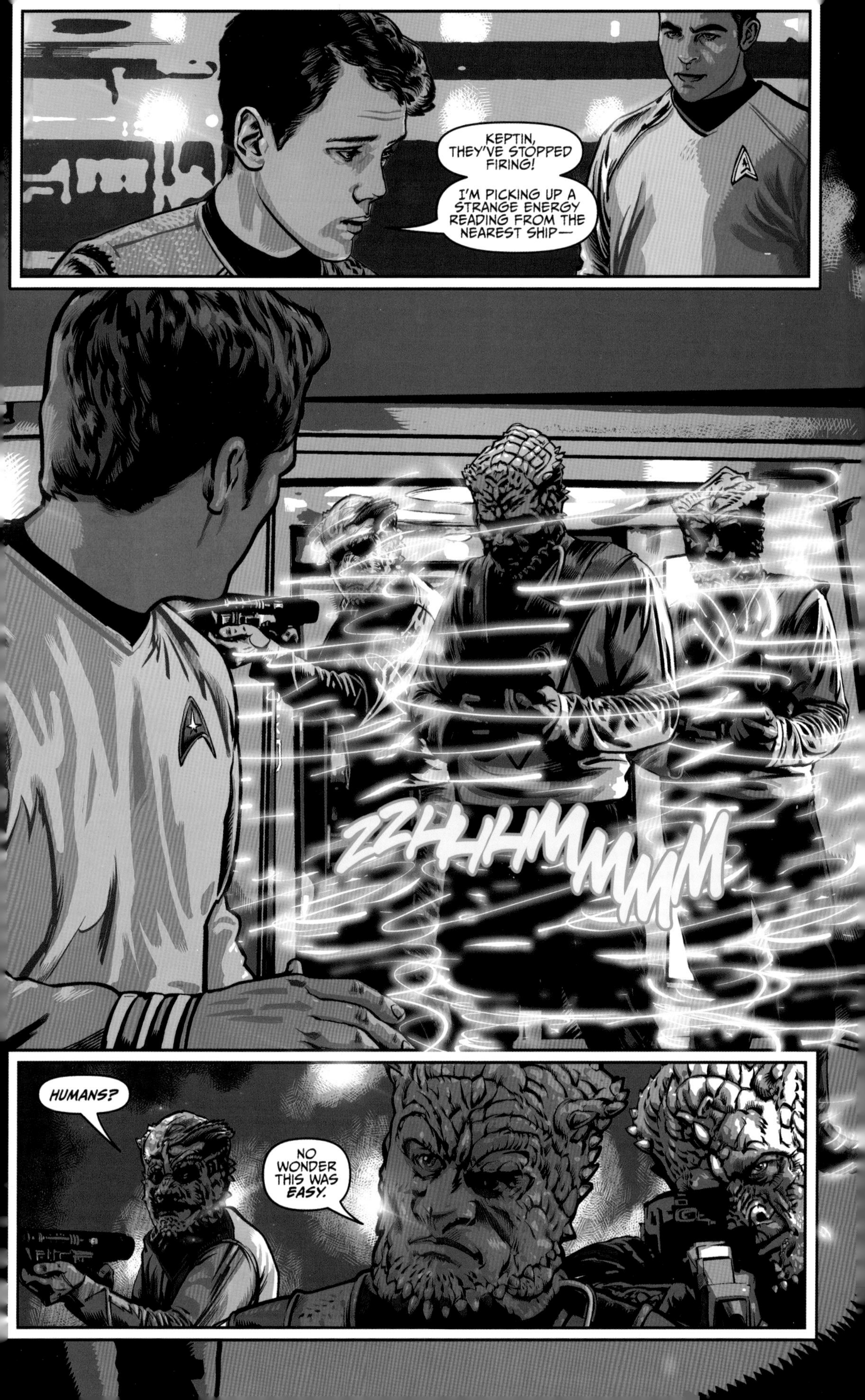
KEPTIN, THEY'VE STOPPED FIRING!
I'M PICKING UP A STRANGE ENERGY READING FROM THE NEAREST SHIP—
ZZHHHMMMM
HUMANS?
NO WONDER THIS WAS EASY.

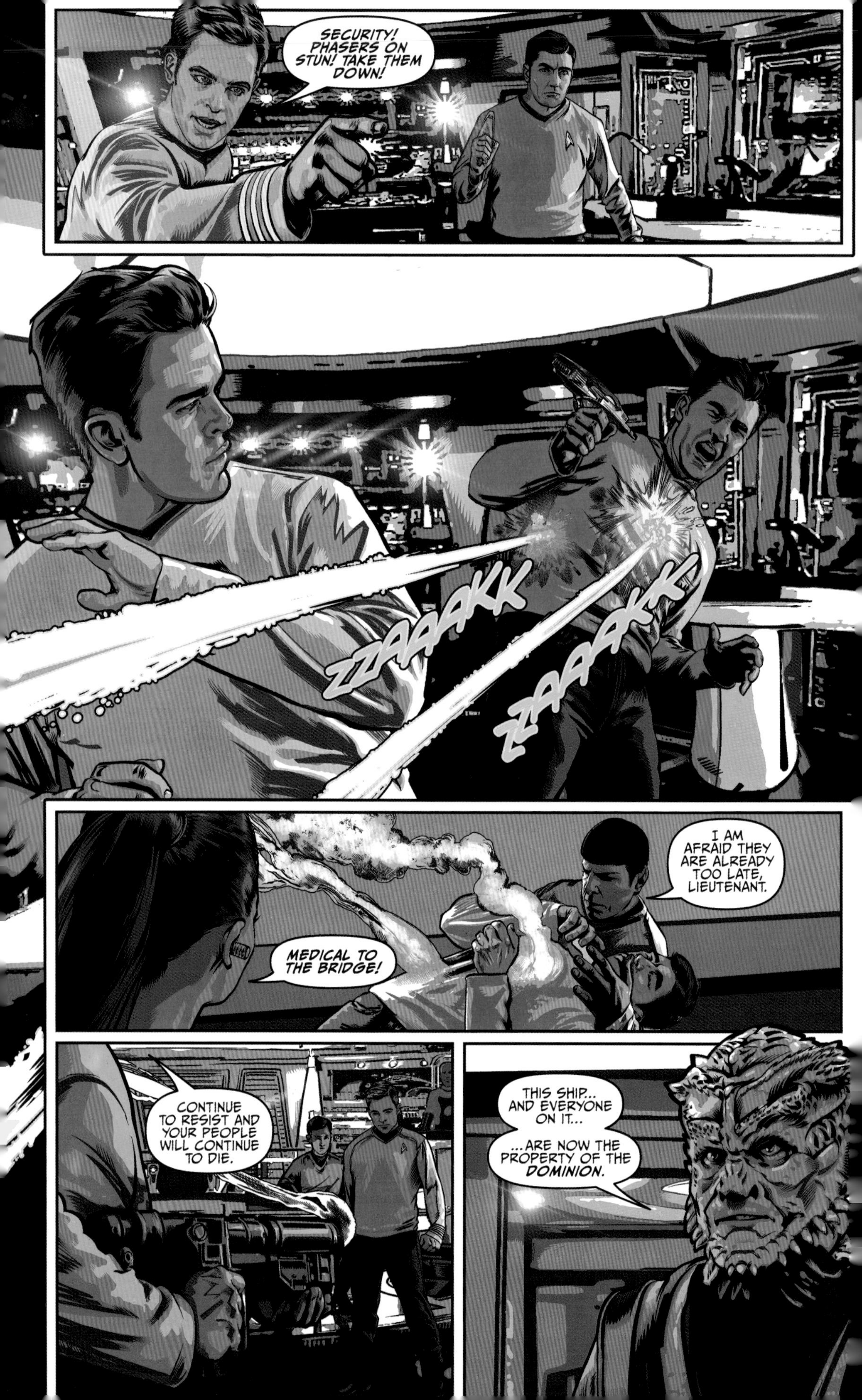
SECURITY! PHASERS ON STUN! TAKE THEM DOWN!
ZZAAAAKK
ZZAAAAKK
MEDICAL TO THE BRIDGE!
I AM AFRAID THEY ARE ALREADY TOO LATE, LIEUTENANT.
CONTINUE TO RESIST AND YOUR PEOPLE WILL CONTINUE TO DIE.
THIS SHIP... AND EVERYONE ON IT...
...ARE NOW THE PROPERTY OF THE *DOMINION*.

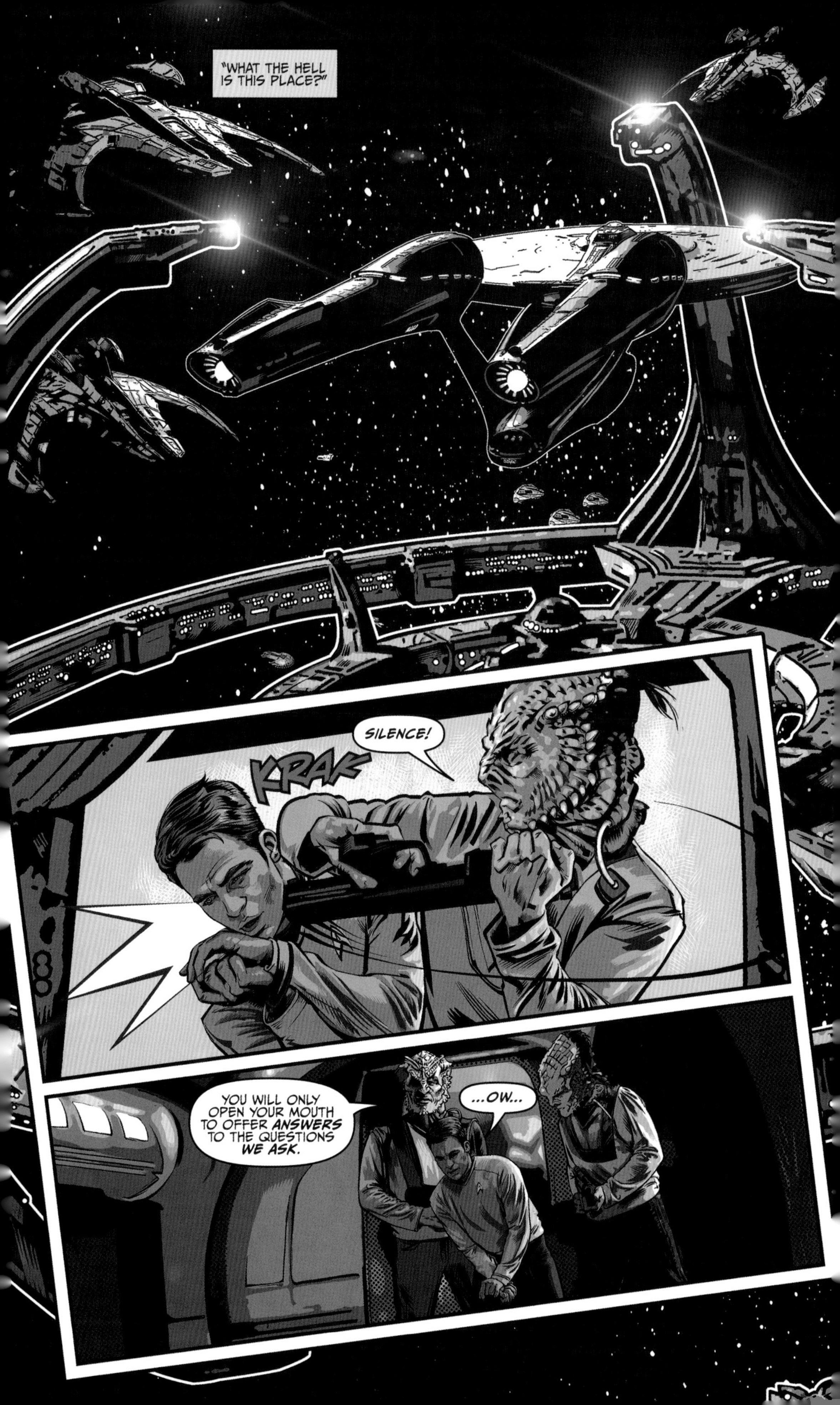

"WHAT THE HELL IS THIS PLACE?"
KRAK
SILENCE!
YOU WILL ONLY OPEN YOUR MOUTH TO OFFER ANSWERS TO THE QUESTIONS WE ASK.
...OW...

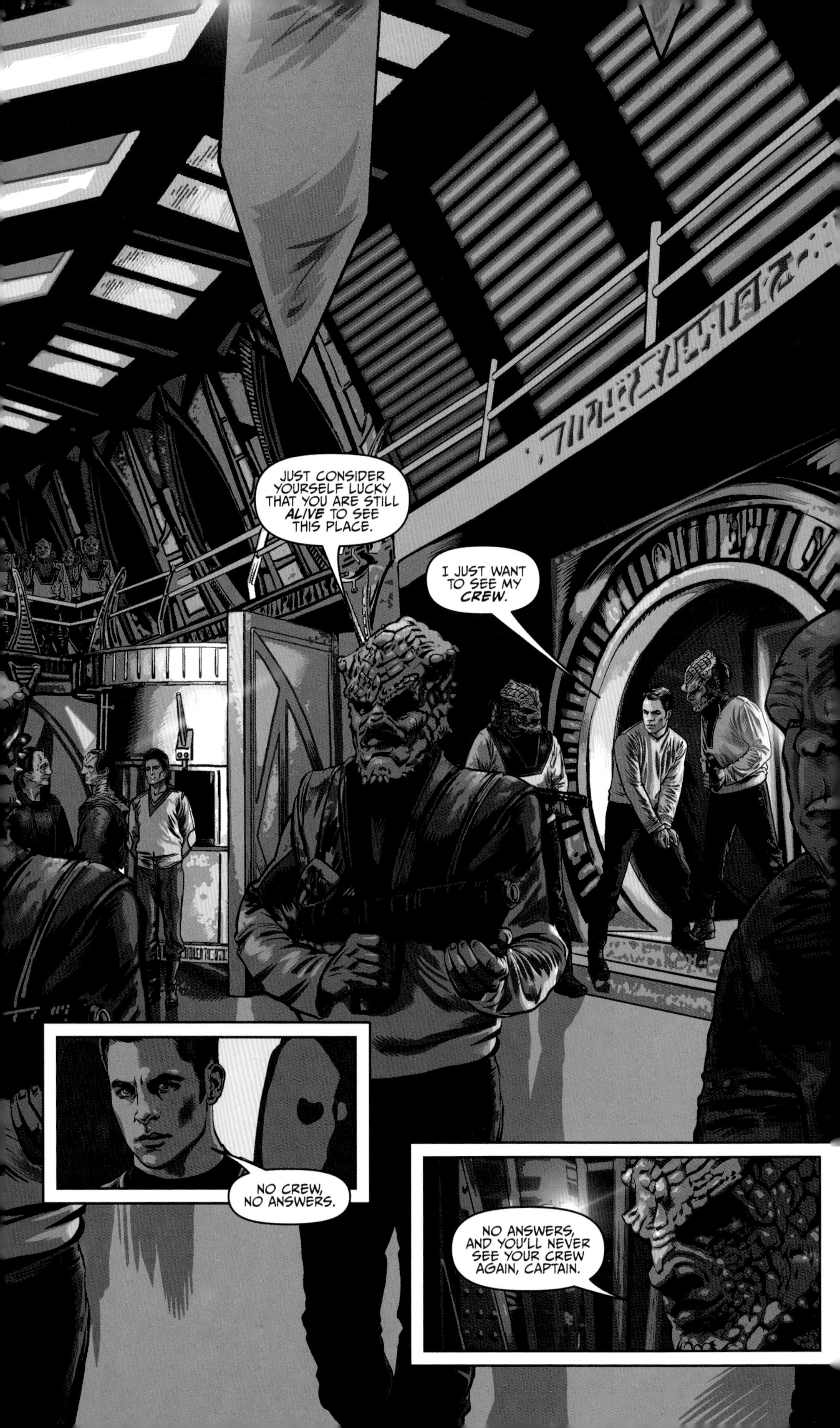
JUST CONSIDER YOURSELF LUCKY THAT YOU ARE STILL *ALIVE* TO SEE THIS PLACE.
I JUST WANT TO SEE MY *CREW*.
NO CREW, NO ANSWERS.
NO ANSWERS, AND YOU'LL NEVER SEE YOUR CREW AGAIN, CAPTAIN.

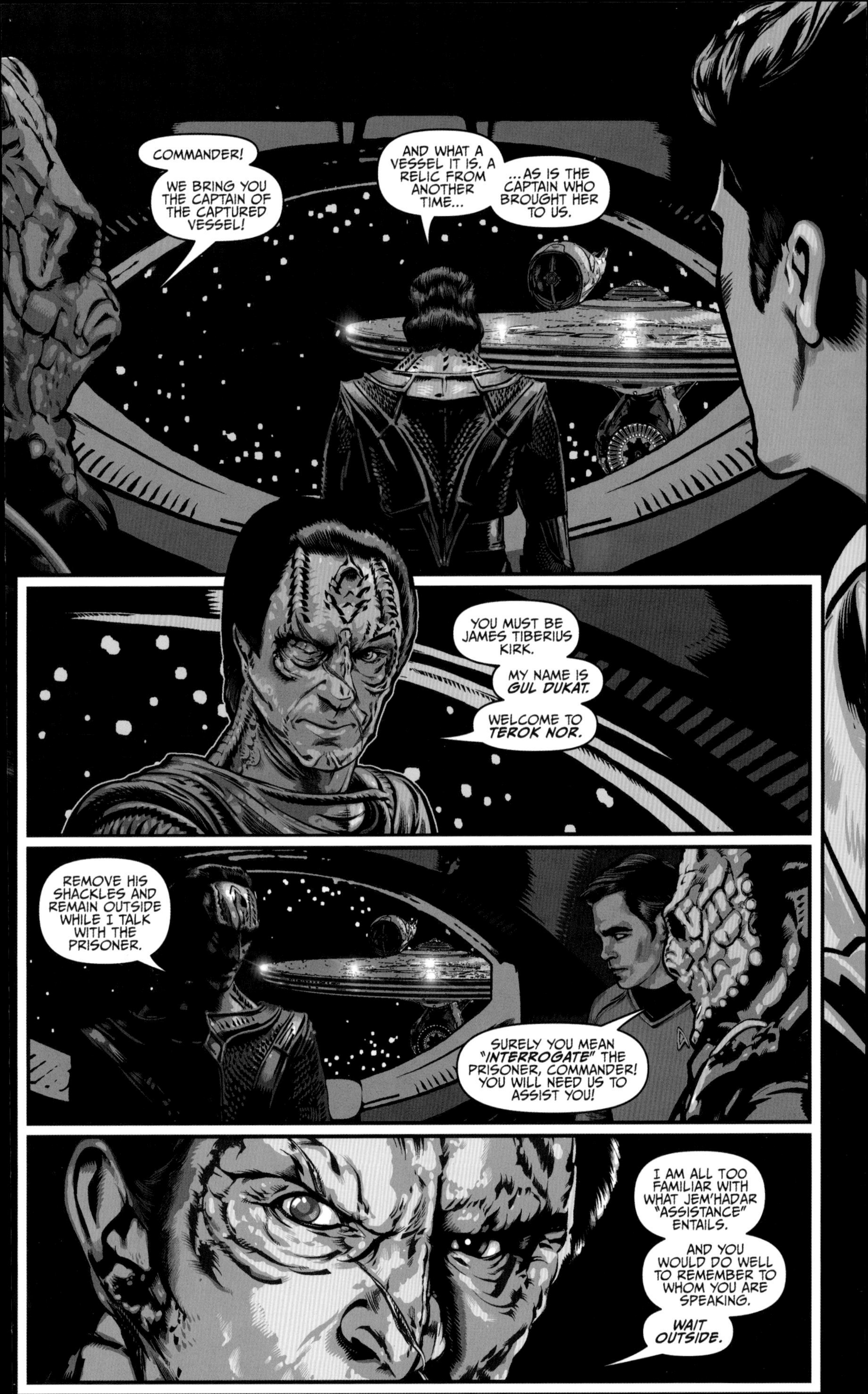
COMMANDER!
WE BRING YOU THE CAPTAIN OF THE CAPTURED VESSEL!
AND WHAT A VESSEL IT IS. A RELIC FROM ANOTHER TIME...
...AS IS THE CAPTAIN WHO BROUGHT HER TO US.
YOU MUST BE JAMES TIBERIUS KIRK.
MY NAME IS *GUL DUKAT.*
WELCOME TO *TEROK NOR.*
REMOVE HIS SHACKLES AND REMAIN OUTSIDE WHILE I TALK WITH THE PRISONER.
SURELY YOU MEAN "*INTERROGATE*" THE PRISONER, COMMANDER! YOU WILL NEED US TO ASSIST YOU!
I AM ALL TOO FAMILIAR WITH WHAT JEM'HADAR "ASSISTANCE" ENTAILS.
AND YOU WOULD DO WELL TO REMEMBER TO WHOM YOU ARE SPEAKING.
WAIT OUTSIDE.

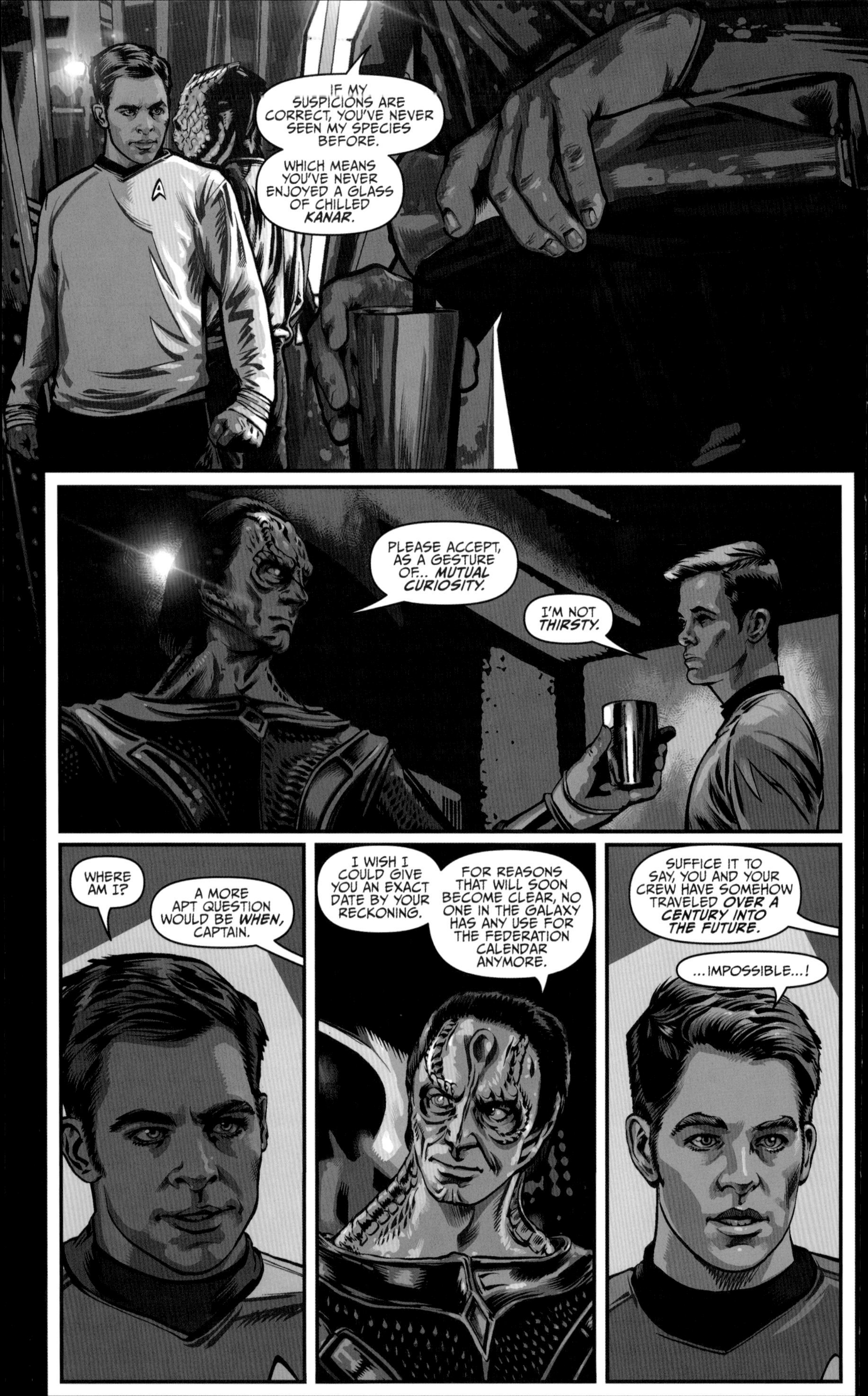
IF MY SUSPICIONS ARE CORRECT, YOU'VE NEVER SEEN MY SPECIES BEFORE.
WHICH MEANS YOU'VE NEVER ENJOYED A GLASS OF CHILLED *KANAR*.
PLEASE ACCEPT, AS A GESTURE OF... *MUTUAL CURIOSITY.*
I'M NOT *THIRSTY.*
WHERE AM I?
A MORE APT QUESTION WOULD BE *WHEN*, CAPTAIN.
I WISH I COULD GIVE YOU AN EXACT DATE BY YOUR RECKONING.
FOR REASONS THAT WILL SOON BECOME CLEAR, NO ONE IN THE GALAXY HAS ANY USE FOR THE FEDERATION CALENDAR ANYMORE.
SUFFICE IT TO SAY, YOU AND YOUR CREW HAVE SOMEHOW TRAVELED *OVER A CENTURY INTO THE FUTURE.*
...IMPOSSIBLE...!

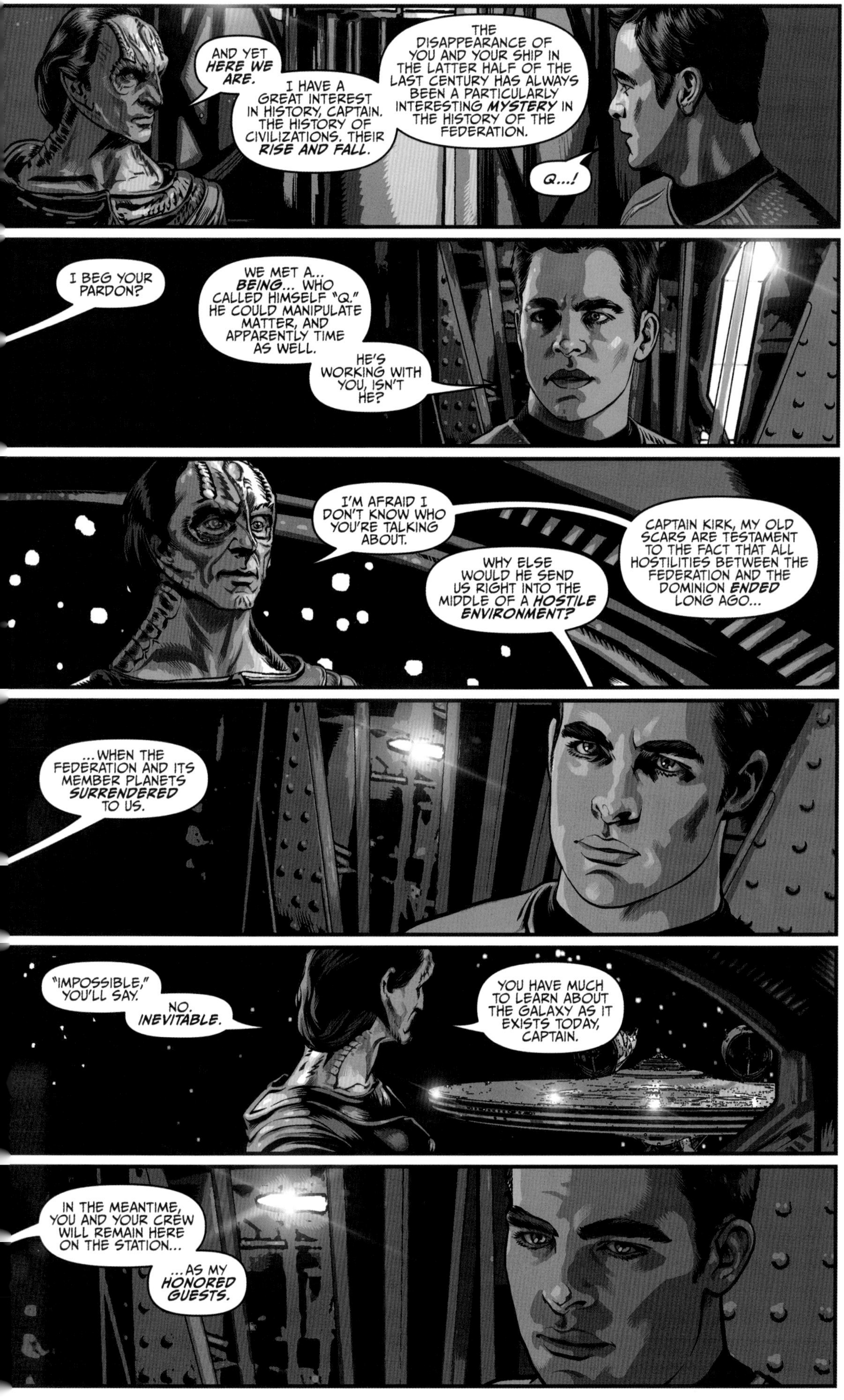
AND YET HERE WE ARE.
I HAVE A GREAT INTEREST IN HISTORY, CAPTAIN. THE HISTORY OF CIVILIZATIONS. THEIR RISE AND FALL.
THE DISAPPEARANCE OF YOU AND YOUR SHIP IN THE LATTER HALF OF THE LAST CENTURY HAS ALWAYS BEEN A PARTICULARLY INTERESTING MYSTERY IN THE HISTORY OF THE FEDERATION.
Q...!
I BEG YOUR PARDON?
WE MET A... BEING... WHO CALLED HIMSELF "Q." HE COULD MANIPULATE MATTER, AND APPARENTLY TIME AS WELL.
HE'S WORKING WITH YOU, ISN'T HE?
I'M AFRAID I DON'T KNOW WHO YOU'RE TALKING ABOUT.
WHY ELSE WOULD HE SEND US RIGHT INTO THE MIDDLE OF A HOSTILE ENVIRONMENT?
CAPTAIN KIRK, MY OLD SCARS ARE TESTAMENT TO THE FACT THAT ALL HOSTILITIES BETWEEN THE FEDERATION AND THE DOMINION ENDED LONG AGO...
...WHEN THE FEDERATION AND ITS MEMBER PLANETS SURRENDERED TO US.
"IMPOSSIBLE," YOU'LL SAY.
NO. INEVITABLE.
YOU HAVE MUCH TO LEARN ABOUT THE GALAXY AS IT EXISTS TODAY, CAPTAIN.
IN THE MEANTIME, YOU AND YOUR CREW WILL REMAIN HERE ON THE STATION...
...AS MY HONORED GUESTS.

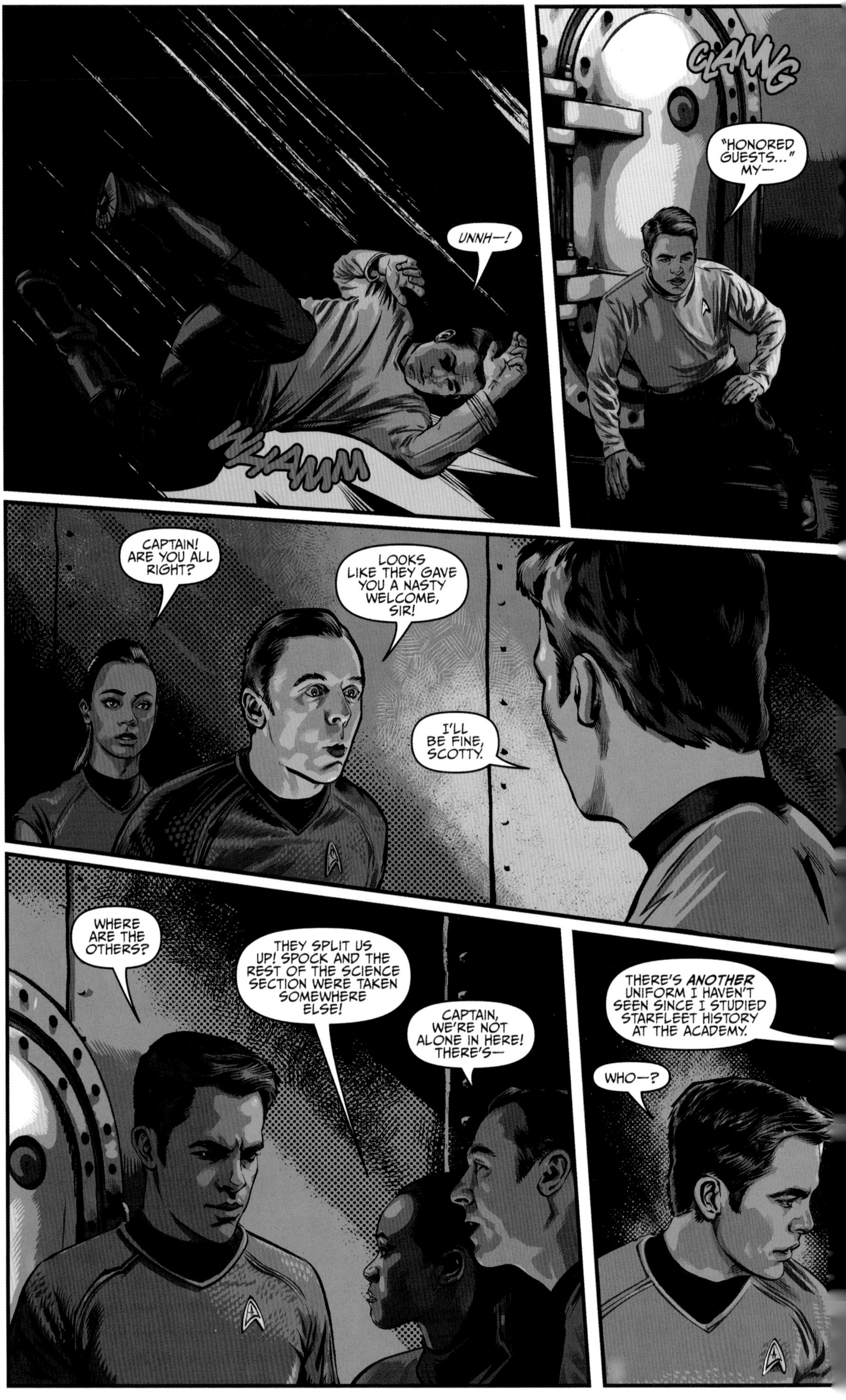
UNNH—!
WHAMM
CLANNG
"HONORED GUESTS..." MY—
CAPTAIN! ARE YOU ALL RIGHT?
LOOKS LIKE THEY GAVE YOU A NASTY WELCOME, SIR!
I'LL BE FINE, SCOTTY.
WHERE ARE THE OTHERS?
THEY SPLIT US UP! SPOCK AND THE REST OF THE SCIENCE SECTION WERE TAKEN SOMEWHERE ELSE!
CAPTAIN, WE'RE NOT ALONE IN HERE! THERE'S—
THERE'S *ANOTHER* UNIFORM I HAVEN'T SEEN SINCE I STUDIED STARFLEET HISTORY AT THE ACADEMY.
WHO—?

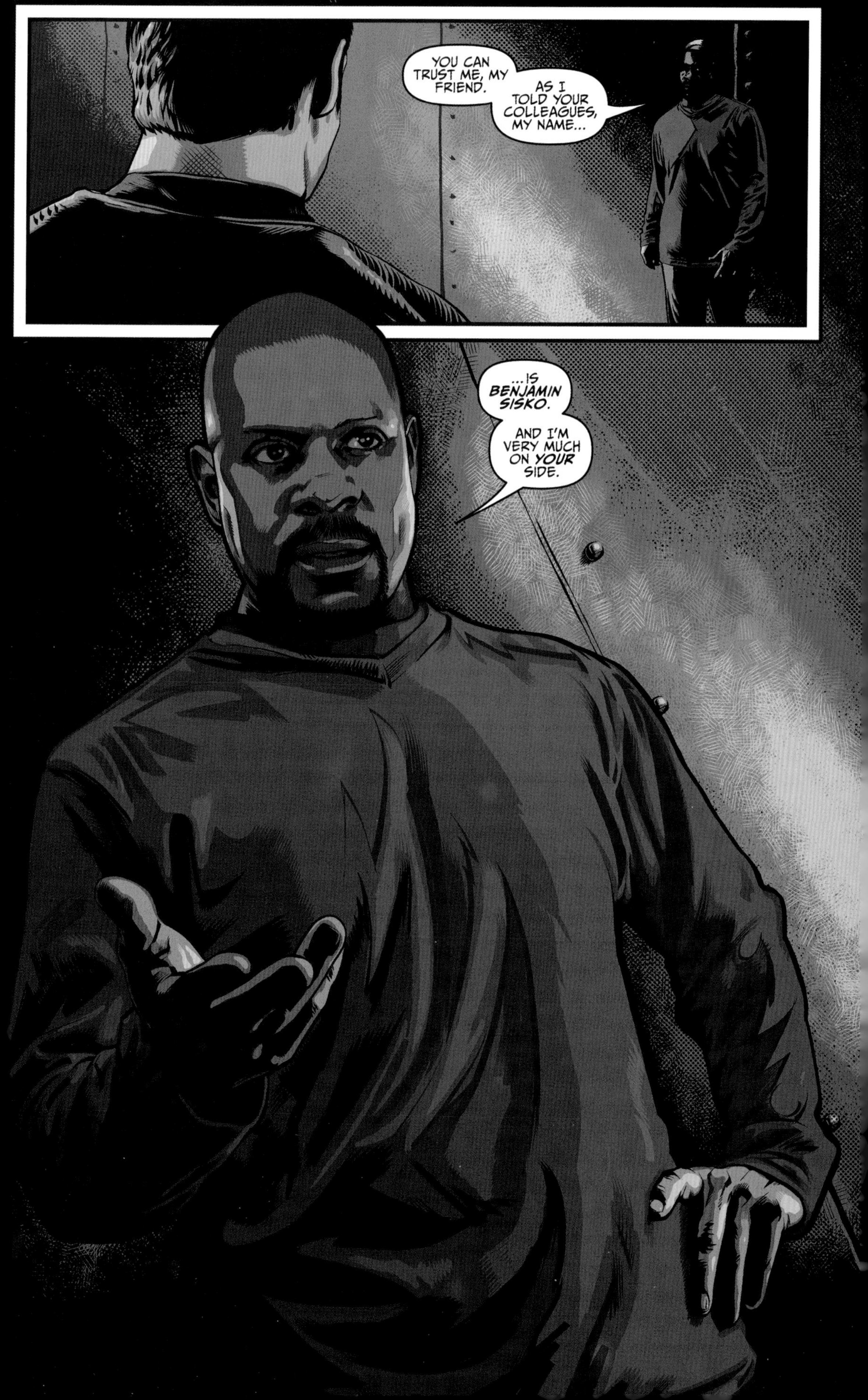

YOU CAN TRUST ME, MY FRIEND.
AS I TOLD YOUR COLLEAGUES, MY NAME...
...IS *BENJAMIN SISKO*.
AND I'M VERY MUCH ON *YOUR* SIDE.

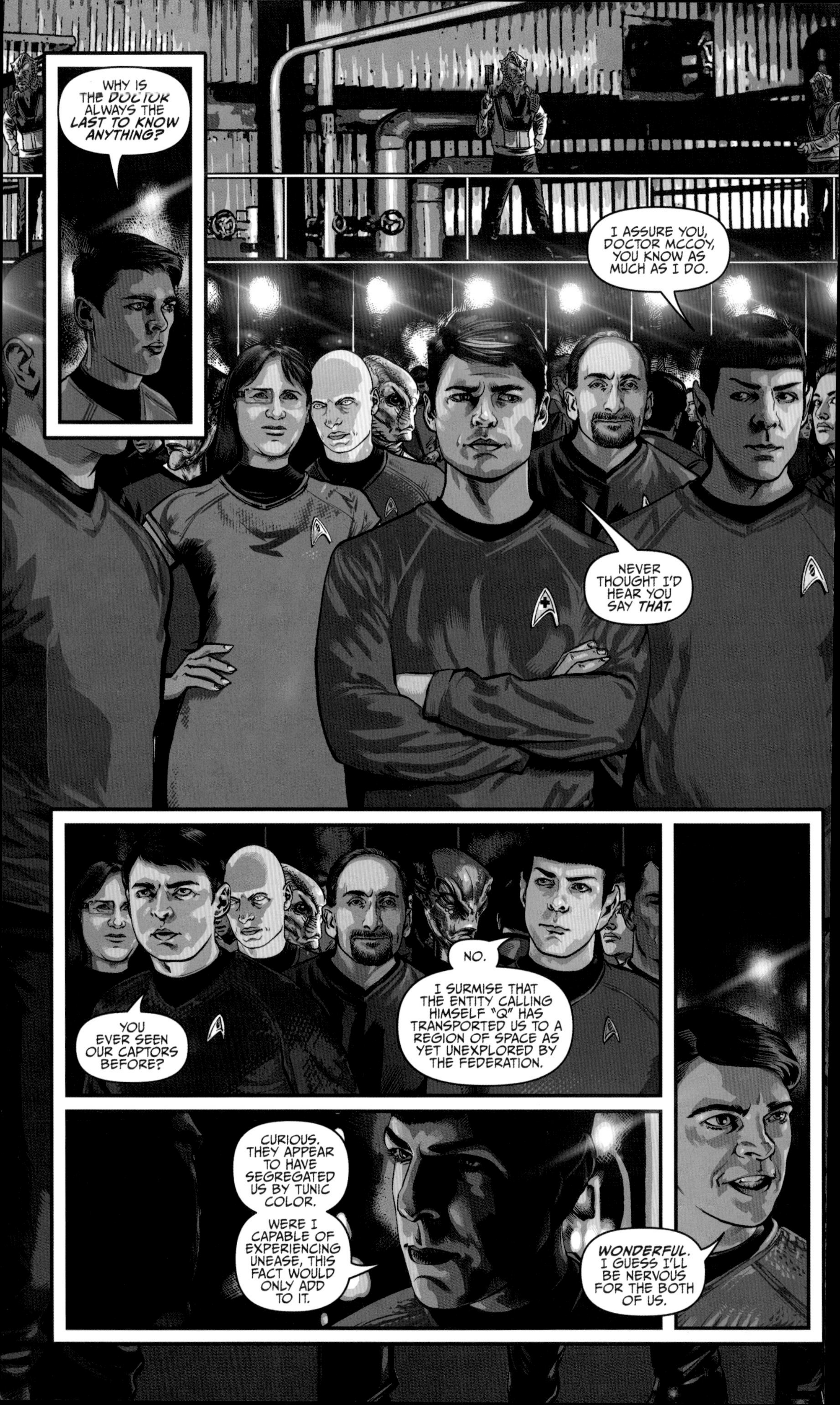
WHY IS THE DOCTOR ALWAYS THE LAST TO KNOW ANYTHING?
I ASSURE YOU, DOCTOR MCCOY, YOU KNOW AS MUCH AS I DO.
NEVER THOUGHT I'D HEAR YOU SAY THAT.
YOU EVER SEEN OUR CAPTORS BEFORE?
NO.
I SURMISE THAT THE ENTITY CALLING HIMSELF "Q" HAS TRANSPORTED US TO A REGION OF SPACE AS YET UNEXPLORED BY THE FEDERATION.
CURIOUS. THEY APPEAR TO HAVE SEGREGATED US BY TUNIC COLOR.
WERE I CAPABLE OF EXPERIENCING UNEASE, THIS FACT WOULD ONLY ADD TO IT.
WONDERFUL. I GUESS I'LL BE NERVOUS FOR THE BOTH OF US.

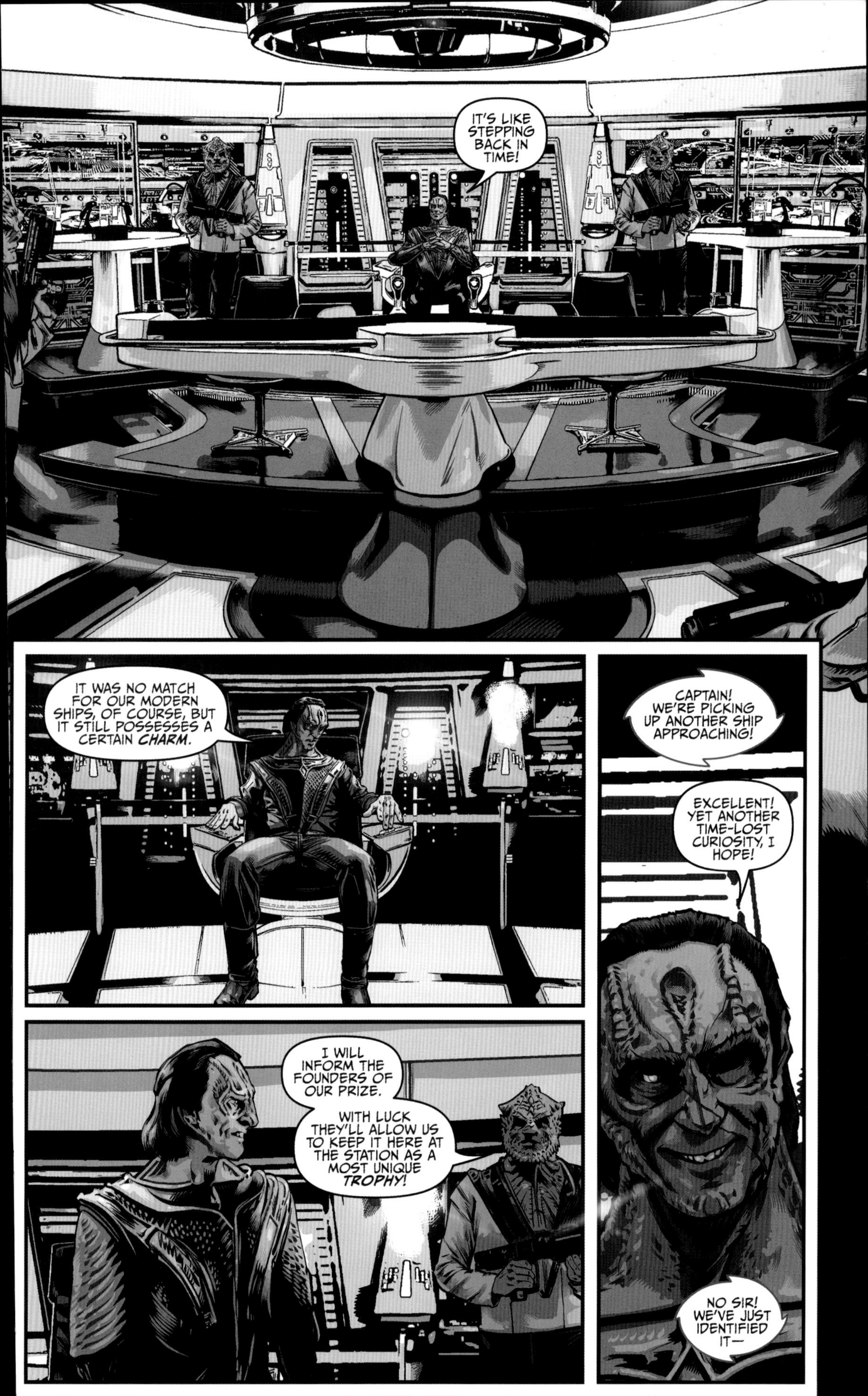
IT'S LIKE STEPPING BACK IN TIME!
IT WAS NO MATCH FOR OUR MODERN SHIPS, OF COURSE, BUT IT STILL POSSESSES A CERTAIN CHARM.
I WILL INFORM THE FOUNDERS OF OUR PRIZE.
WITH LUCK THEY'LL ALLOW US TO KEEP IT HERE AT THE STATION AS A MOST UNIQUE TROPHY!
CAPTAIN! WE'RE PICKING UP ANOTHER SHIP APPROACHING!
EXCELLENT! YET ANOTHER TIME-LOST CURIOSITY, I HOPE!
NO SIR! WE'VE JUST IDENTIFIED IT—

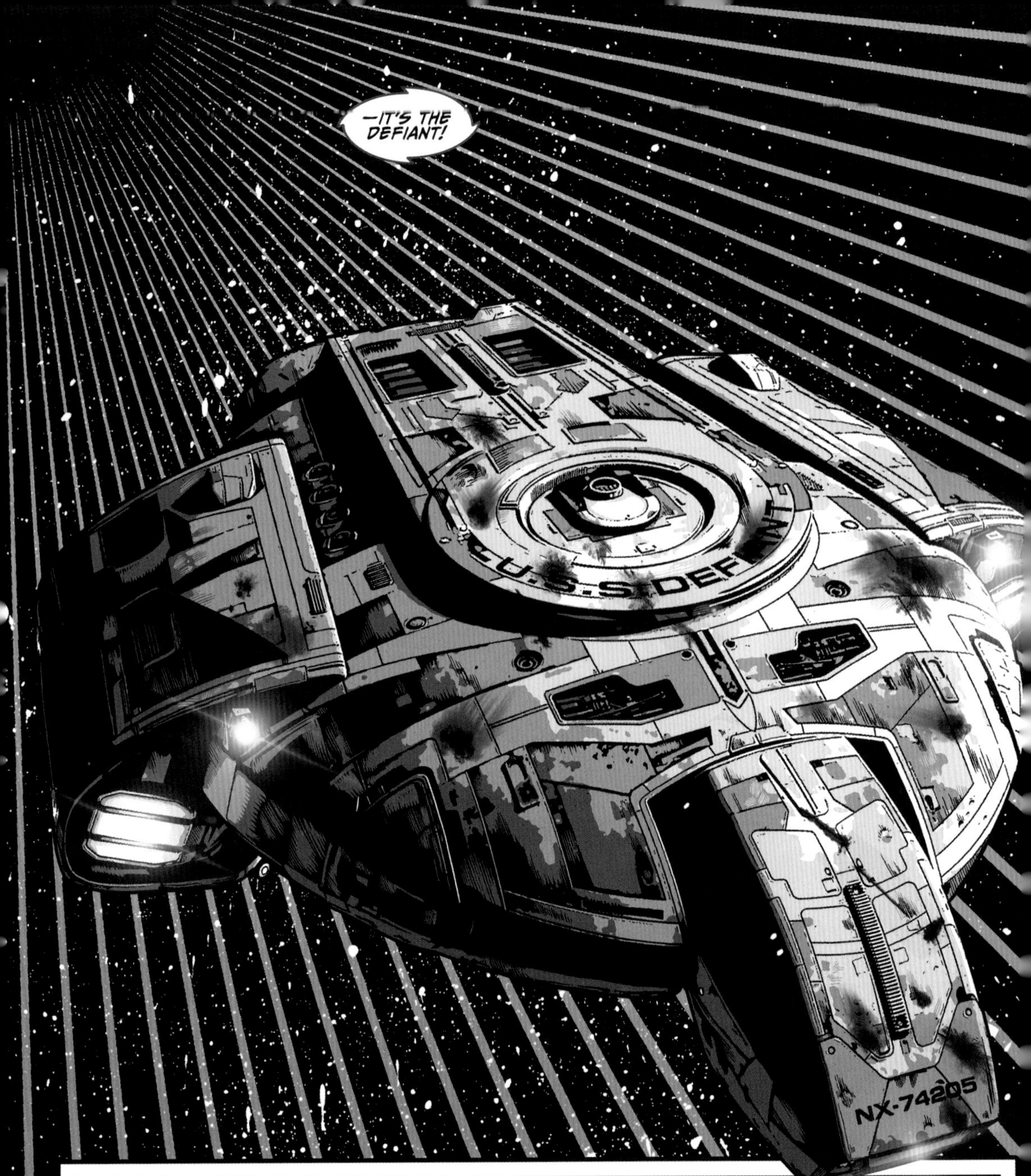
—IT'S THE DEFIANT!
U.S.S. DEF
NX-74205
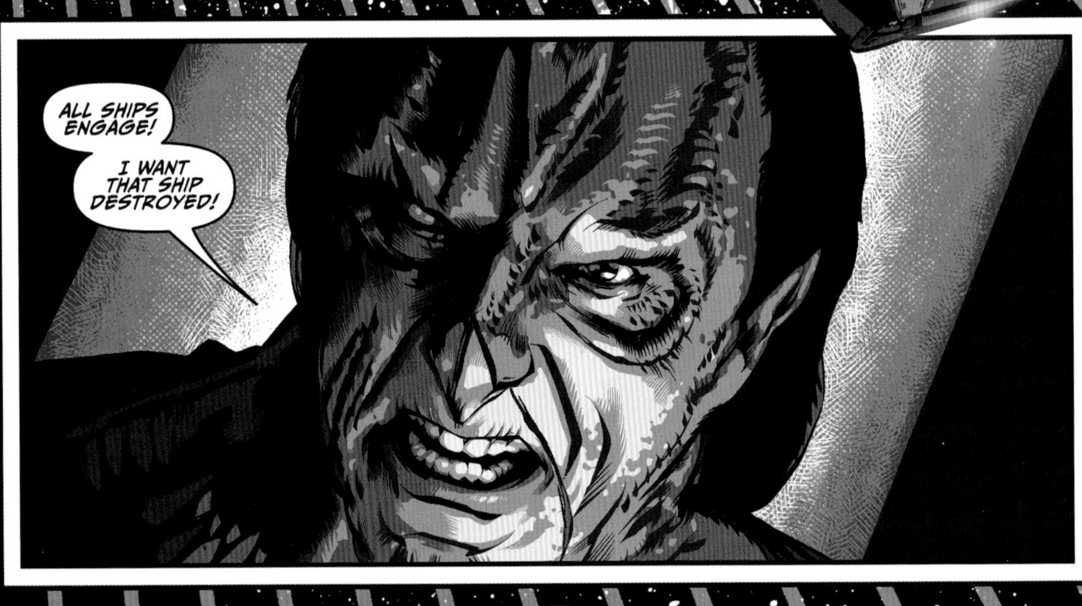
ALL SHIPS ENGAGE!
I WANT THAT SHIP DESTROYED!

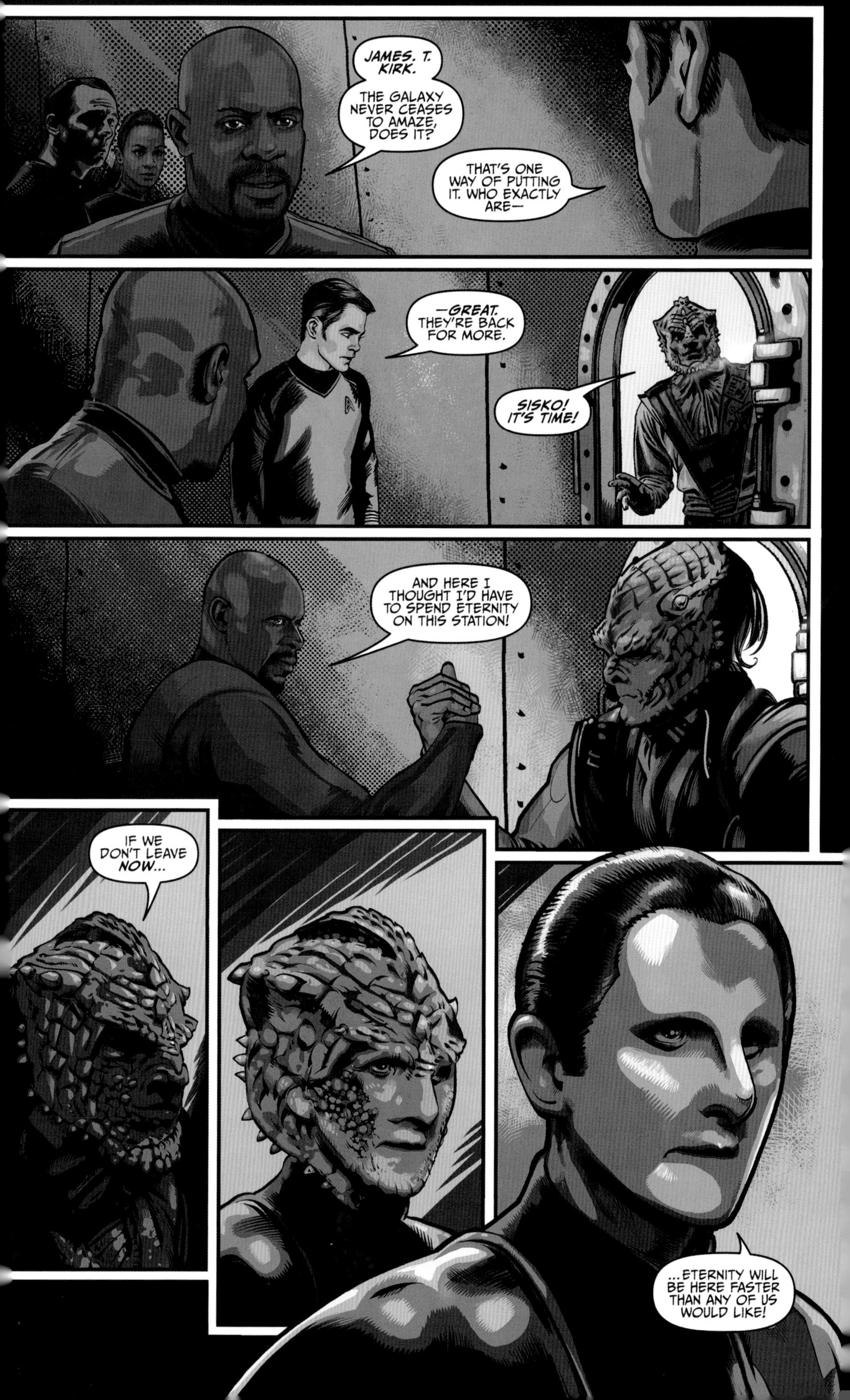
JAMES. T. KIRK.
THE GALAXY NEVER CEASES TO AMAZE, DOES IT?
THAT'S ONE WAY OF PUTTING IT. WHO EXACTLY ARE—
—GREAT. THEY'RE BACK FOR MORE.
SISKO! IT'S TIME!
AND HERE I THOUGHT I'D HAVE TO SPEND ETERNITY ON THIS STATION!
IF WE DON'T LEAVE NOW...
...ETERNITY WILL BE HERE FASTER THAN ANY OF US WOULD LIKE!

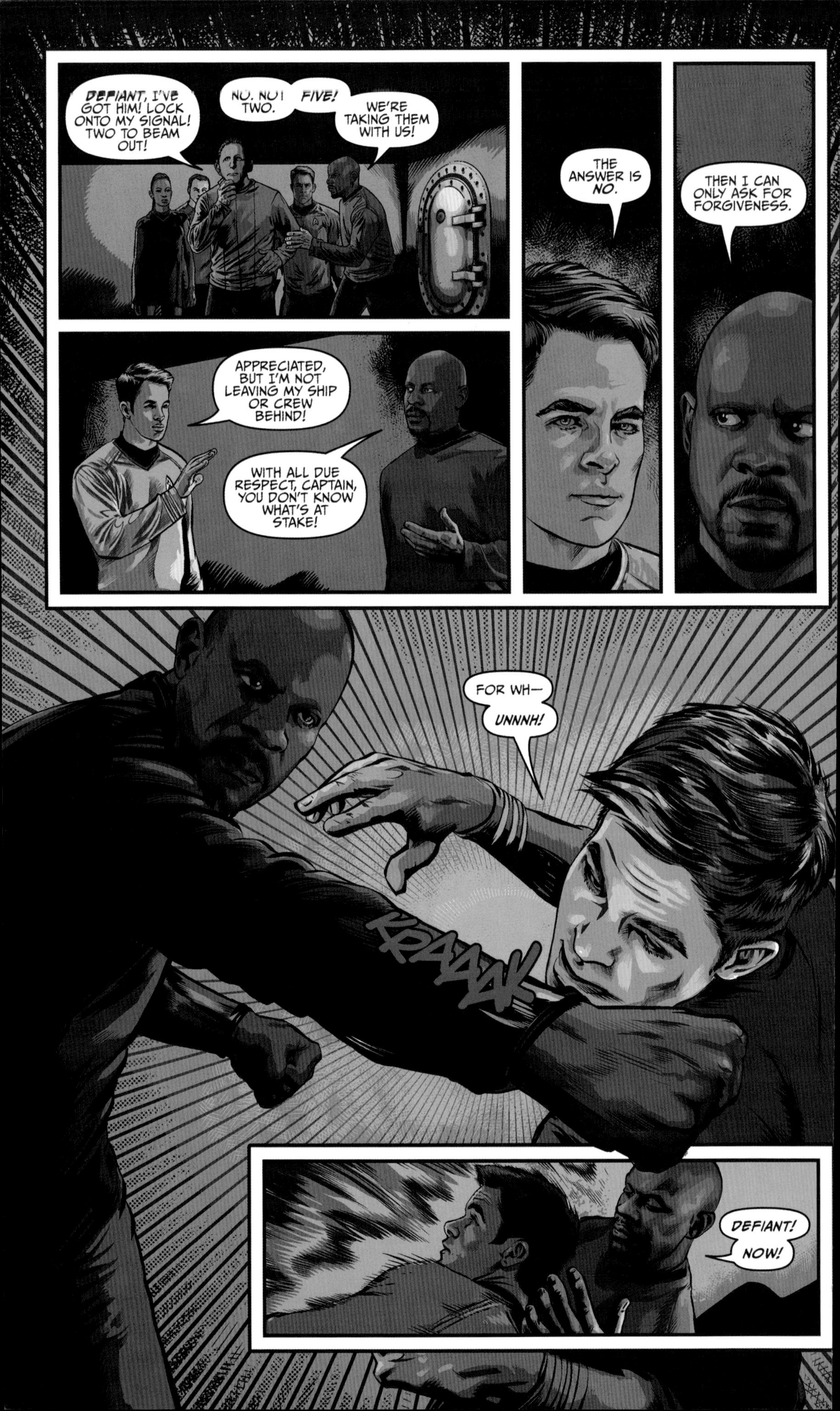

DEFIANT, I'VE GOT HIM! LOCK ONTO MY SIGNAL! TWO TO BEAM OUT!
NO. NOT TWO.
FIVE!
WE'RE TAKING THEM WITH US!
THE ANSWER IS NO.
THEN I CAN ONLY ASK FOR FORGIVENESS.
APPRECIATED, BUT I'M NOT LEAVING MY SHIP OR CREW BEHIND!
WITH ALL DUE RESPECT, CAPTAIN, YOU DON'T KNOW WHAT'S AT STAKE!
FOR WH—
UNNNH!
KRAAAK
DEFIANT!
NOW!

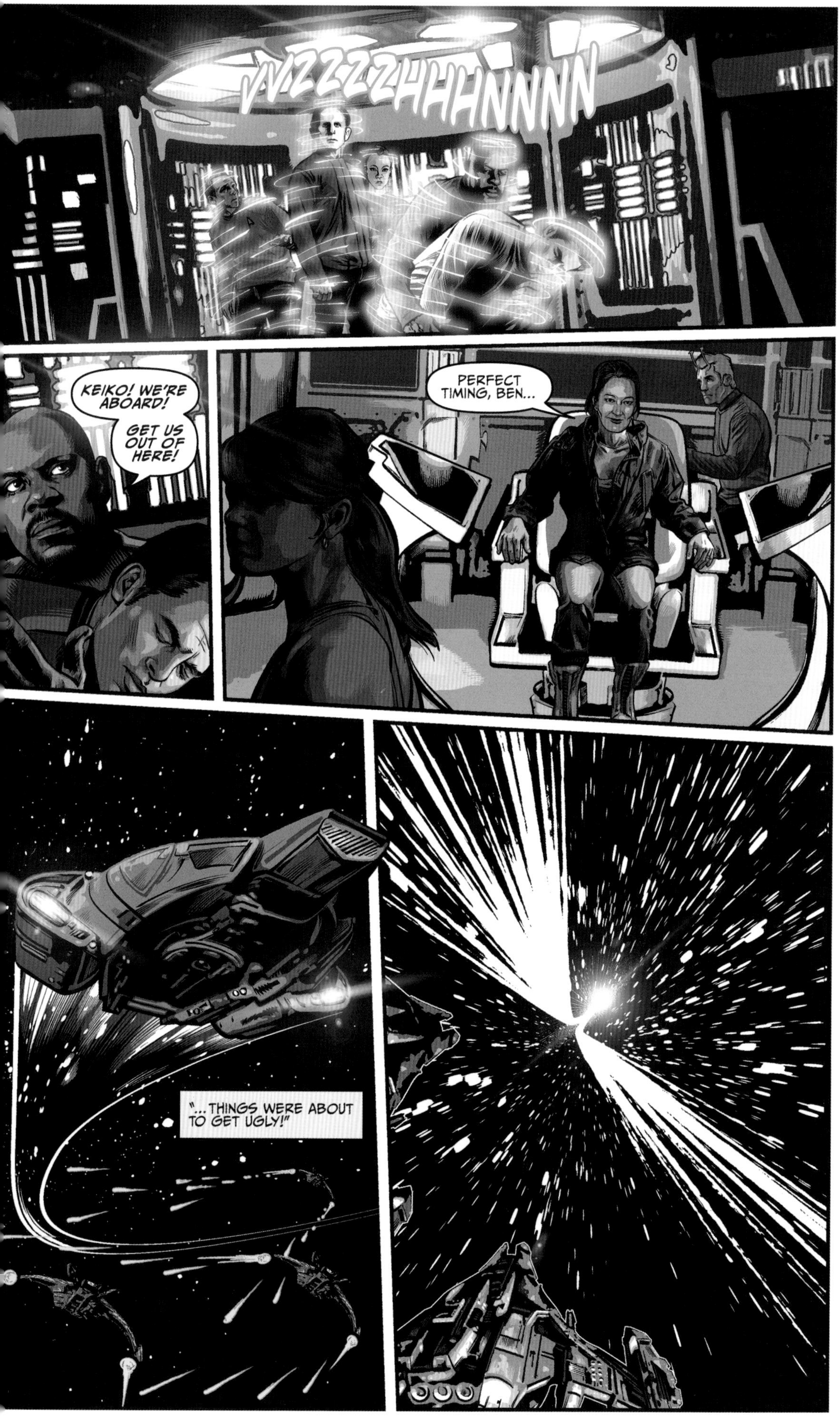
VVZZZZZHHHNNNNN
KEIKO! WE'RE ABOARD!
GET US OUT OF HERE!
PERFECT TIMING, BEN...
"...THINGS WERE ABOUT TO GET UGLY!"

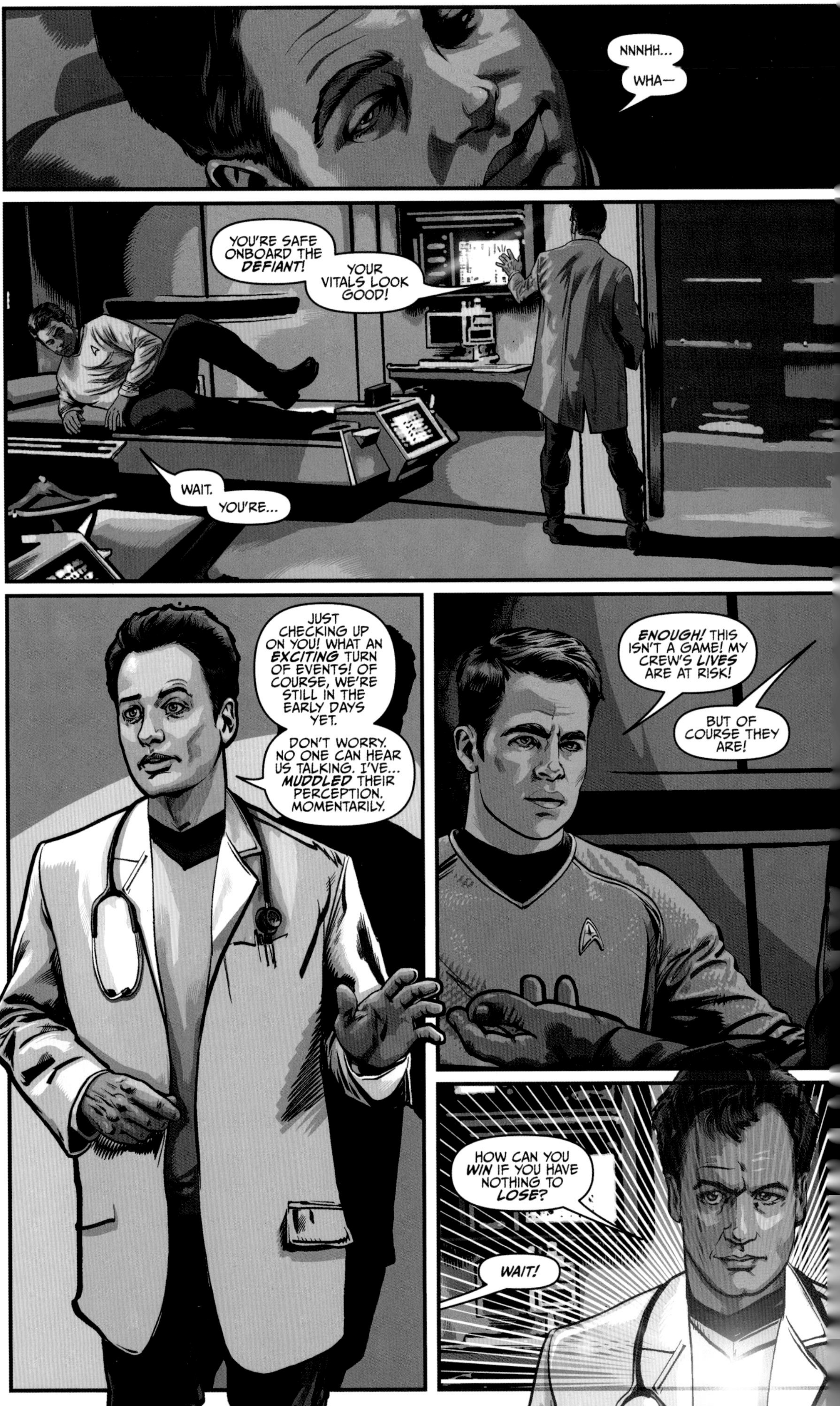
NNNHH...
WHA—
YOU'RE SAFE ONBOARD THE DEFIANT!
YOUR VITALS LOOK GOOD!
WAIT.
YOU'RE...
JUST CHECKING UP ON YOU! WHAT AN EXCITING TURN OF EVENTS! OF COURSE, WE'RE STILL IN THE EARLY DAYS YET.
DON'T WORRY. NO ONE CAN HEAR US TALKING. I'VE... MUDDLED THEIR PERCEPTION. MOMENTARILY.
ENOUGH! THIS ISN'T A GAME! MY CREW'S LIVES ARE AT RISK!
BUT OF COURSE THEY ARE!
HOW CAN YOU WIN IF YOU HAVE NOTHING TO LOSE?
WAIT!

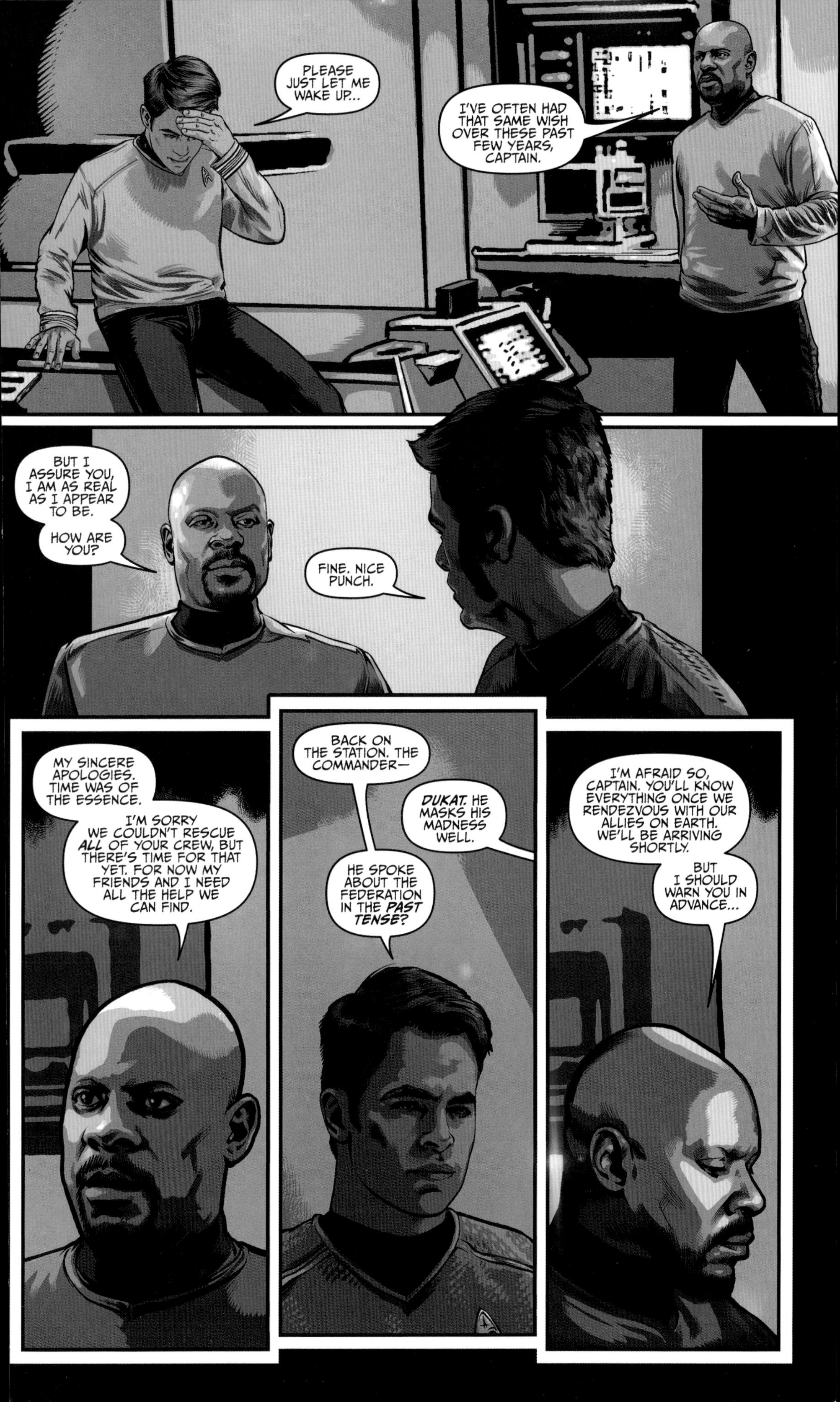
PLEASE JUST LET ME WAKE UP...
I'VE OFTEN HAD THAT SAME WISH OVER THESE PAST FEW YEARS, CAPTAIN.
BUT I ASSURE YOU, I AM AS REAL AS I APPEAR TO BE.
HOW ARE YOU?
FINE. NICE PUNCH.
MY SINCERE APOLOGIES. TIME WAS OF THE ESSENCE.
I'M SORRY WE COULDN'T RESCUE ALL OF YOUR CREW, BUT THERE'S TIME FOR THAT YET. FOR NOW MY FRIENDS AND I NEED ALL THE HELP WE CAN FIND.
BACK ON THE STATION. THE COMMANDER—
DUKAT. HE MASKS HIS MADNESS WELL.
HE SPOKE ABOUT THE FEDERATION IN THE PAST TENSE?
I'M AFRAID SO, CAPTAIN. YOU'LL KNOW EVERYTHING ONCE WE RENDEZVOUS WITH OUR ALLIES ON EARTH. WE'LL BE ARRIVING SHORTLY.
BUT I SHOULD WARN YOU IN ADVANCE...

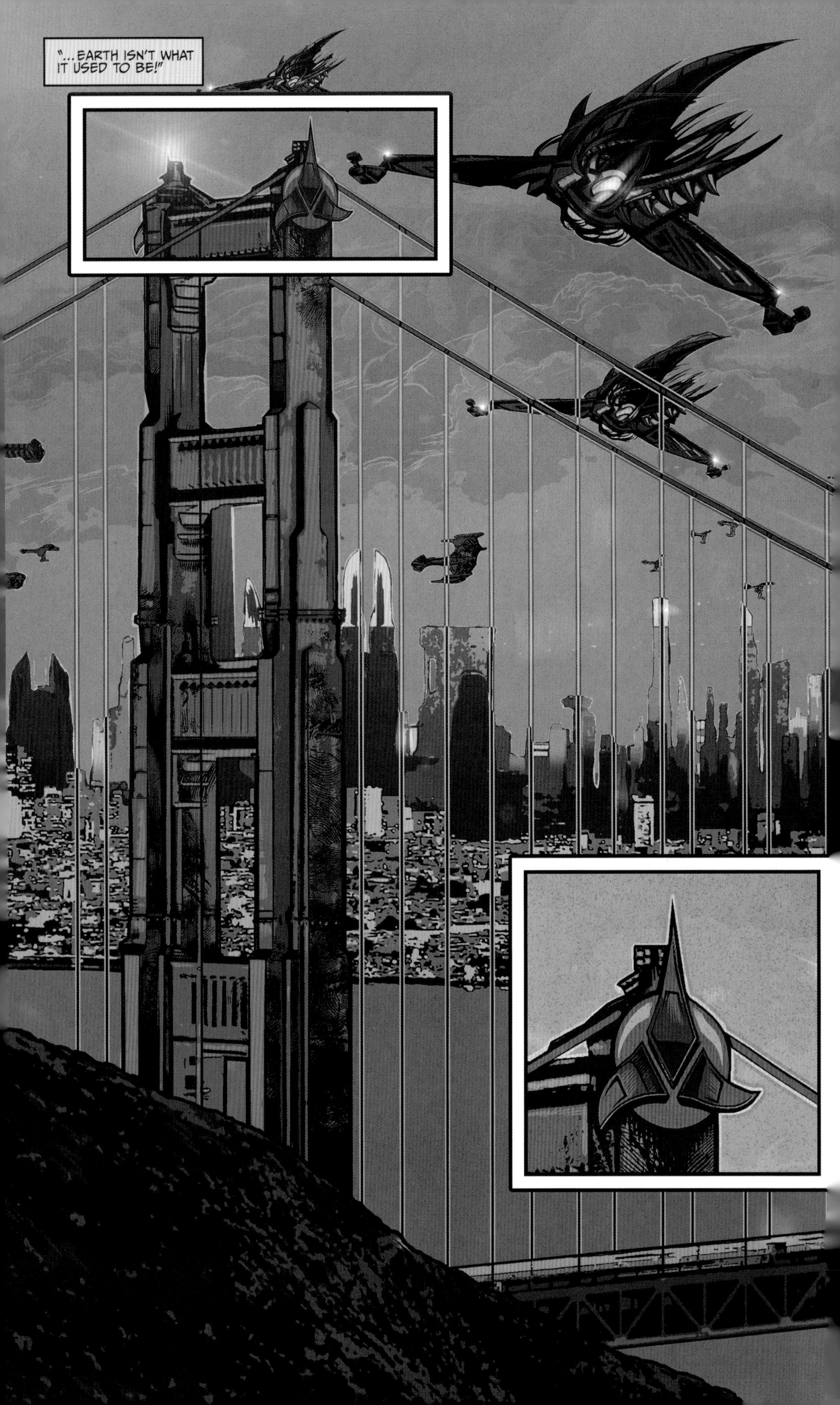

"...EARTH ISN'T WHAT IT USED TO BE!"

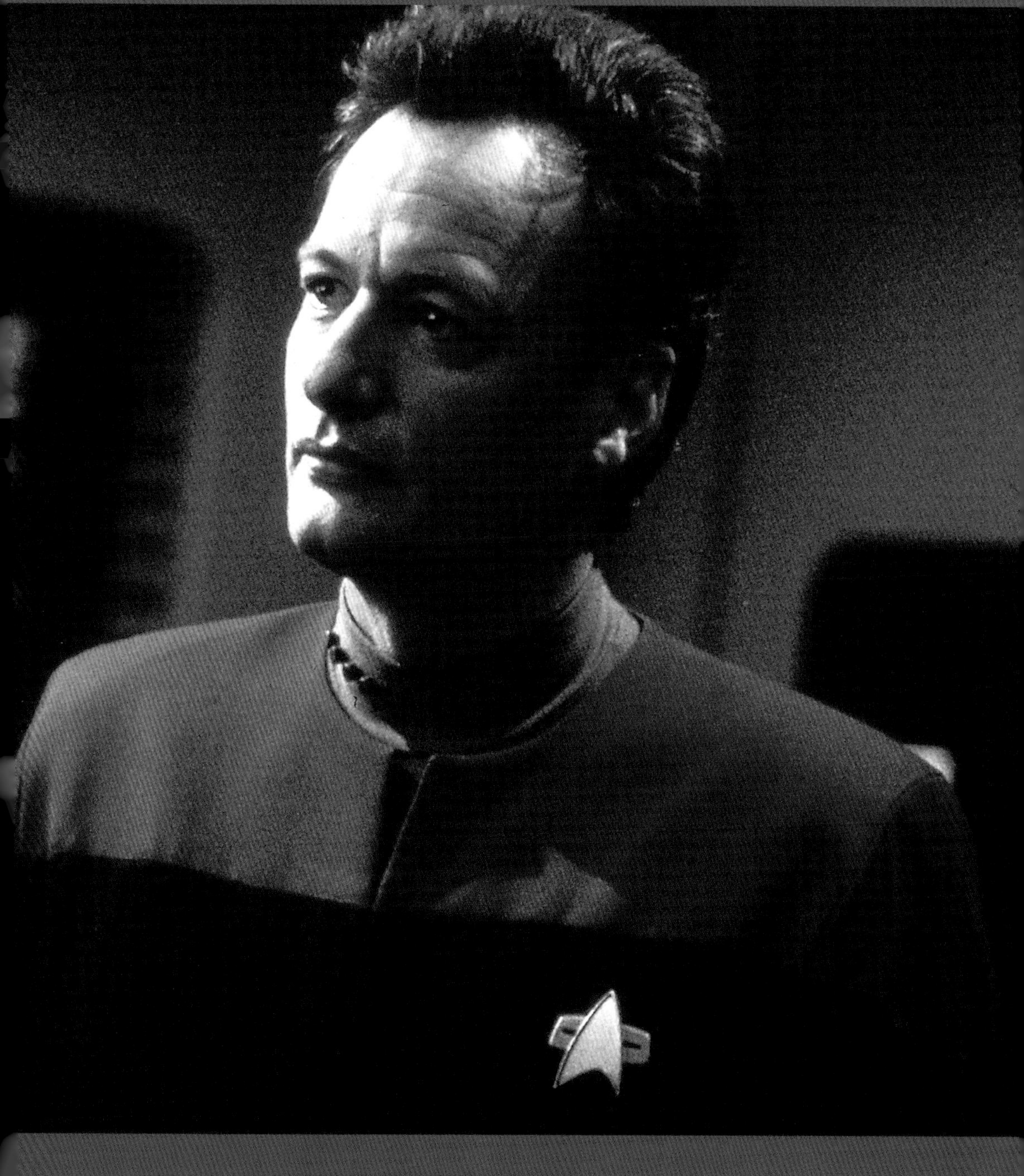

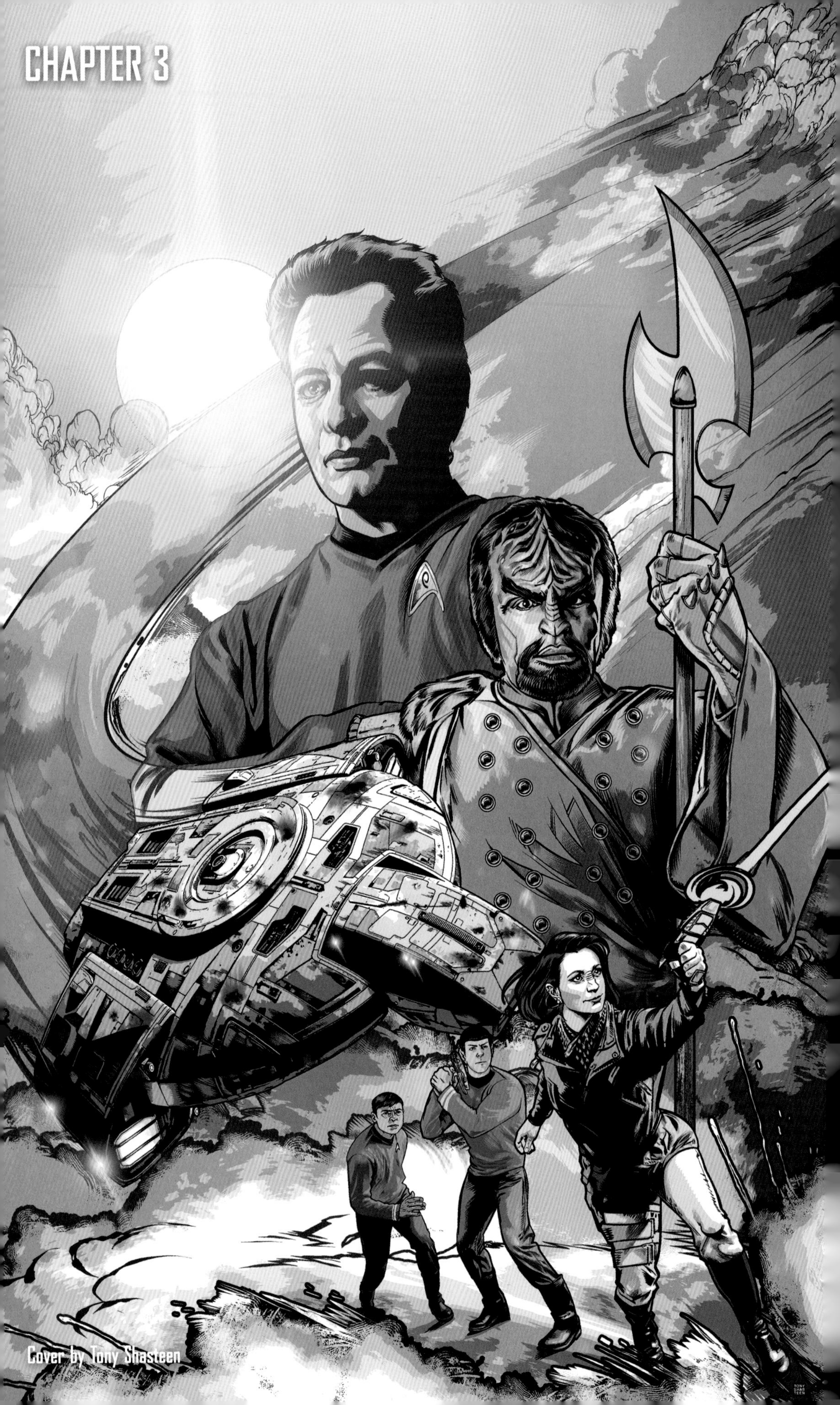
CHAPTER 3
Cover by Tony Shasteen

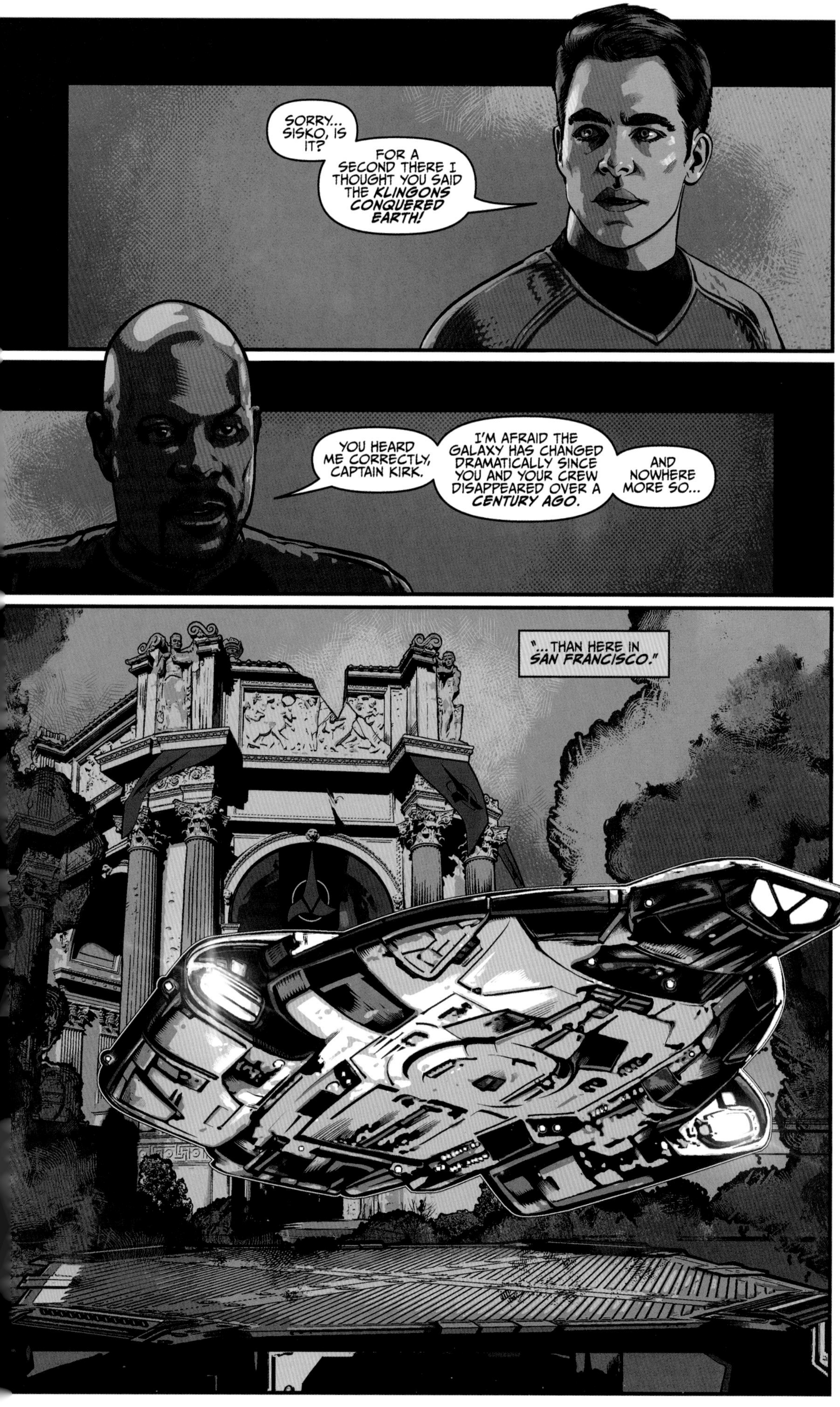
SORRY... SISKO, IS IT?
FOR A SECOND THERE I THOUGHT YOU SAID THE KLINGONS CONQUERED EARTH!
YOU HEARD ME CORRECTLY, CAPTAIN KIRK.
I'M AFRAID THE GALAXY HAS CHANGED DRAMATICALLY SINCE YOU AND YOUR CREW DISAPPEARED OVER A CENTURY AGO.
AND NOWHERE MORE SO...
"...THAN HERE IN SAN FRANCISCO."

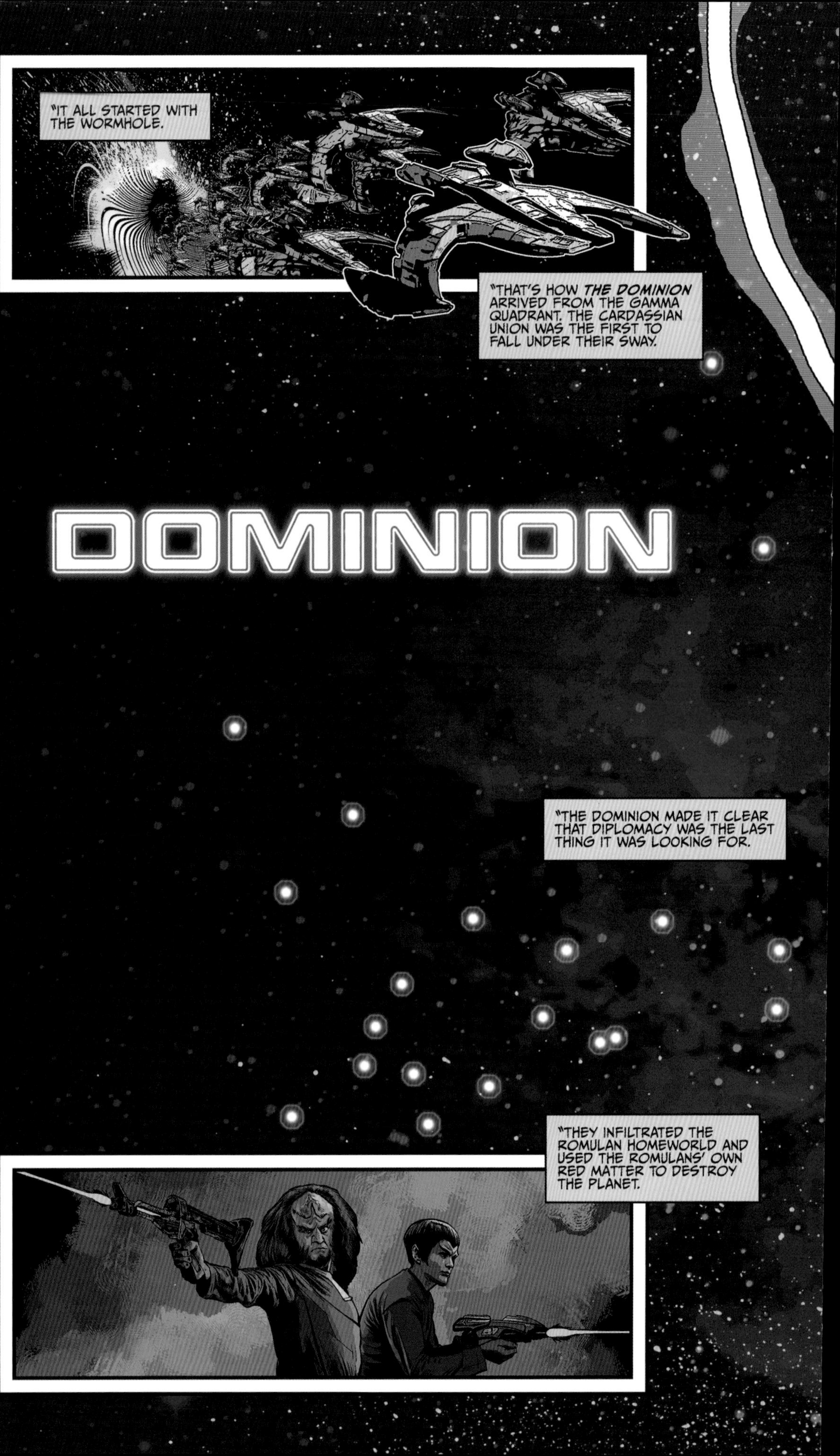

"IT ALL STARTED WITH THE WORMHOLE.
"THAT'S HOW *THE DOMINION* ARRIVED FROM THE GAMMA QUADRANT. THE CARDASSIAN UNION WAS THE FIRST TO FALL UNDER THEIR SWAY.
DOMINION
"THE DOMINION MADE IT CLEAR THAT DIPLOMACY WAS THE LAST THING IT WAS LOOKING FOR.
"THEY INFILTRATED THE ROMULAN HOMEWORLD AND USED THE ROMULANS' OWN RED MATTER TO DESTROY THE PLANET.

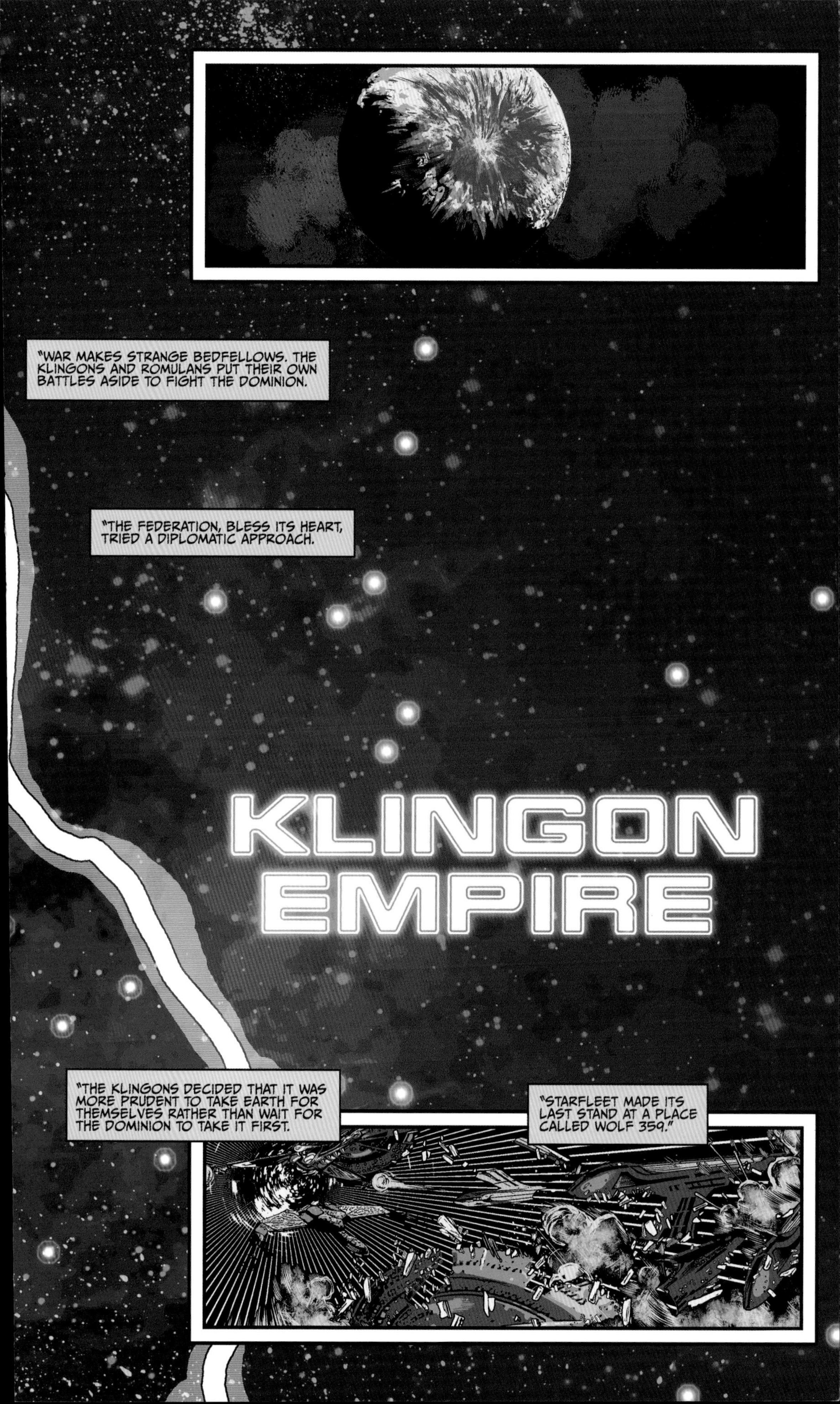
"WAR MAKES STRANGE BEDFELLOWS. THE KLINGONS AND ROMULANS PUT THEIR OWN BATTLES ASIDE TO FIGHT THE DOMINION.
"THE FEDERATION, BLESS ITS HEART, TRIED A DIPLOMATIC APPROACH.
KLINGON EMPIRE
"THE KLINGONS DECIDED THAT IT WAS MORE PRUDENT TO TAKE EARTH FOR THEMSELVES RATHER THAN WAIT FOR THE DOMINION TO TAKE IT FIRST.
"STARFLEET MADE ITS LAST STAND AT A PLACE CALLED WOLF 359."

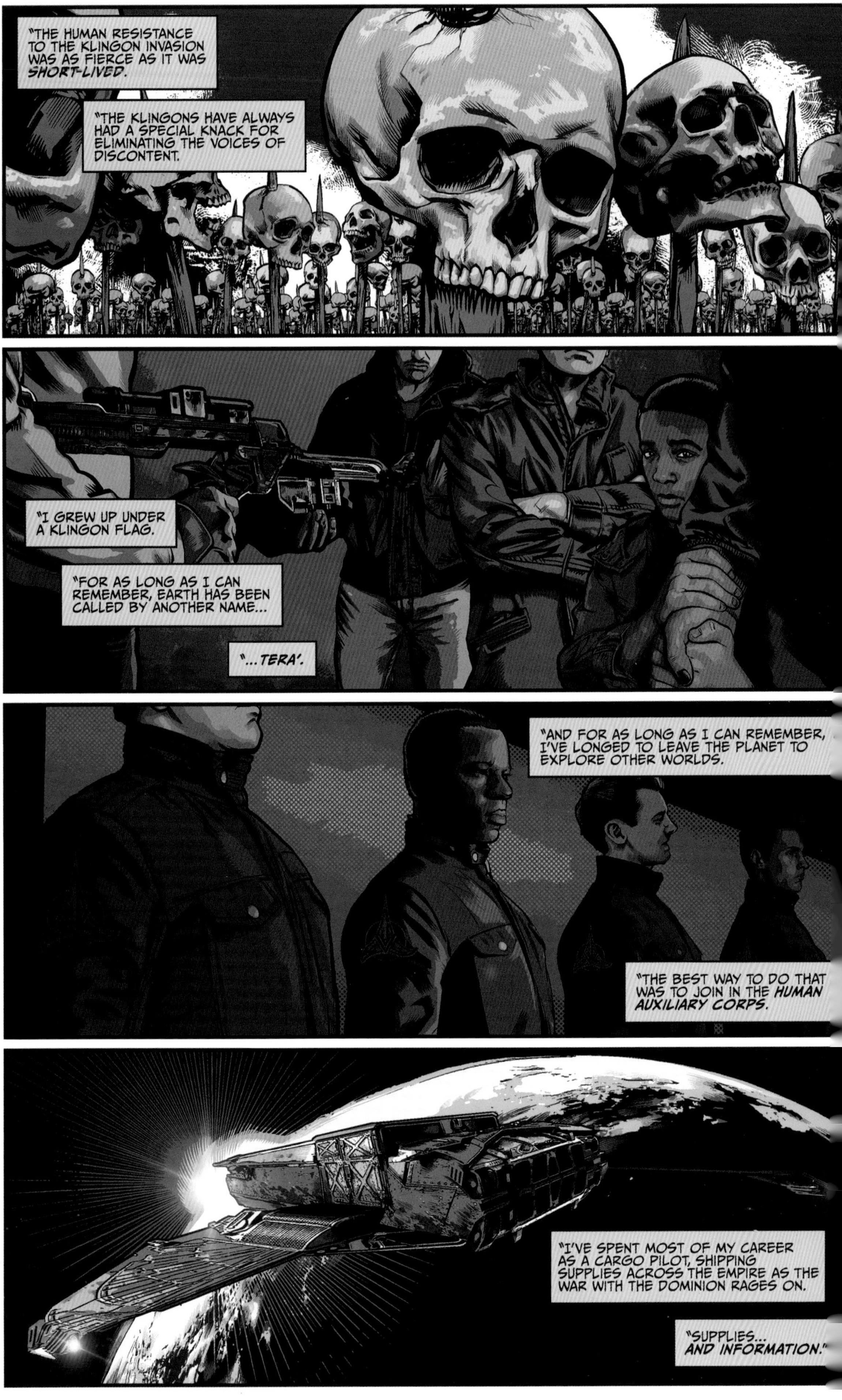
"THE HUMAN RESISTANCE TO THE KLINGON INVASION WAS AS FIERCE AS IT WAS SHORT-LIVED.
"THE KLINGONS HAVE ALWAYS HAD A SPECIAL KNACK FOR ELIMINATING THE VOICES OF DISCONTENT.
"I GREW UP UNDER A KLINGON FLAG.
"FOR AS LONG AS I CAN REMEMBER, EARTH HAS BEEN CALLED BY ANOTHER NAME...
"...TERA'.
"AND FOR AS LONG AS I CAN REMEMBER, I'VE LONGED TO LEAVE THE PLANET TO EXPLORE OTHER WORLDS.
"THE BEST WAY TO DO THAT WAS TO JOIN IN THE HUMAN AUXILIARY CORPS.
"I'VE SPENT MOST OF MY CAREER AS A CARGO PILOT, SHIPPING SUPPLIES ACROSS THE EMPIRE AS THE WAR WITH THE DOMINION RAGES ON.
"SUPPLIES... AND INFORMATION."

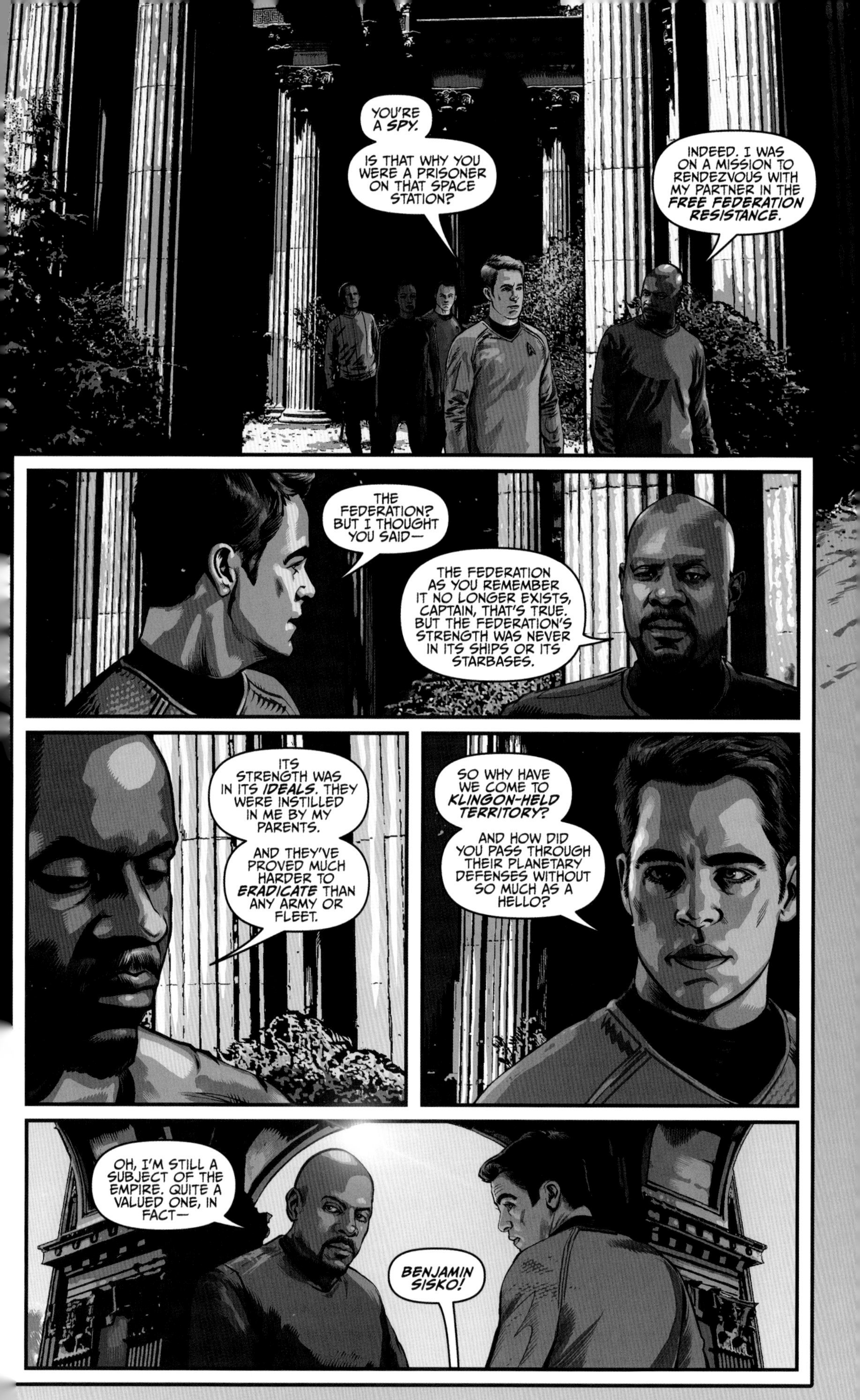

YOU'RE A SPY.
IS THAT WHY YOU WERE A PRISONER ON THAT SPACE STATION?
INDEED. I WAS ON A MISSION TO RENDEZVOUS WITH MY PARTNER IN THE FREE FEDERATION RESISTANCE.
THE FEDERATION? BUT I THOUGHT YOU SAID—
THE FEDERATION AS YOU REMEMBER IT NO LONGER EXISTS, CAPTAIN, THAT'S TRUE. BUT THE FEDERATION'S STRENGTH WAS NEVER IN ITS SHIPS OR ITS STARBASES.
ITS STRENGTH WAS IN ITS IDEALS. THEY WERE INSTILLED IN ME BY MY PARENTS.
AND THEY'VE PROVED MUCH HARDER TO ERADICATE THAN ANY ARMY OR FLEET.
SO WHY HAVE WE COME TO KLINGON-HELD TERRITORY?
AND HOW DID YOU PASS THROUGH THEIR PLANETARY DEFENSES WITHOUT SO MUCH AS A HELLO?
OH, I'M STILL A SUBJECT OF THE EMPIRE. QUITE A VALUED ONE, IN FACT—
BENJAMIN SISKO!

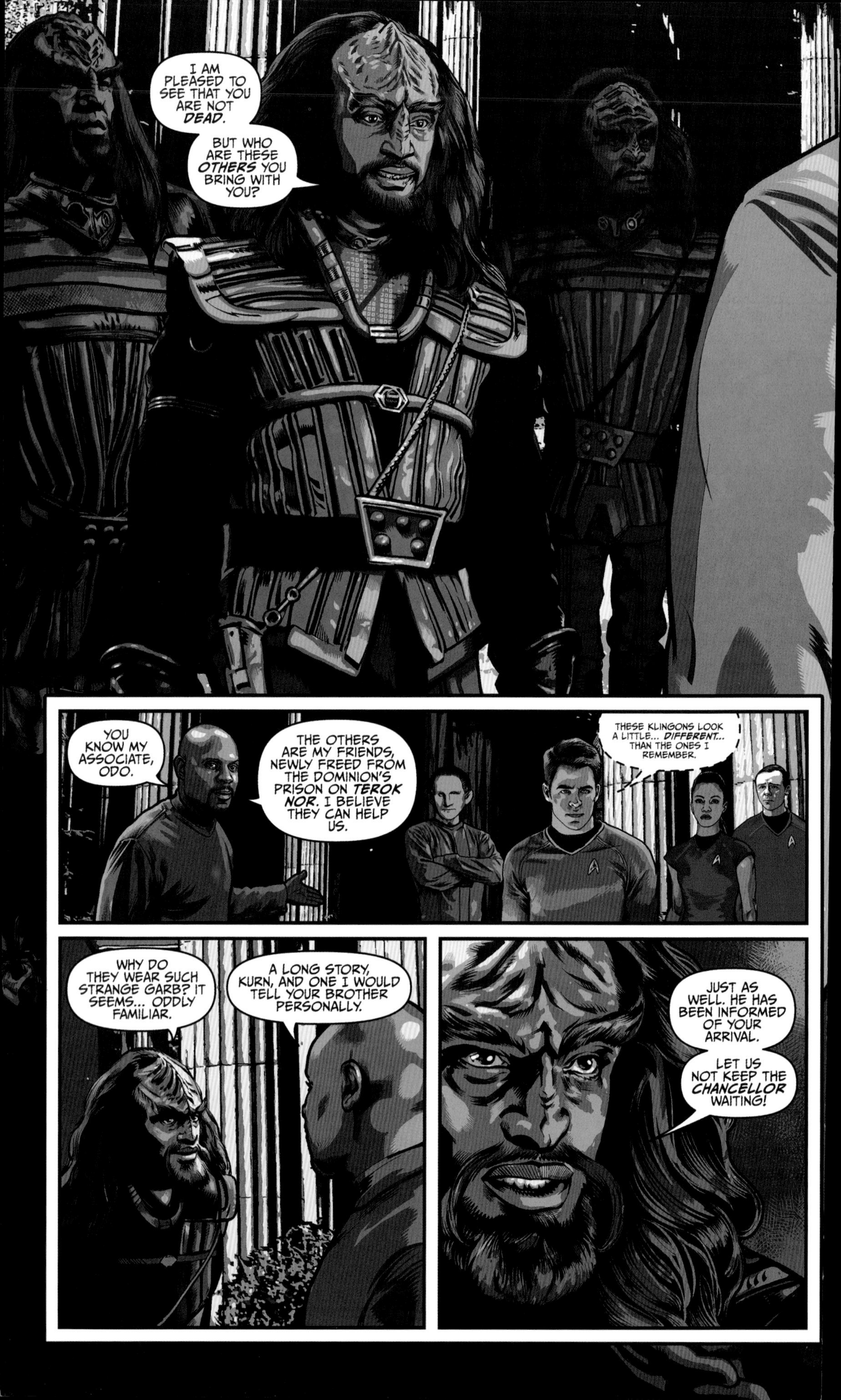
I AM PLEASED TO SEE THAT YOU ARE NOT DEAD.
BUT WHO ARE THESE OTHERS YOU BRING WITH YOU?
YOU KNOW MY ASSOCIATE, ODO.
THE OTHERS ARE MY FRIENDS, NEWLY FREED FROM THE DOMINION'S PRISON ON TEROK NOR. I BELIEVE THEY CAN HELP US.
THESE KLINGONS LOOK A LITTLE... DIFFERENT... THAN THE ONES I REMEMBER.
WHY DO THEY WEAR SUCH STRANGE GARB? IT SEEMS... ODDLY FAMILIAR.
A LONG STORY, KURN, AND ONE I WOULD TELL YOUR BROTHER PERSONALLY.
JUST AS WELL. HE HAS BEEN INFORMED OF YOUR ARRIVAL.
LET US NOT KEEP THE CHANCELLOR WAITING!

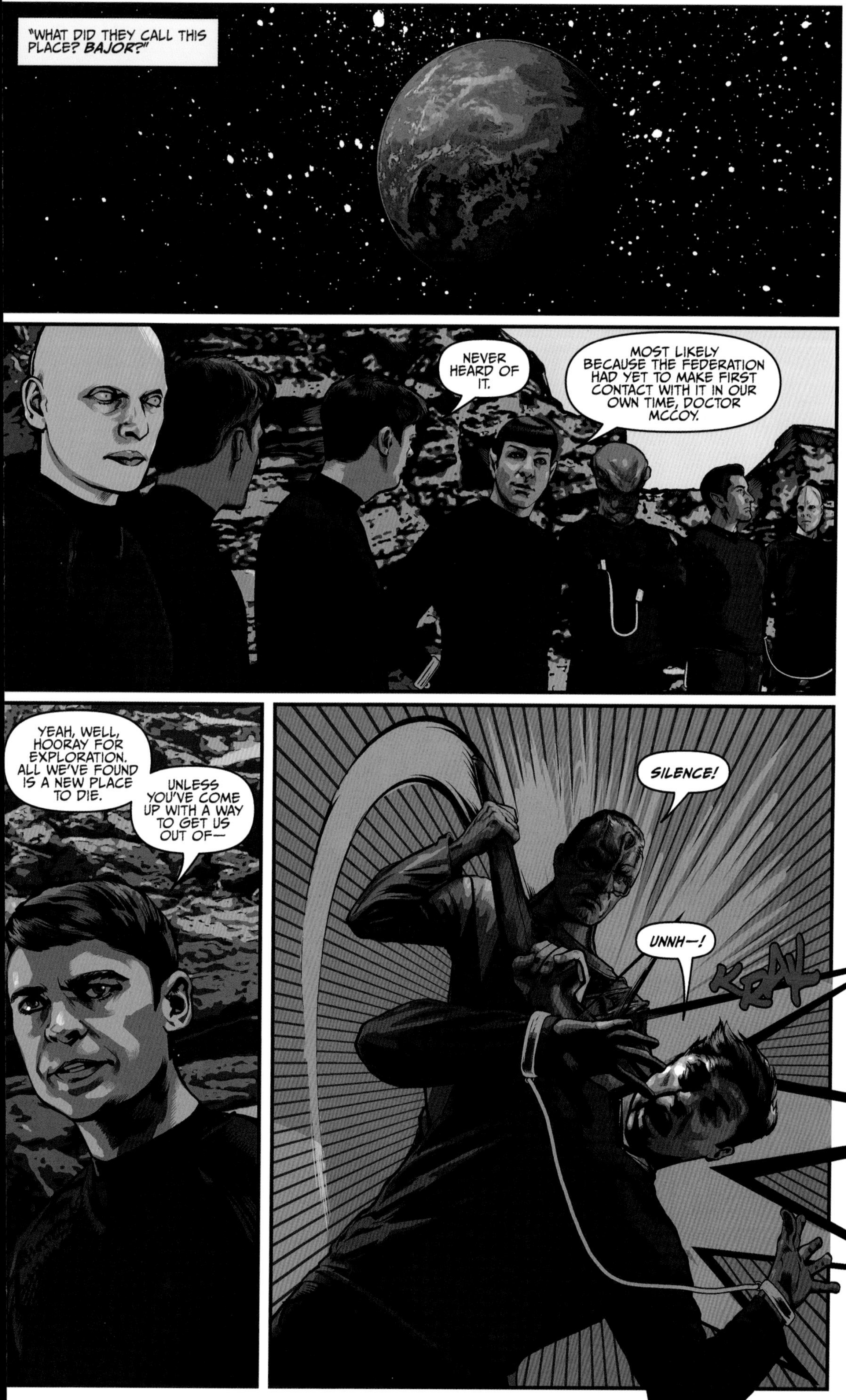
"WHAT DID THEY CALL THIS PLACE? *BAJOR?*"
NEVER HEARD OF IT.
MOST LIKELY BECAUSE THE FEDERATION HAD YET TO MAKE FIRST CONTACT WITH IT IN OUR OWN TIME, DOCTOR MCCOY.
YEAH, WELL, HOORAY FOR EXPLORATION. ALL WE'VE FOUND IS A NEW PLACE TO DIE.
UNLESS YOU'VE COME UP WITH A WAY TO GET US OUT OF—
SILENCE!
UNNH—!
KRAK

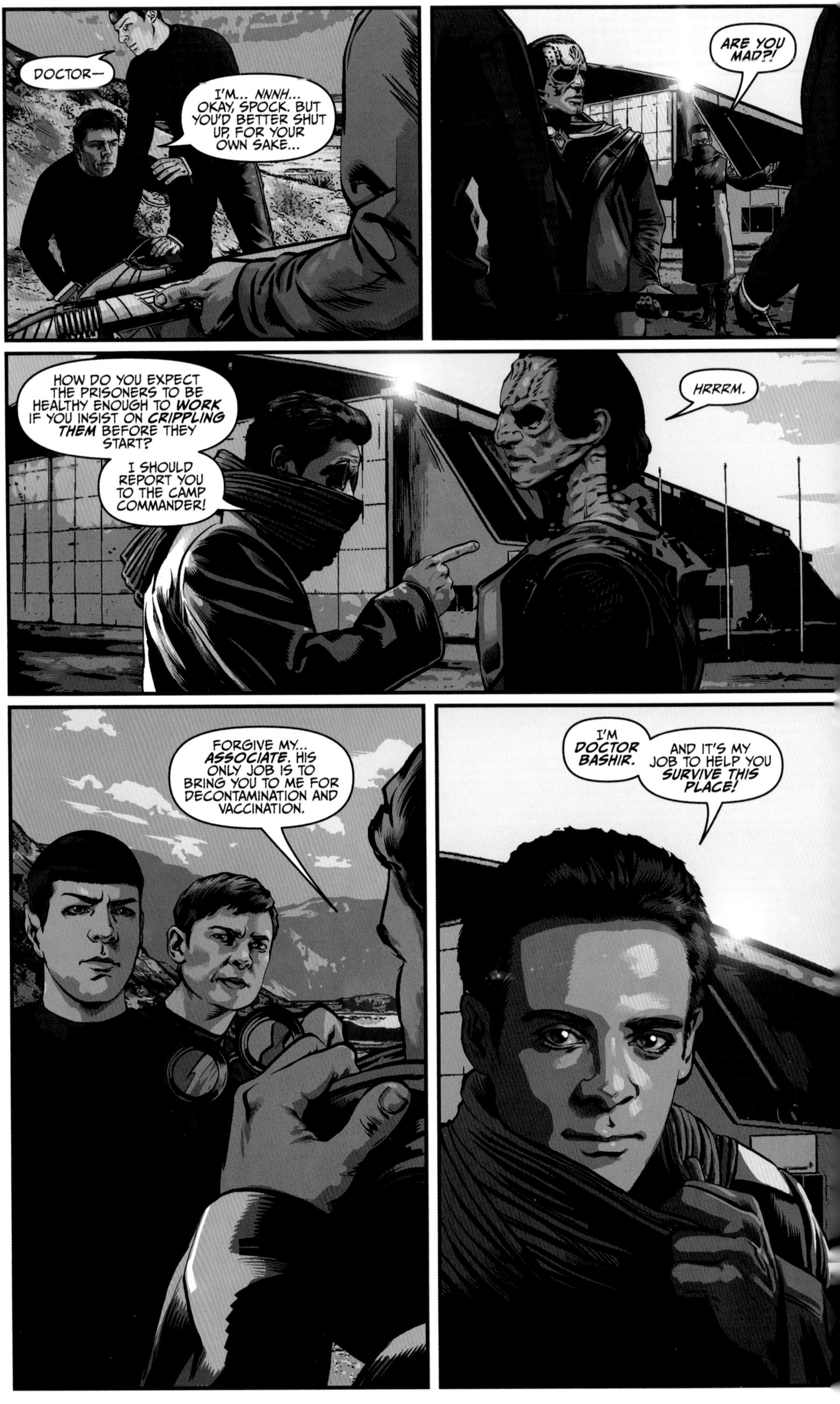
DOCTOR—
I'M... NNNH... OKAY, SPOCK. BUT YOU'D BETTER SHUT UP, FOR YOUR OWN SAKE...
ARE YOU MAD?!
HOW DO YOU EXPECT THE PRISONERS TO BE HEALTHY ENOUGH TO WORK IF YOU INSIST ON CRIPPLING THEM BEFORE THEY START?
I SHOULD REPORT YOU TO THE CAMP COMMANDER!
HRRRM.
FORGIVE MY... ASSOCIATE. HIS ONLY JOB IS TO BRING YOU TO ME FOR DECONTAMINATION AND VACCINATION.
I'M DOCTOR BASHIR.
AND IT'S MY JOB TO HELP YOU SURVIVE THIS PLACE!

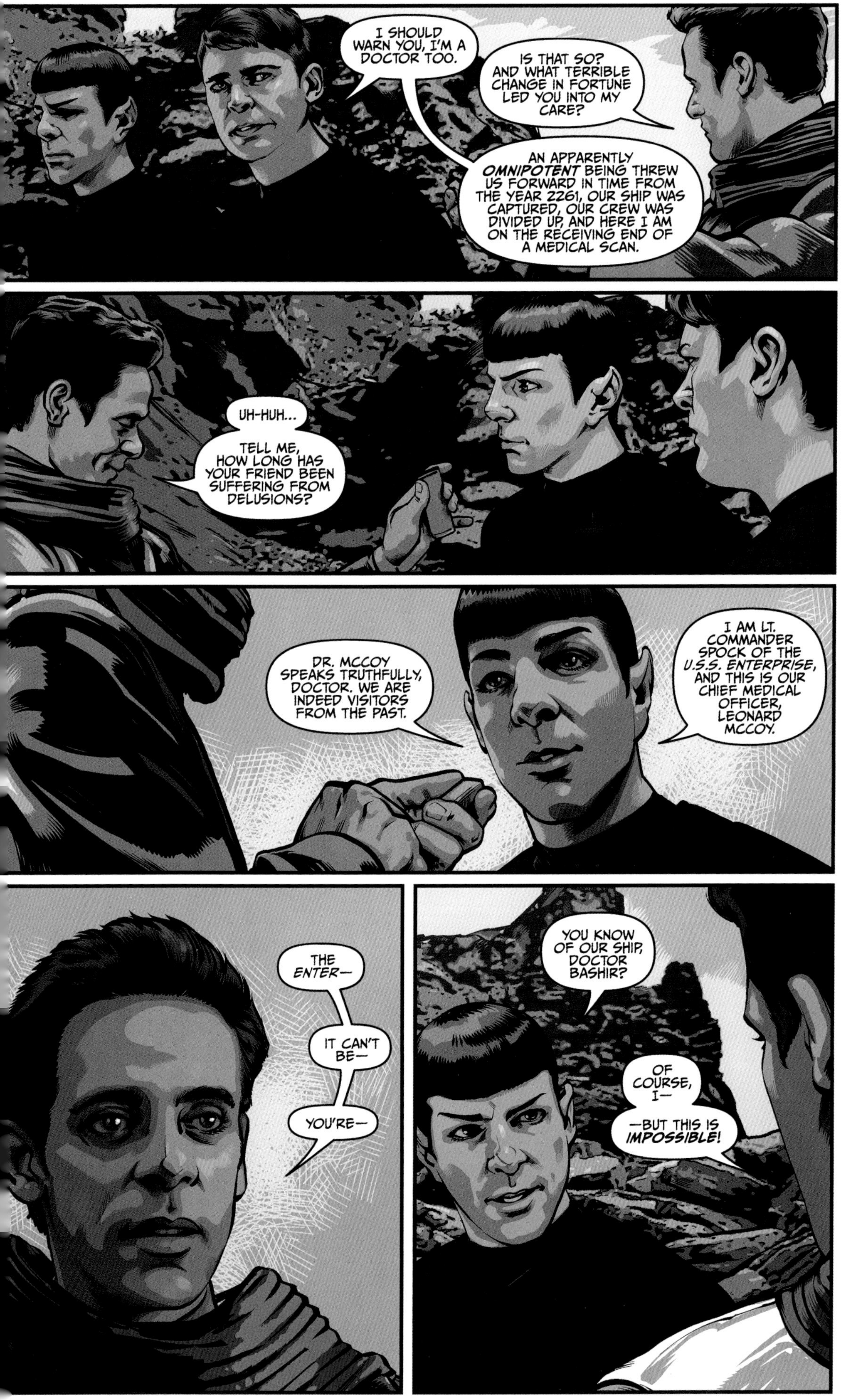
I SHOULD WARN YOU, I'M A DOCTOR TOO.
IS THAT SO? AND WHAT TERRIBLE CHANGE IN FORTUNE LED YOU INTO MY CARE?
AN APPARENTLY *OMNIPOTENT* BEING THREW US FORWARD IN TIME FROM THE YEAR 2261, OUR SHIP WAS CAPTURED, OUR CREW WAS DIVIDED UP, AND HERE I AM ON THE RECEIVING END OF A MEDICAL SCAN.
UH-HUH...
TELL ME, HOW LONG HAS YOUR FRIEND BEEN SUFFERING FROM DELUSIONS?
DR. MCCOY SPEAKS TRUTHFULLY, DOCTOR. WE ARE INDEED VISITORS FROM THE PAST.
I AM LT. COMMANDER SPOCK OF THE *U.S.S. ENTERPRISE*, AND THIS IS OUR CHIEF MEDICAL OFFICER, LEONARD MCCOY.
THE *ENTER*—
IT CAN'T BE—
YOU'RE—
YOU KNOW OF OUR SHIP, DOCTOR BASHIR?
OF COURSE, I—
—BUT THIS IS *IMPOSSIBLE*!

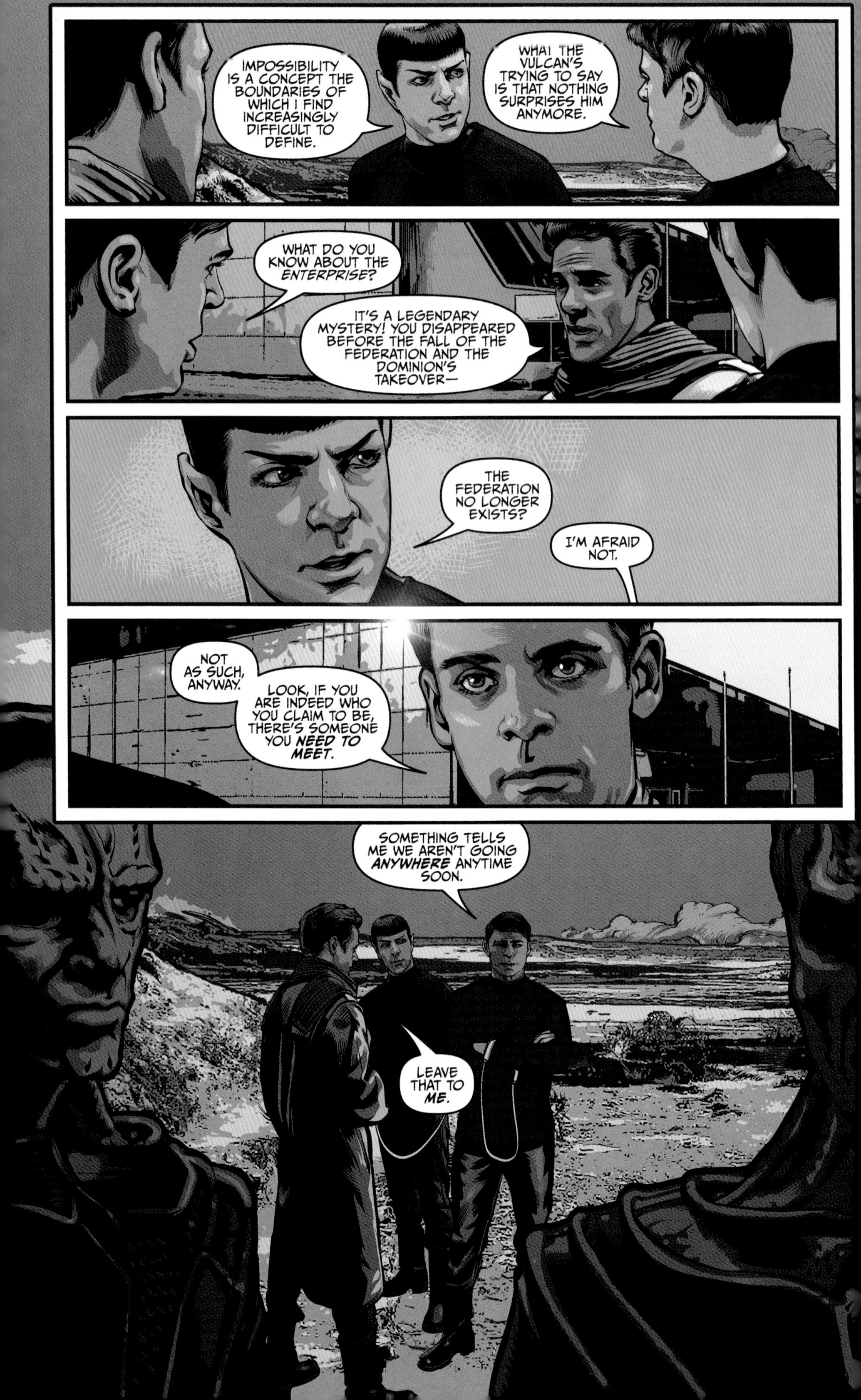
IMPOSSIBILITY IS A CONCEPT THE BOUNDARIES OF WHICH I FIND INCREASINGLY DIFFICULT TO DEFINE.
WHAT THE VULCAN'S TRYING TO SAY IS THAT NOTHING SURPRISES HIM ANYMORE.
WHAT DO YOU KNOW ABOUT THE *ENTERPRISE*?
IT'S A LEGENDARY MYSTERY! YOU DISAPPEARED BEFORE THE FALL OF THE FEDERATION AND THE DOMINION'S TAKEOVER—
THE FEDERATION NO LONGER EXISTS?
I'M AFRAID NOT.
NOT AS SUCH, ANYWAY.
LOOK, IF YOU ARE INDEED WHO YOU CLAIM TO BE, THERE'S SOMEONE YOU ***NEED TO MEET***.
SOMETHING TELLS ME WE AREN'T GOING ***ANYWHERE*** ANYTIME SOON.
LEAVE THAT TO ***ME***.

SAN FRANCISCO.

"LET ME GUESS.

THEY DIDN'T KEEP STARFLEET ACADEMY INTACT."

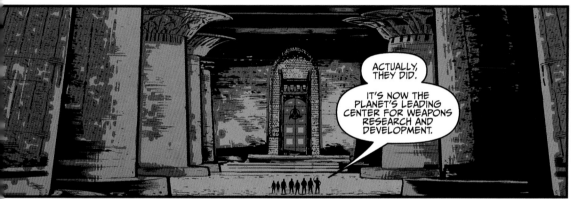

ACTUALLY, THEY DID.

IT'S NOW THE PLANET'S LEADING CENTER FOR WEAPONS RESEARCH AND DEVELOPMENT.

WHY AM I NOT SURPRISED?

PLANETARY DOMINATION ASIDE... IT'S REALLY RATHER AN IMPRESSIVE BUILDING, ISN'T IT?

BENJAMIN. I SENSE SOMETHING...

...AMISS.

I GET THE SAME PIT IN MY STOMACH WHENEVER I'M HERE, OLD FRIEND. DON'T WORRY.

BENJAMIN SISKO, ASSORTED GUESTS, IT IS TIME FOR YOU TO HUMBLE YOURSELF BEFORE THE *SUPREME COMMANDER* OF THE EMPIRE'S *TERA' COLONY*, HIS EMINENCE—

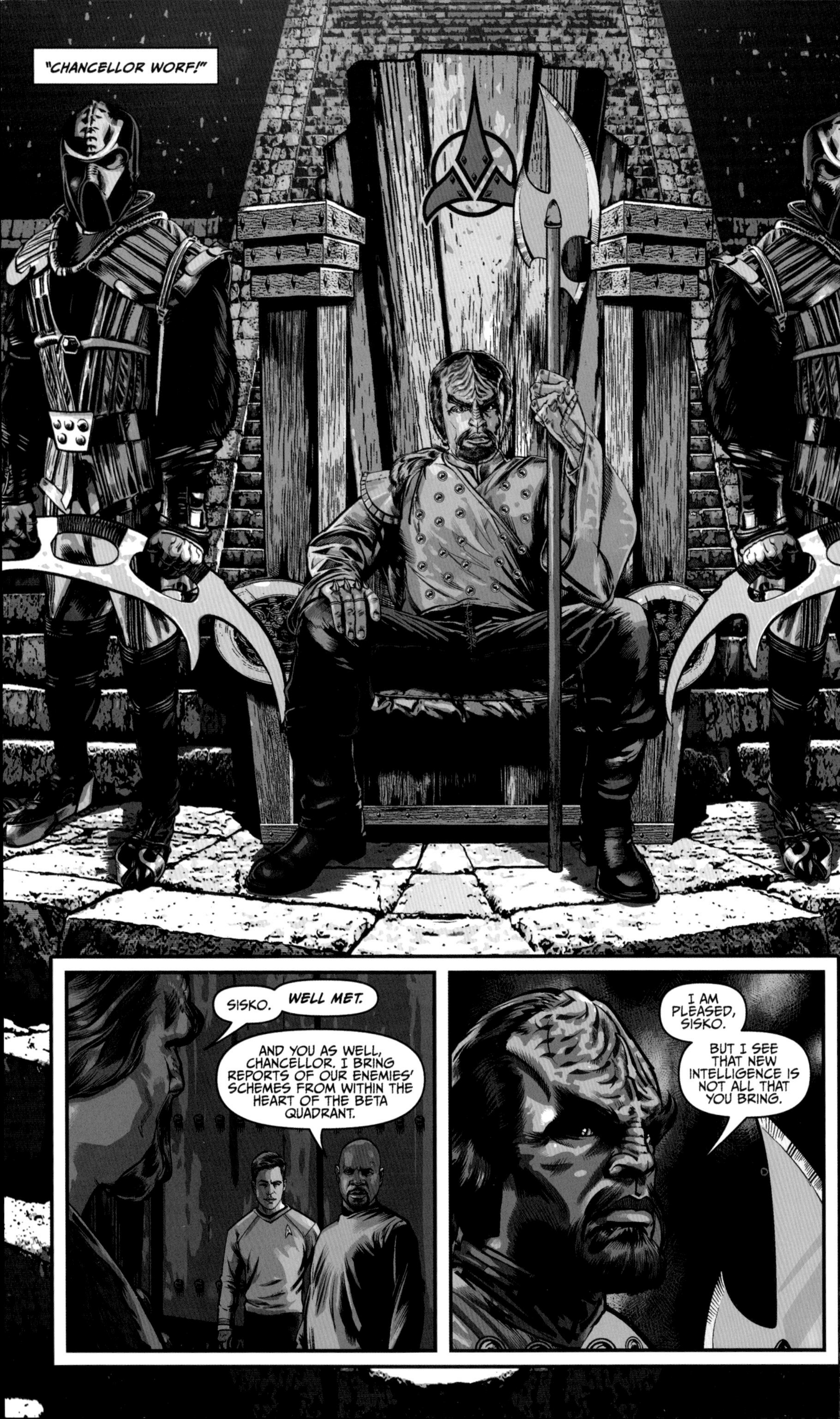
"CHANCELLOR WORF!"
SISKO. WELL MET.
AND YOU AS WELL, CHANCELLOR. I BRING REPORTS OF OUR ENEMIES' SCHEMES FROM WITHIN THE HEART OF THE BETA QUADRANT.
I AM PLEASED, SISKO.
BUT I SEE THAT NEW INTELLIGENCE IS NOT ALL THAT YOU BRING.

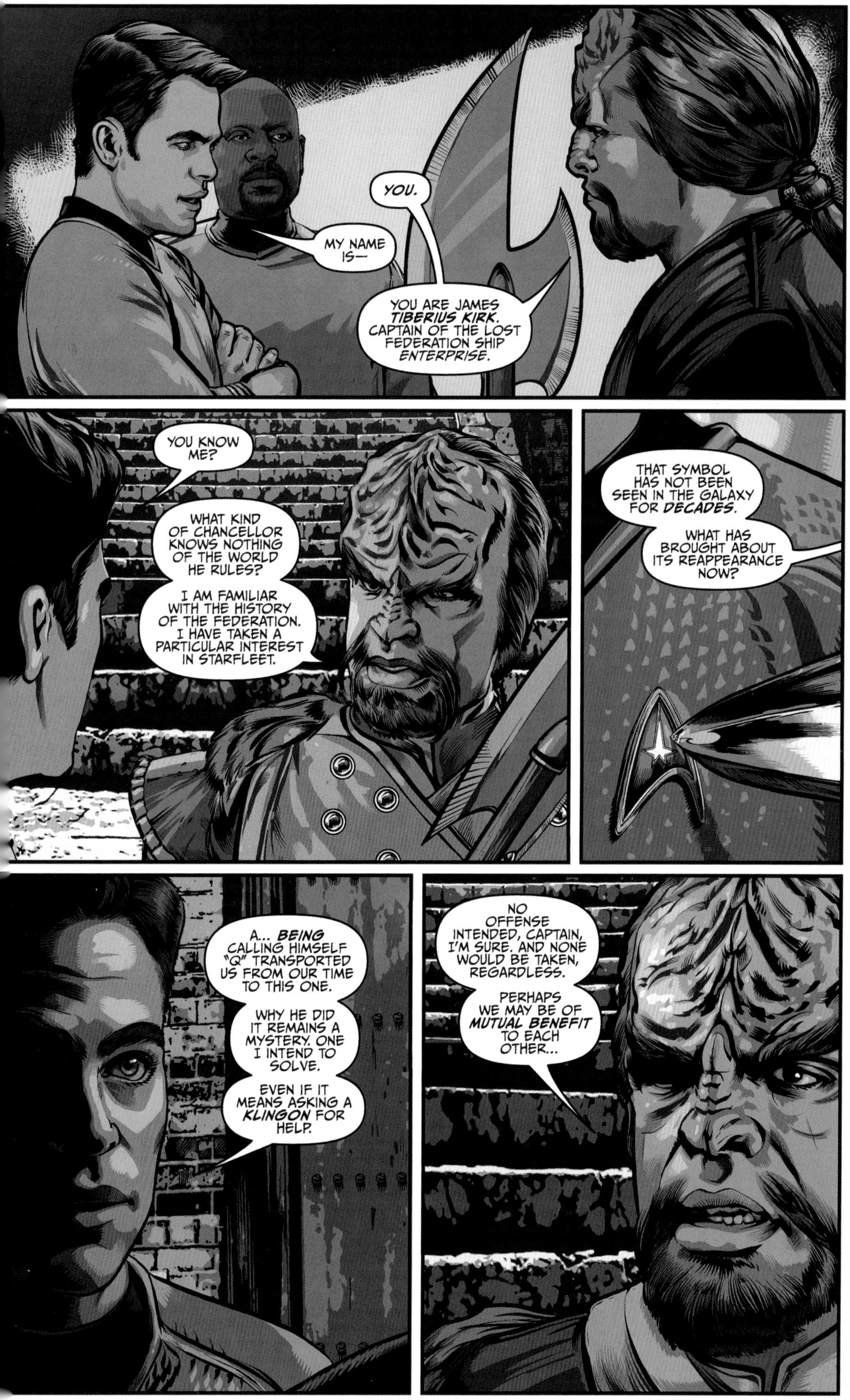
YOU.
MY NAME IS—
YOU ARE JAMES TIBERIUS KIRK. CAPTAIN OF THE LOST FEDERATION SHIP ENTERPRISE.
YOU KNOW ME?
WHAT KIND OF CHANCELLOR KNOWS NOTHING OF THE WORLD HE RULES?
I AM FAMILIAR WITH THE HISTORY OF THE FEDERATION. I HAVE TAKEN A PARTICULAR INTEREST IN STARFLEET.
THAT SYMBOL HAS NOT BEEN SEEN IN THE GALAXY FOR DECADES.
WHAT HAS BROUGHT ABOUT ITS REAPPEARANCE NOW?
A... BEING CALLING HIMSELF "Q" TRANSPORTED US FROM OUR TIME TO THIS ONE.
WHY HE DID IT REMAINS A MYSTERY. ONE I INTEND TO SOLVE.
EVEN IF IT MEANS ASKING A KLINGON FOR HELP.
NO OFFENSE INTENDED, CAPTAIN, I'M SURE. AND NONE WOULD BE TAKEN, REGARDLESS.
PERHAPS WE MAY BE OF MUTUAL BENEFIT TO EACH OTHER...

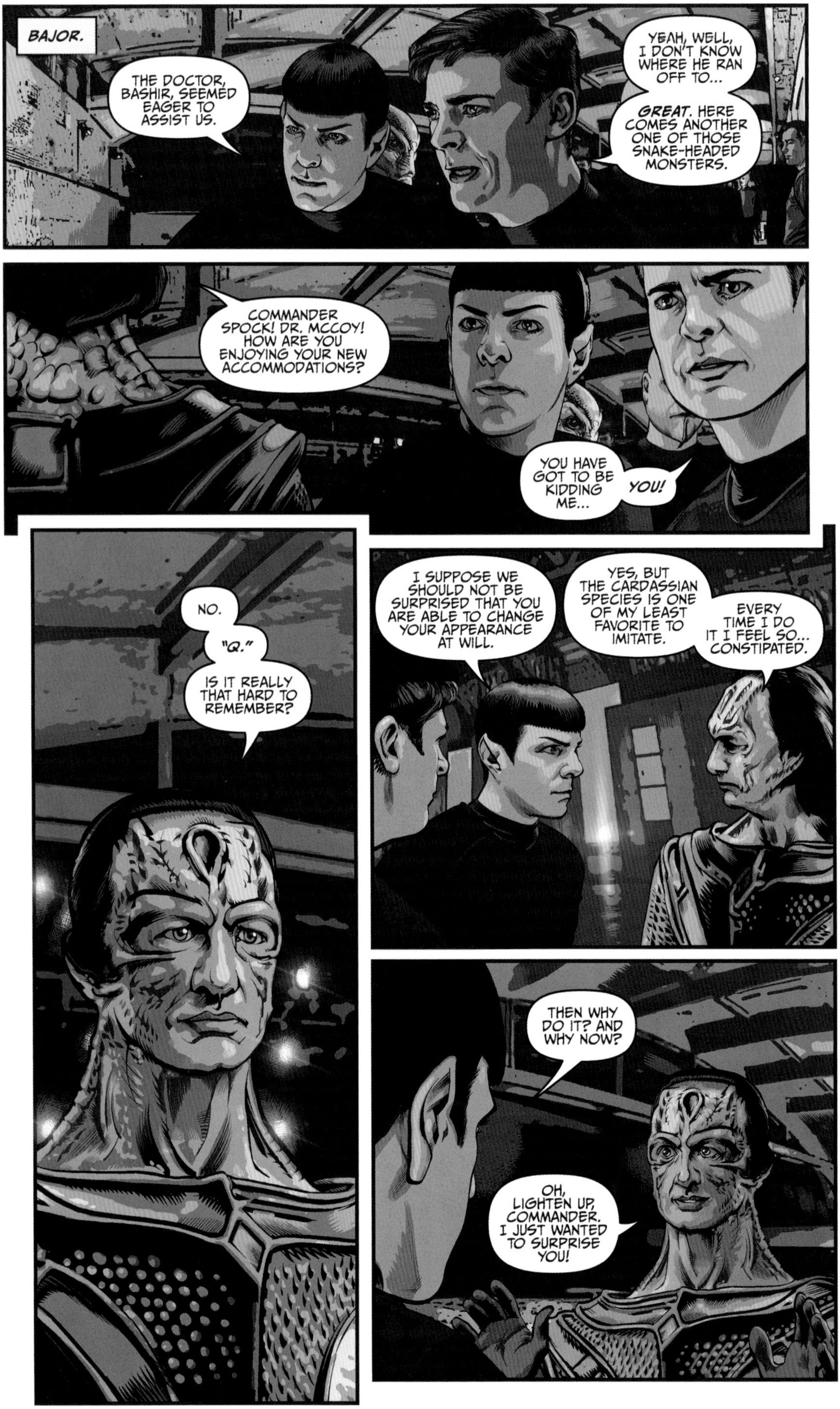
BAJOR.
THE DOCTOR, BASHIR, SEEMED EAGER TO ASSIST US.
YEAH, WELL, I DON'T KNOW WHERE HE RAN OFF TO...
GREAT. HERE COMES ANOTHER ONE OF THOSE SNAKE-HEADED MONSTERS.
COMMANDER SPOCK! DR. MCCOY! HOW ARE YOU ENJOYING YOUR NEW ACCOMMODATIONS?
YOU HAVE GOT TO BE KIDDING ME...
YOU!
NO.
"Q."
IS IT REALLY THAT HARD TO REMEMBER?
I SUPPOSE WE SHOULD NOT BE SURPRISED THAT YOU ARE ABLE TO CHANGE YOUR APPEARANCE AT WILL.
YES, BUT THE CARDASSIAN SPECIES IS ONE OF MY LEAST FAVORITE TO IMITATE.
EVERY TIME I DO IT I FEEL SO... CONSTIPATED.
THEN WHY DO IT? AND WHY NOW?
OH, LIGHTEN UP, COMMANDER. I JUST WANTED TO SURPRISE YOU!

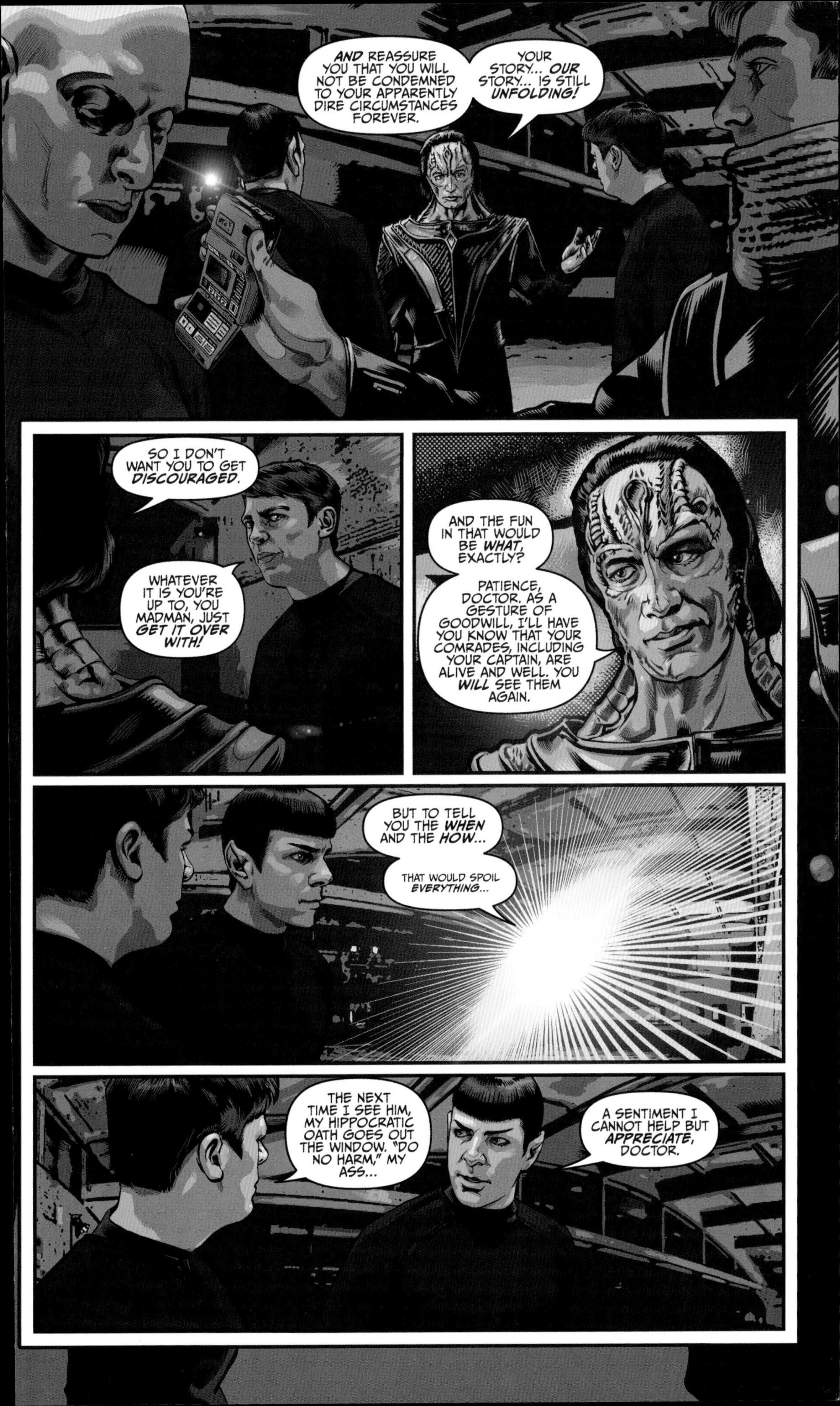
AND REASSURE YOU THAT YOU WILL NOT BE CONDEMNED TO YOUR APPARENTLY DIRE CIRCUMSTANCES FOREVER.
YOUR STORY... OUR STORY... IS STILL UNFOLDING!
SO I DON'T WANT YOU TO GET DISCOURAGED.
WHATEVER IT IS YOU'RE UP TO, YOU MADMAN, JUST GET IT OVER WITH!
AND THE FUN IN THAT WOULD BE WHAT, EXACTLY?
PATIENCE, DOCTOR. AS A GESTURE OF GOODWILL, I'LL HAVE YOU KNOW THAT YOUR COMRADES, INCLUDING YOUR CAPTAIN, ARE ALIVE AND WELL. YOU WILL SEE THEM AGAIN.
BUT TO TELL YOU THE WHEN AND THE HOW...
THAT WOULD SPOIL EVERYTHING...
THE NEXT TIME I SEE HIM, MY HIPPOCRATIC OATH GOES OUT THE WINDOW. "DO NO HARM," MY ASS...
A SENTIMENT I CANNOT HELP BUT APPRECIATE, DOCTOR.

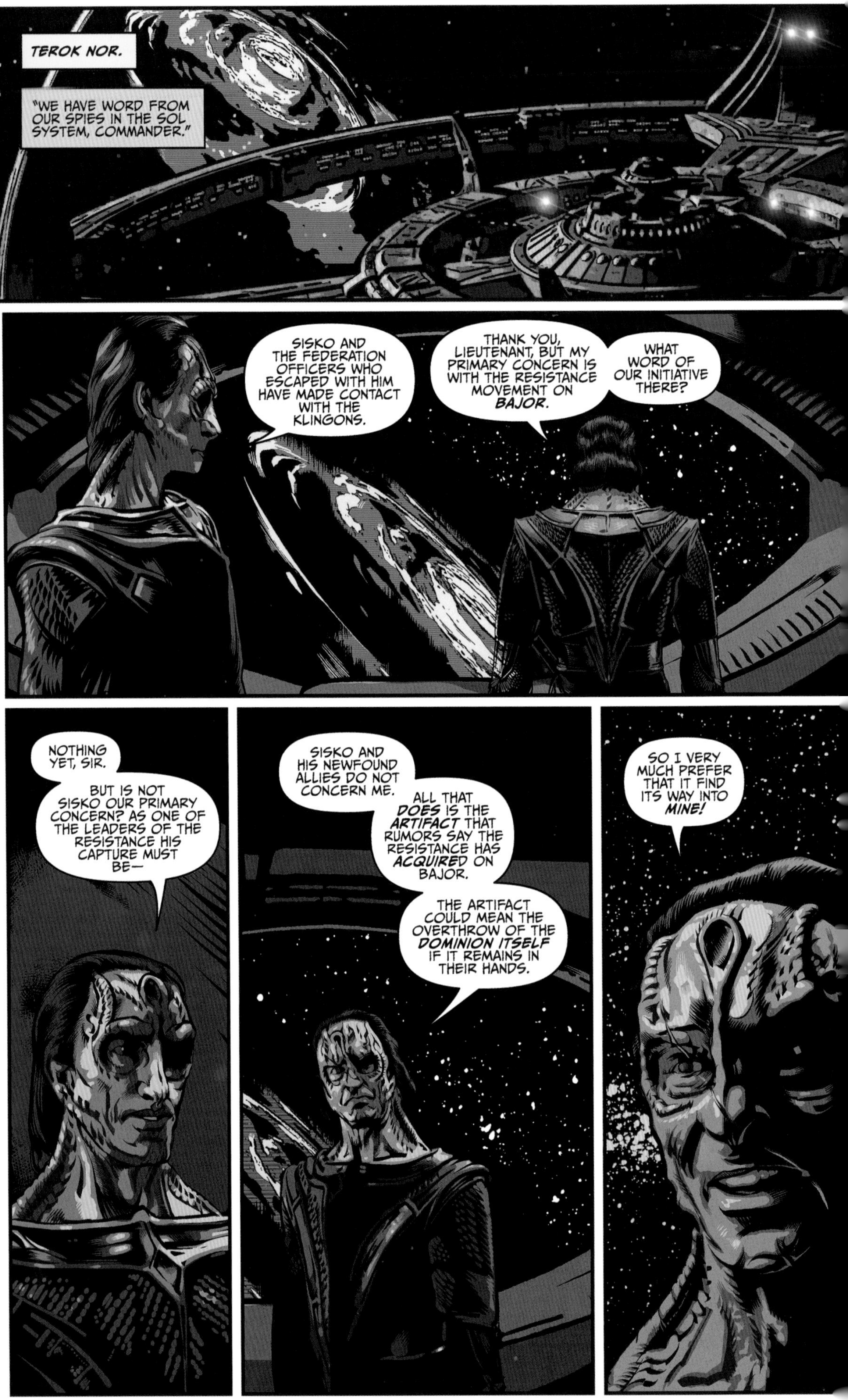
TEROK NOR.
"WE HAVE WORD FROM OUR SPIES IN THE SOL SYSTEM, COMMANDER."
SISKO AND THE FEDERATION OFFICERS WHO ESCAPED WITH HIM HAVE MADE CONTACT WITH THE KLINGONS.
THANK YOU, LIEUTENANT, BUT MY PRIMARY CONCERN IS WITH THE RESISTANCE MOVEMENT ON BAJOR.
WHAT WORD OF OUR INITIATIVE THERE?
NOTHING YET, SIR.
BUT IS NOT SISKO OUR PRIMARY CONCERN? AS ONE OF THE LEADERS OF THE RESISTANCE HIS CAPTURE MUST BE—
SISKO AND HIS NEWFOUND ALLIES DO NOT CONCERN ME.
ALL THAT DOES IS THE ARTIFACT THAT RUMORS SAY THE RESISTANCE HAS ACQUIRED ON BAJOR.
THE ARTIFACT COULD MEAN THE OVERTHROW OF THE DOMINION ITSELF IF IT REMAINS IN THEIR HANDS.
SO I VERY MUCH PREFER THAT IT FIND ITS WAY INTO MINE!

BAJOR.

THIS IS COMPLETELY UNACCEPTABLE! A CONTRACT IS A CONTRACT!

EXACTLY! AND THE CONTRACT CALLED FOR TWO ORDERS OF *VIABLE* VACCINE!

THIS USELESS SWILL YOU DELIVERED WOULD KILL ANYONE I GAVE IT TO, QUARK! I *DEMAND* THAT YOU TAKE IT BACK AND PROVIDE RESTITUTION!

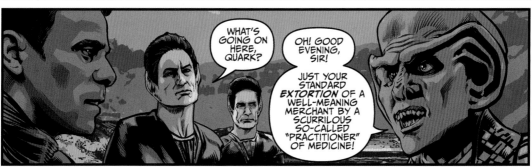

WHAT'S GOING ON HERE, QUARK?

OH! GOOD EVENING, SIR!

JUST YOUR STANDARD *EXTORTION* OF A WELL-MEANING MERCHANT BY A SCURRILOUS SO-CALLED "PRACTITIONER" OF MEDICINE!

THAT'S RIDICULOUS! I'VE BEEN DELIVERED *SUB-STANDARD* SUPPLIES!

IF THEY AREN'T REPLACED WITH THE PROPER VACCINE, HALF THE PRISONERS IN THE LABOR CAMP WILL BE SUBJECT TO INFECTION BY NATIVE PATHOGENS!

SO?

SO HOW WOULD YOUR COMMANDING OFFICER REACT IF HE KNEW THAT YOU IMPEDED THE FULL HEALTH AND FUNCTIONING OF A LABOR FORCE VITAL TO THE PROCUREMENT AND REFINING OF NATURAL RESOURCES CRITICAL TO THE DOMINION'S WAR EFFORT?

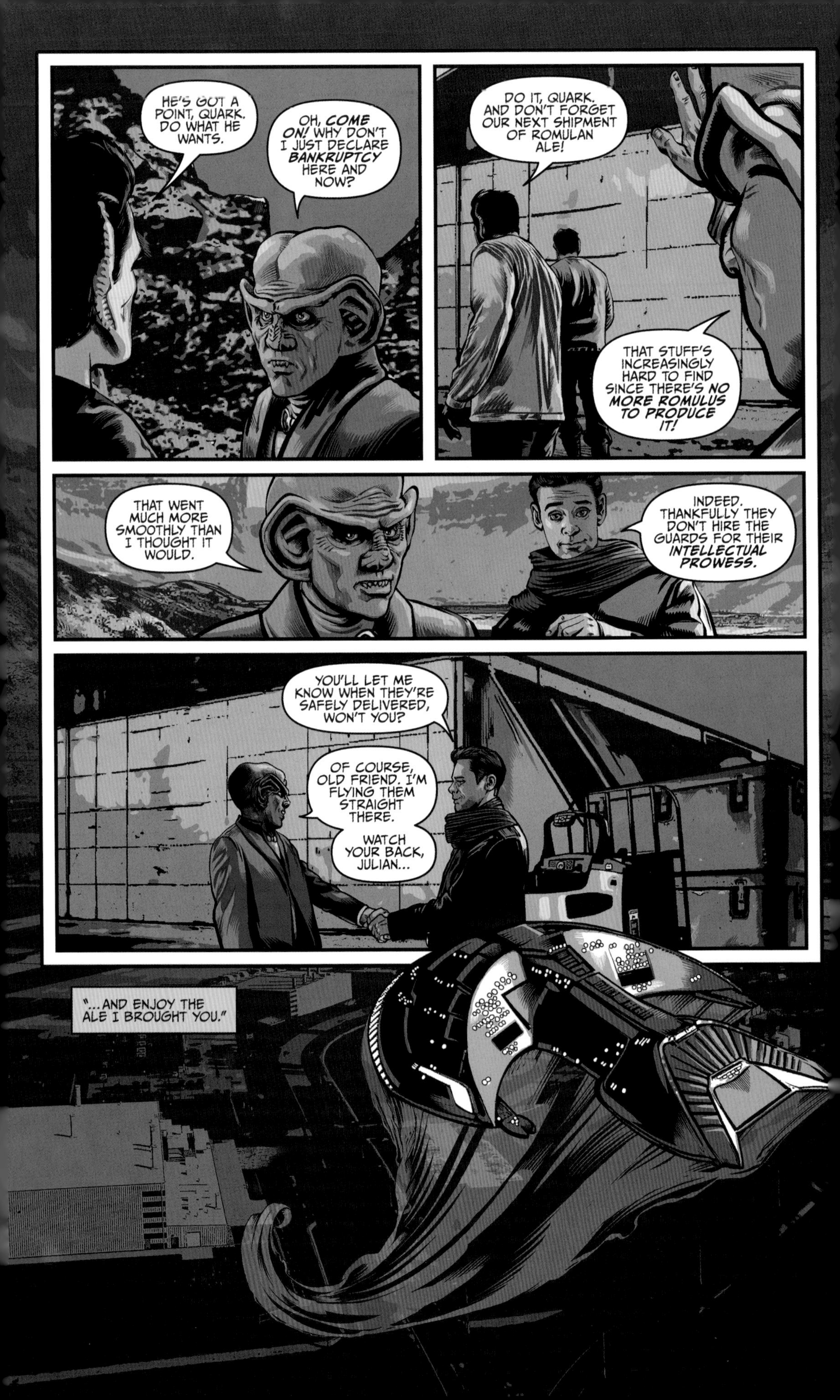

HE'S GOT A POINT, QUARK. DO WHAT HE WANTS.
OH, COME ON! WHY DON'T I JUST DECLARE BANKRUPTCY HERE AND NOW?
DO IT, QUARK. AND DON'T FORGET OUR NEXT SHIPMENT OF ROMULAN ALE!
THAT STUFF'S INCREASINGLY HARD TO FIND SINCE THERE'S NO MORE ROMULUS TO PRODUCE IT!
THAT WENT MUCH MORE SMOOTHLY THAN I THOUGHT IT WOULD.
INDEED. THANKFULLY THEY DON'T HIRE THE GUARDS FOR THEIR INTELLECTUAL PROWESS.
YOU'LL LET ME KNOW WHEN THEY'RE SAFELY DELIVERED, WON'T YOU?
OF COURSE, OLD FRIEND. I'M FLYING THEM STRAIGHT THERE.
WATCH YOUR BACK, JULIAN...
"...AND ENJOY THE ALE I BROUGHT YOU."

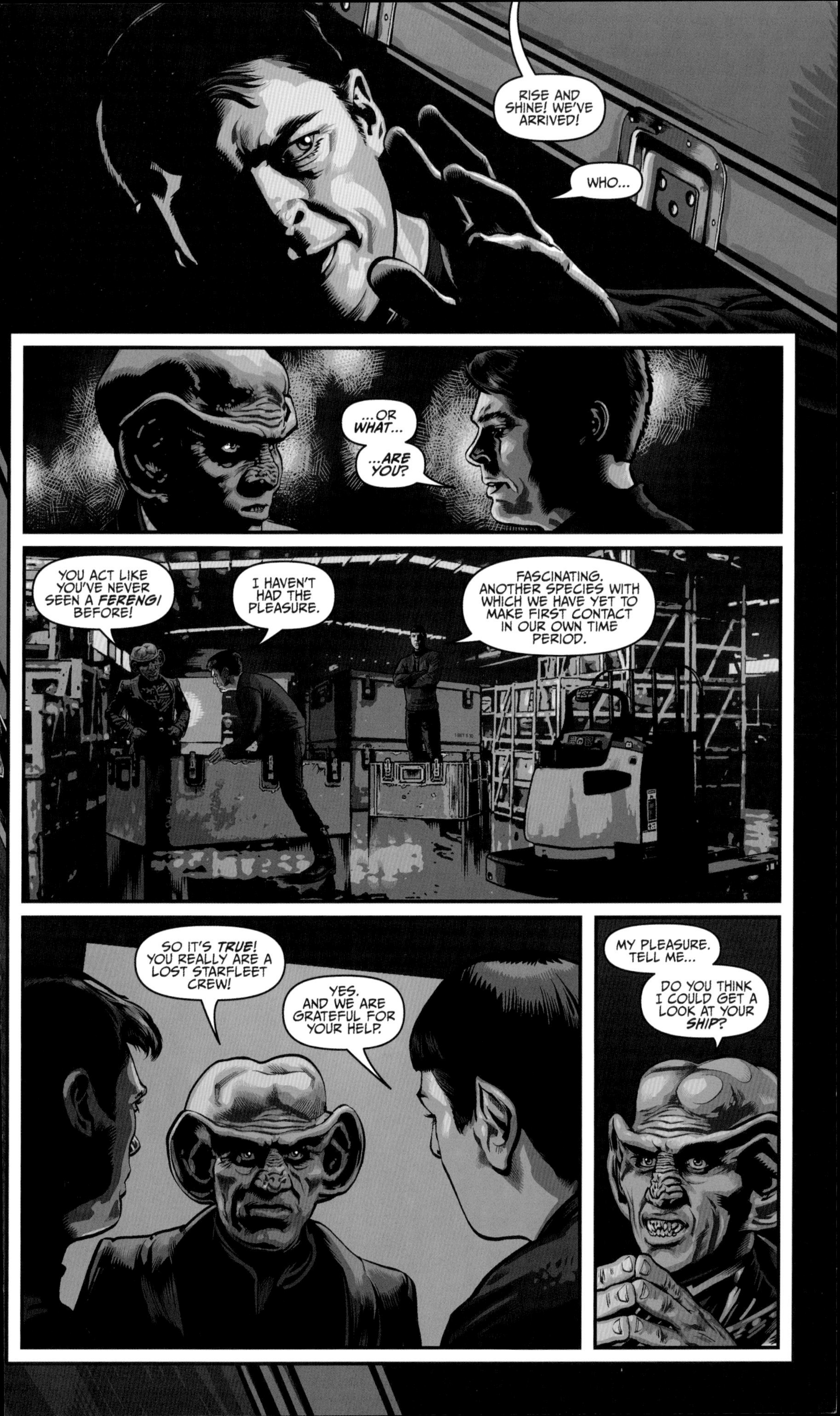
RISE AND SHINE! WE'VE ARRIVED!
WHO...
...OR WHAT...
...ARE YOU?
YOU ACT LIKE YOU'VE NEVER SEEN A FERENGI BEFORE!
I HAVEN'T HAD THE PLEASURE.
FASCINATING. ANOTHER SPECIES WITH WHICH WE HAVE YET TO MAKE FIRST CONTACT IN OUR OWN TIME PERIOD.
SO IT'S TRUE! YOU REALLY ARE A LOST STARFLEET CREW!
YES. AND WE ARE GRATEFUL FOR YOUR HELP.
MY PLEASURE. TELL ME...
DO YOU THINK I COULD GET A LOOK AT YOUR SHIP?

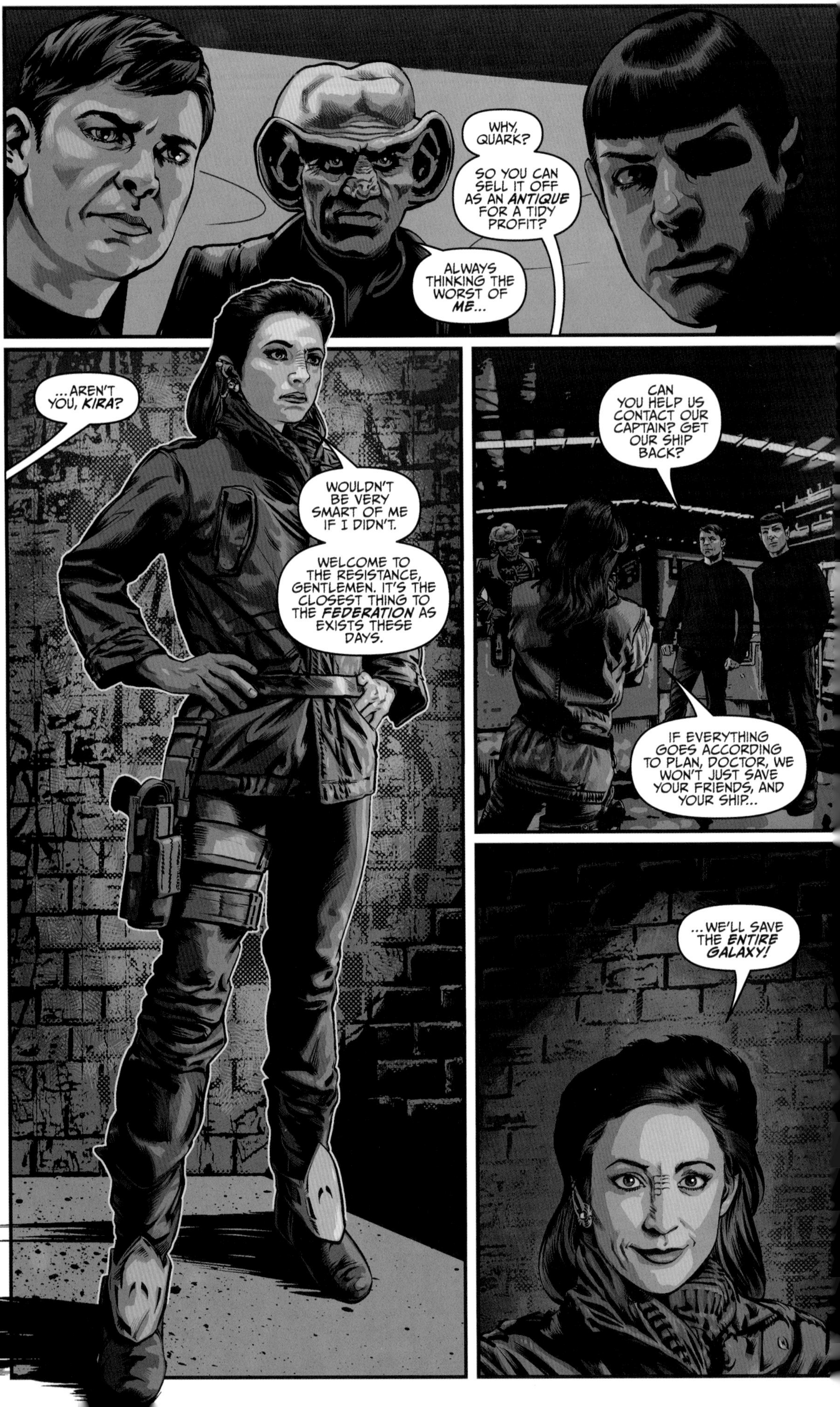
WHY, QUARK?
SO YOU CAN SELL IT OFF AS AN *ANTIQUE* FOR A TIDY PROFIT?
ALWAYS THINKING THE WORST OF *ME*...
...AREN'T YOU, *KIRA*?
WOULDN'T BE VERY SMART OF ME IF I DIDN'T.
WELCOME TO THE RESISTANCE, GENTLEMEN. IT'S THE CLOSEST THING TO THE *FEDERATION* AS EXISTS THESE DAYS.
CAN YOU HELP US CONTACT OUR CAPTAIN? GET OUR SHIP BACK?
IF EVERYTHING GOES ACCORDING TO PLAN, DOCTOR, WE WON'T JUST SAVE YOUR FRIENDS, AND YOUR SHIP...
...WE'LL SAVE THE *ENTIRE GALAXY!*

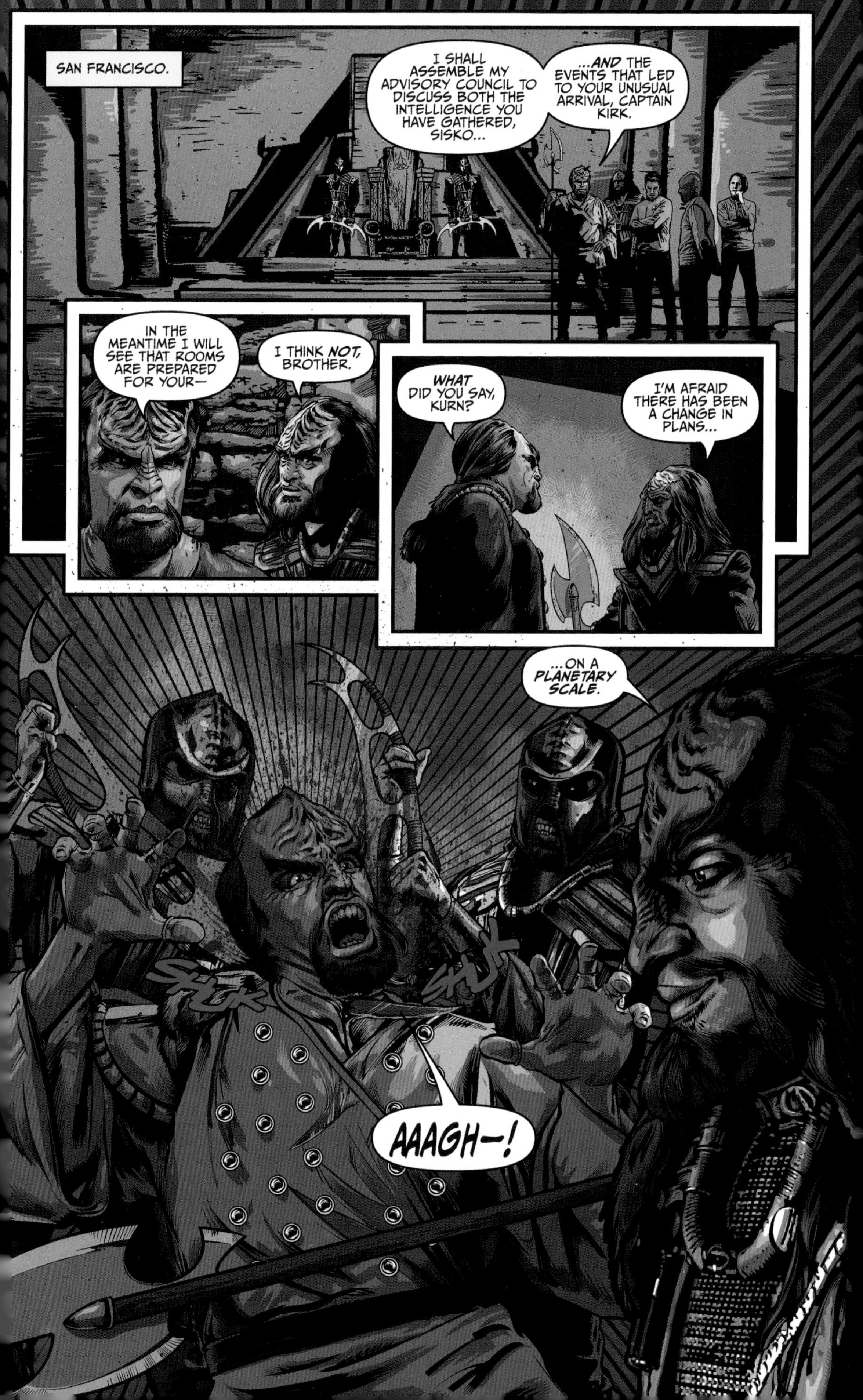
SAN FRANCISCO.
I SHALL ASSEMBLE MY ADVISORY COUNCIL TO DISCUSS BOTH THE INTELLIGENCE YOU HAVE GATHERED, SISKO...
...AND THE EVENTS THAT LED TO YOUR UNUSUAL ARRIVAL, CAPTAIN KIRK.
IN THE MEANTIME I WILL SEE THAT ROOMS ARE PREPARED FOR YOUR—
I THINK NOT, BROTHER.
WHAT DID YOU SAY, KURN?
I'M AFRAID THERE HAS BEEN A CHANGE IN PLANS...
...ON A PLANETARY SCALE.
SHUK
SHUK
AAAGH—!

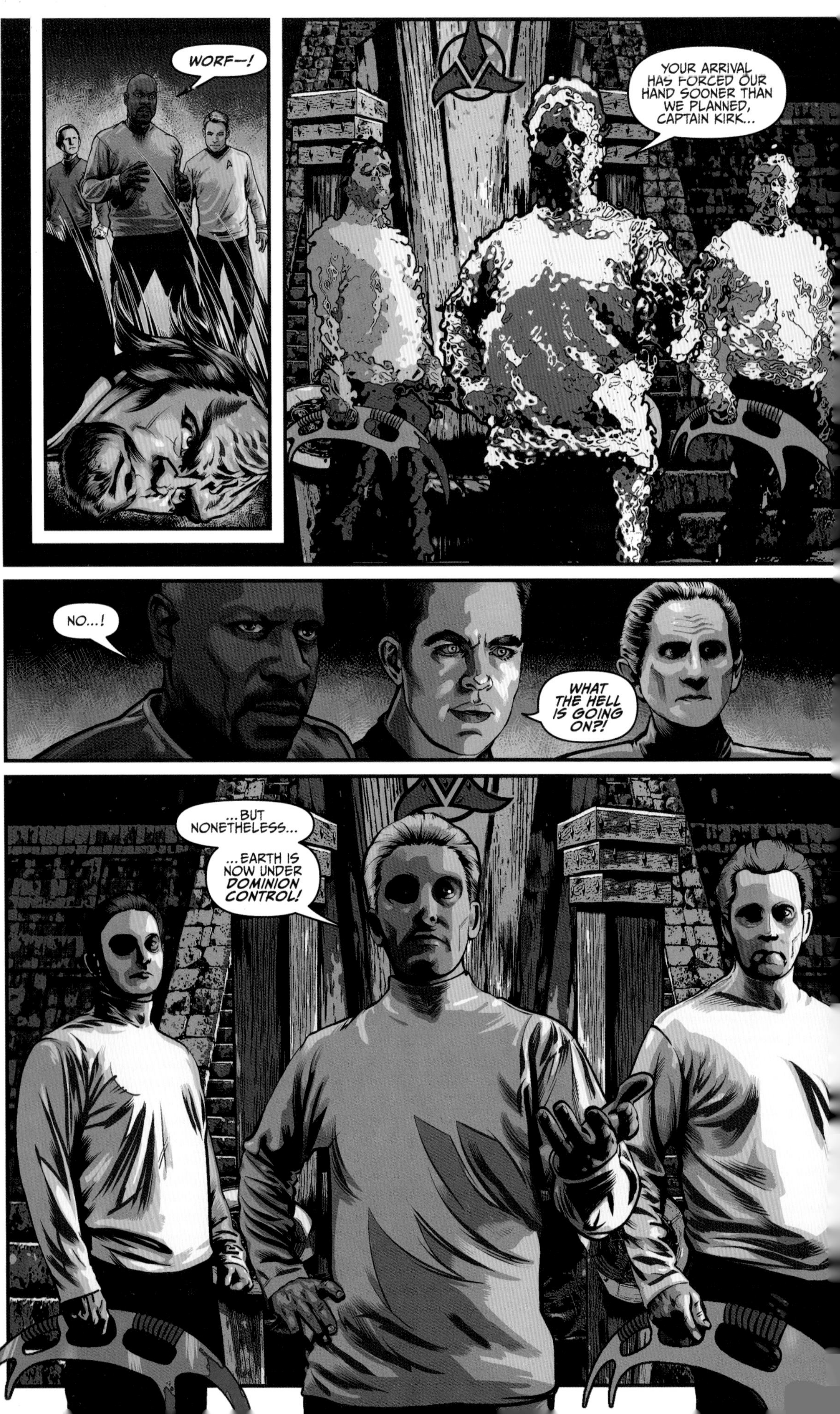
WORF—!
YOUR ARRIVAL HAS FORCED OUR HAND SOONER THAN WE PLANNED, CAPTAIN KIRK...
NO...!
WHAT THE HELL IS GOING ON?!
...BUT NONETHELESS...
...EARTH IS NOW UNDER DOMINION CONTROL!

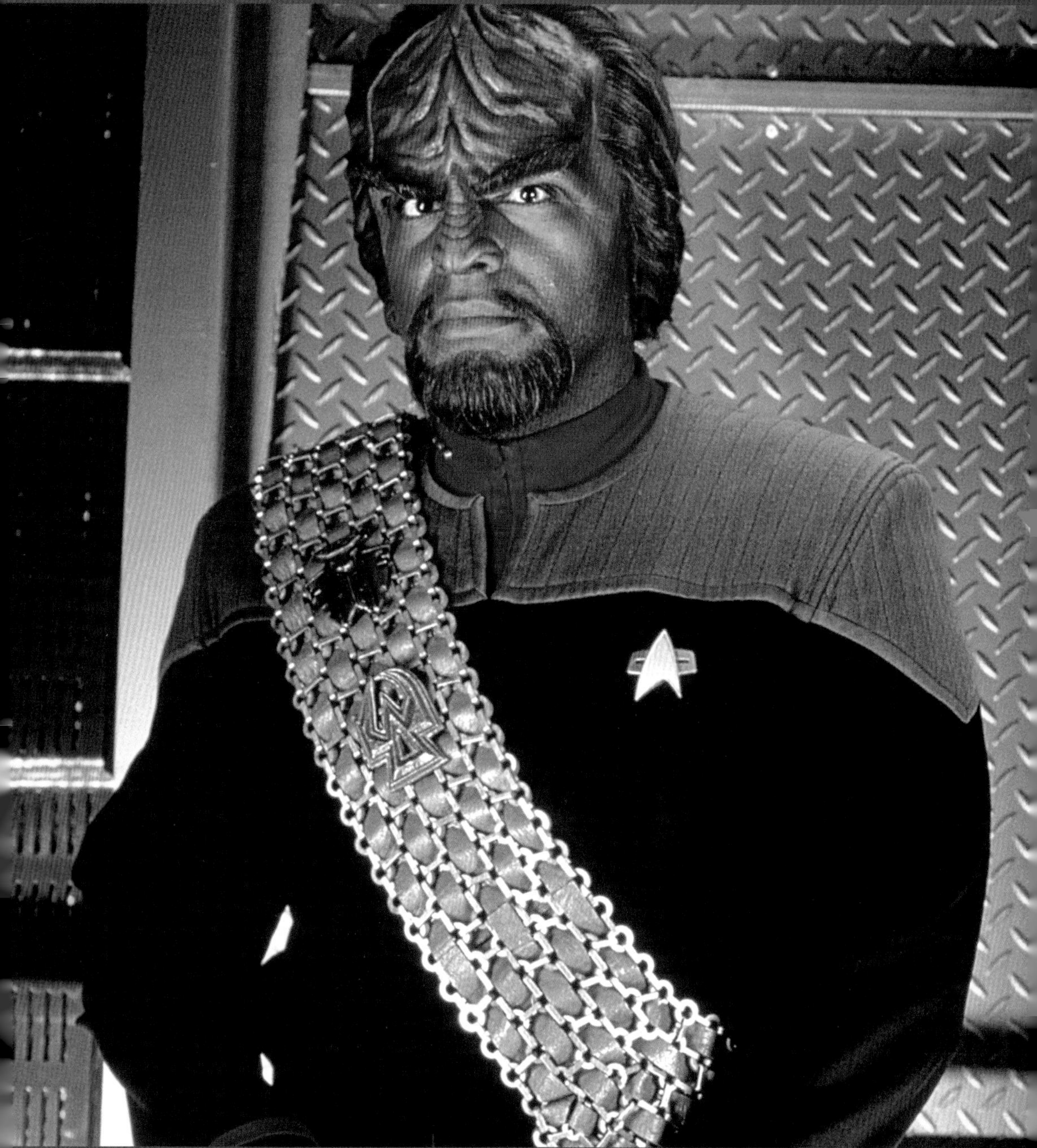

CHAPTER 4

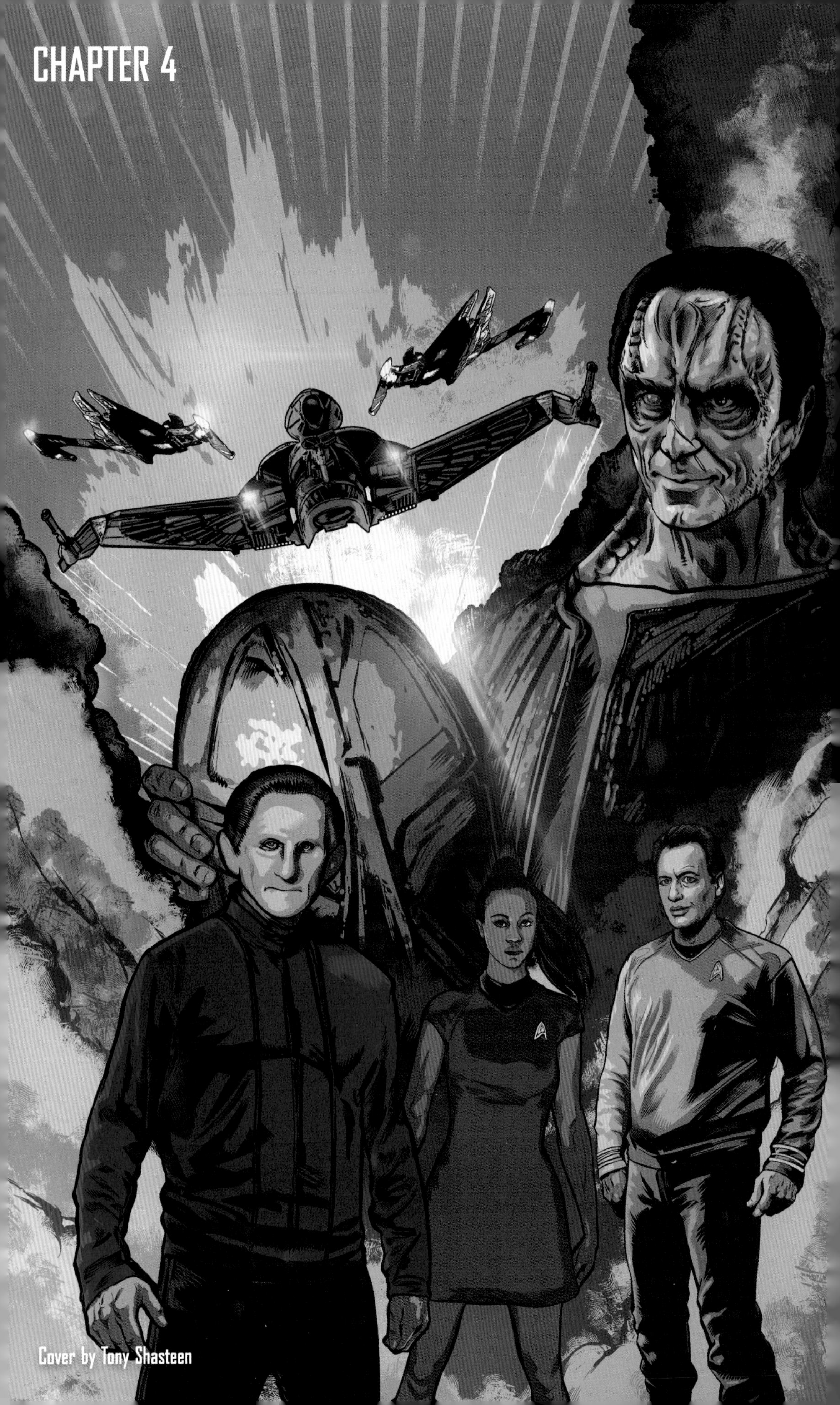

Cover by Tony Shasteen

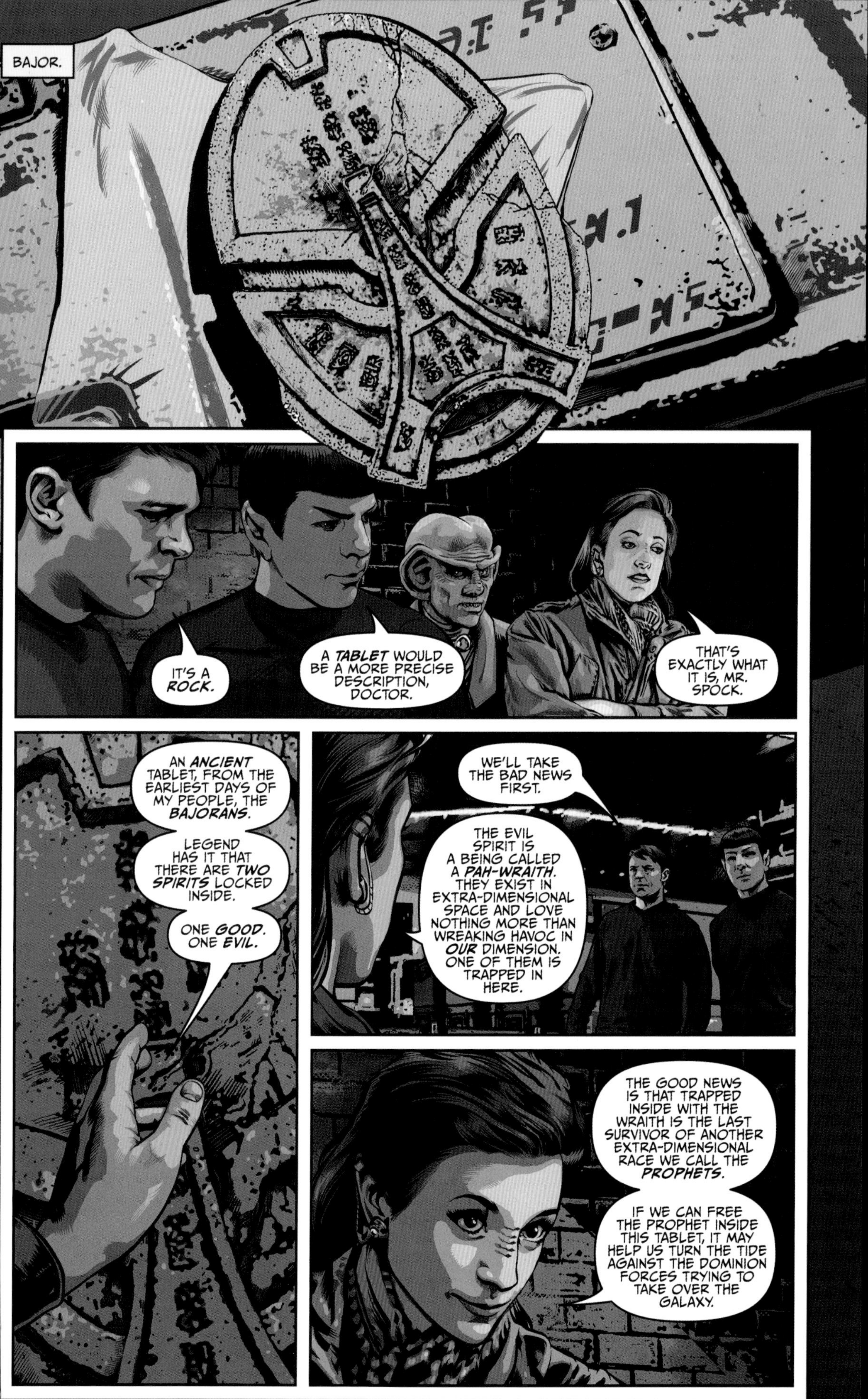

BAJOR.
IT'S A ROCK.
A TABLET WOULD BE A MORE PRECISE DESCRIPTION, DOCTOR.
THAT'S EXACTLY WHAT IT IS, MR. SPOCK.
AN ANCIENT TABLET, FROM THE EARLIEST DAYS OF MY PEOPLE, THE BAJORANS.
LEGEND HAS IT THAT THERE ARE TWO SPIRITS LOCKED INSIDE.
ONE GOOD. ONE EVIL.
WE'LL TAKE THE BAD NEWS FIRST.
THE EVIL SPIRIT IS A BEING CALLED A PAH-WRAITH. THEY EXIST IN EXTRA-DIMENSIONAL SPACE AND LOVE NOTHING MORE THAN WREAKING HAVOC IN OUR DIMENSION. ONE OF THEM IS TRAPPED IN HERE.
THE GOOD NEWS IS THAT TRAPPED INSIDE WITH THE WRAITH IS THE LAST SURVIVOR OF ANOTHER EXTRA-DIMENSIONAL RACE WE CALL THE PROPHETS.
IF WE CAN FREE THE PROPHET INSIDE THIS TABLET, IT MAY HELP US TURN THE TIDE AGAINST THE DOMINION FORCES TRYING TO TAKE OVER THE GALAXY.

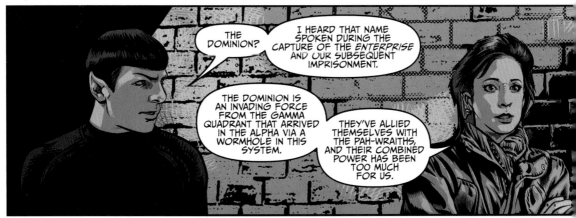

THE DOMINION?

I HEARD THAT NAME SPOKEN DURING THE CAPTURE OF THE *ENTERPRISE* AND OUR SUBSEQUENT IMPRISONMENT.

THE DOMINION IS AN INVADING FORCE FROM THE GAMMA QUADRANT THAT ARRIVED IN THE ALPHA VIA A WORMHOLE IN THIS SYSTEM.

THEY'VE ALLIED THEMSELVES WITH THE PAH-WRAITHS, AND THEIR COMBINED POWER HAS BEEN TOO MUCH FOR US.

"DOMINION"? "WRAITHS"? "PROPHETS"?

I PREFER THE GOOD OLD DAYS, WHEN WE JUST HAD TO WORRY ABOUT KLINGONS.

CONFUSING, I KNOW. BUT AS MY WISE OLD GRANDMOTHER USED TO SAY, THE MORE FACTIONS IN THE FIGHT, THE MORE PROFIT IN YOUR POCKET!

SOUNDS LIKE A CHARMING WOMAN.

FERENGI!

GESUNDHEIT.

HOW DO YOU INTEND TO FREE THIS "PROPHET" INSIDE THE TABLET?

VERY CAREFULLY.

I WAS SUPPOSED TO RENDEZVOUS WITH MY PARTNER—*BEN SISKO*—AND DELIVER THE TABLET TO OUR BASE ON A PLANET HIDDEN FROM THE DOMINION'S PRYING EYES. THAT'S WHERE WE'LL TRY TO FREE THE PROPHET.

BUT SISKO WAS CAPTURED. THE REBELLION WAS A MAN DOWN...

...UNTIL *YOU TWO* DROPPED INTO MY LAP FROM THE LONG-LOST PAST.

SO WHAT DO YOU SAY, BOYS? READY TO GET *REBELLIOUS?*

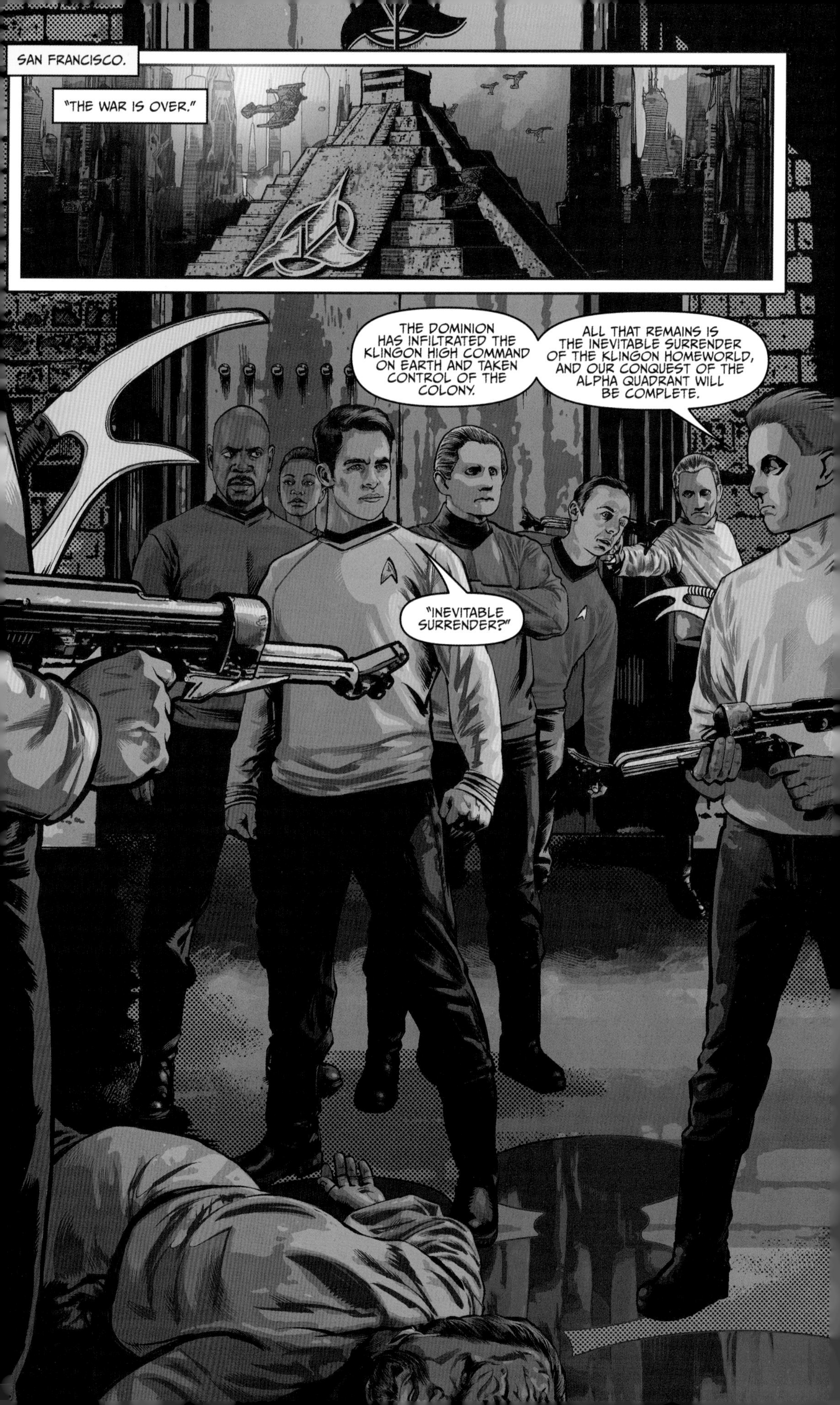
SAN FRANCISCO.
"THE WAR IS OVER."
THE DOMINION HAS INFILTRATED THE KLINGON HIGH COMMAND ON EARTH AND TAKEN CONTROL OF THE COLONY.
ALL THAT REMAINS IS THE INEVITABLE SURRENDER OF THE KLINGON HOMEWORLD, AND OUR CONQUEST OF THE ALPHA QUADRANT WILL BE COMPLETE.
"INEVITABLE SURRENDER?"

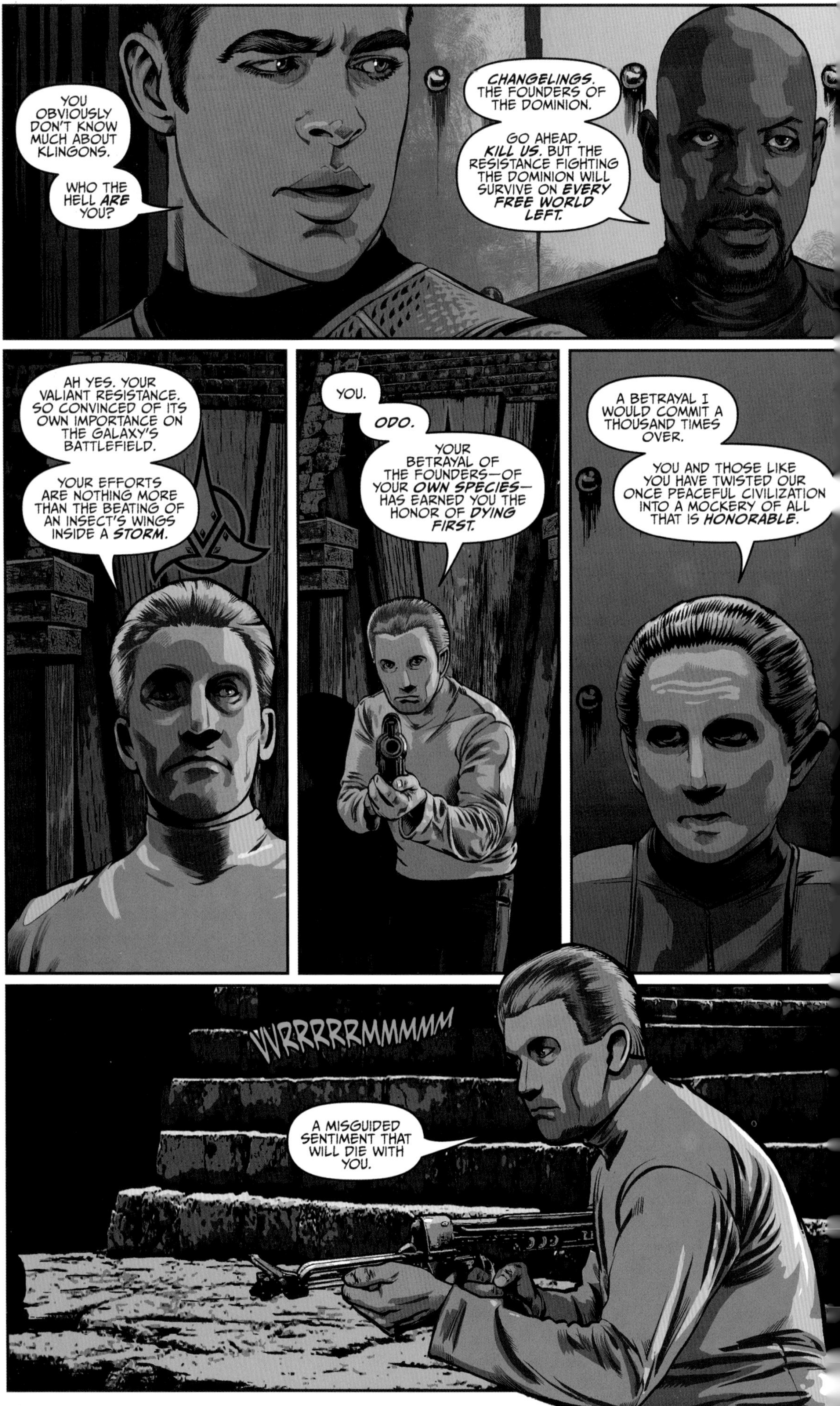

YOU OBVIOUSLY DON'T KNOW MUCH ABOUT KLINGONS.
WHO THE HELL *ARE* YOU?
CHANGELINGS. THE FOUNDERS OF THE DOMINION.
GO AHEAD. *KILL US.* BUT THE RESISTANCE FIGHTING THE DOMINION WILL SURVIVE ON *EVERY FREE WORLD LEFT.*
AH YES. YOUR VALIANT RESISTANCE. SO CONVINCED OF ITS OWN IMPORTANCE ON THE GALAXY'S BATTLEFIELD.
YOUR EFFORTS ARE NOTHING MORE THAN THE BEATING OF AN INSECT'S WINGS INSIDE A *STORM.*
YOU.
ODO.
YOUR BETRAYAL OF THE FOUNDERS—OF YOUR *OWN SPECIES*—HAS EARNED YOU THE HONOR OF *DYING FIRST.*
A BETRAYAL I WOULD COMMIT A THOUSAND TIMES OVER.
YOU AND THOSE LIKE YOU HAVE TWISTED OUR ONCE PEACEFUL CIVILIZATION INTO A MOCKERY OF ALL THAT IS *HONORABLE.*
VVRRRRRMMMMM
A MISGUIDED SENTIMENT THAT WILL DIE WITH YOU.

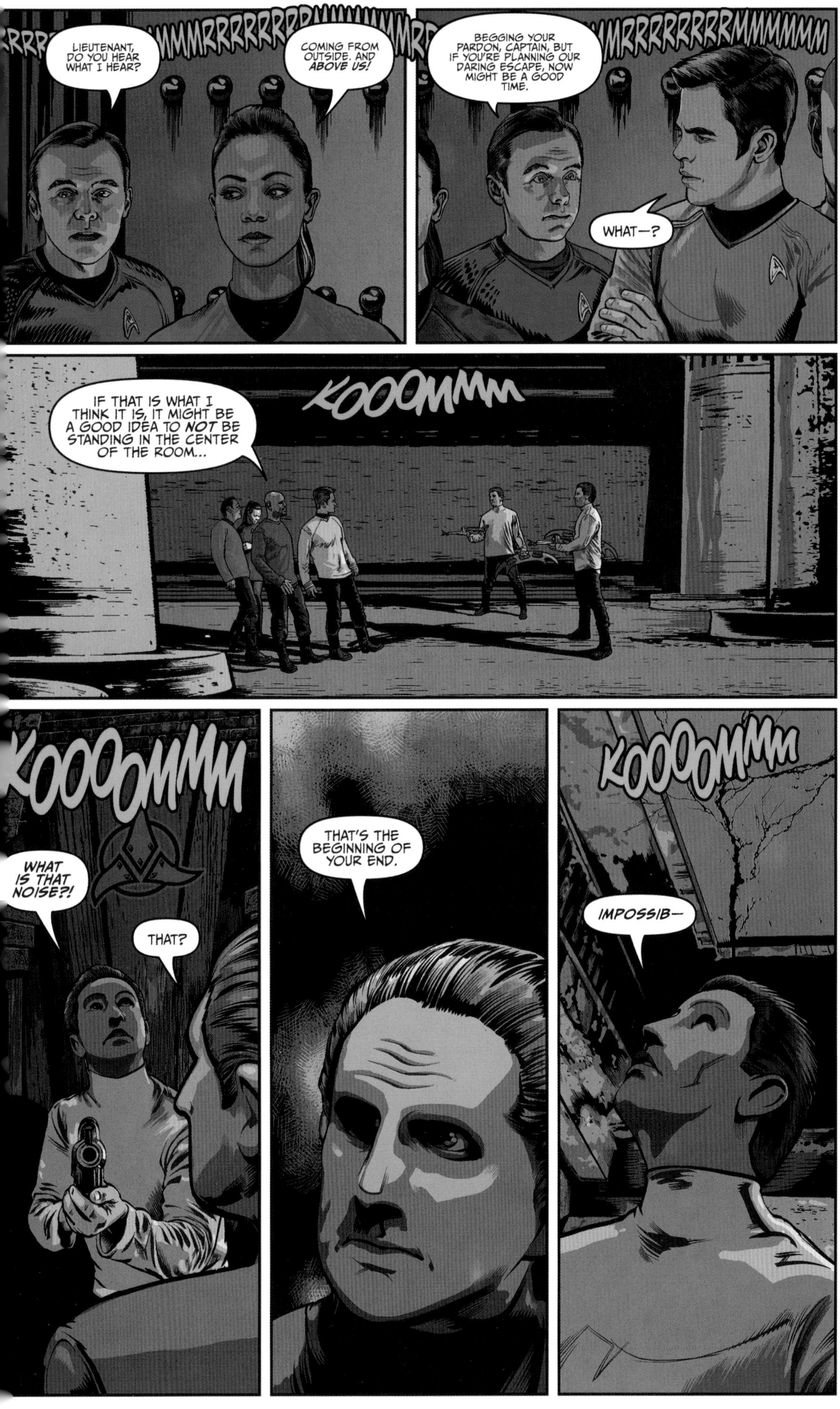
RRRRRRRRMMMMRRRRRRRRMMMMMMMRRRRRRRRRMMMMMMM
LIEUTENANT, DO YOU HEAR WHAT I HEAR?
COMING FROM OUTSIDE. AND *ABOVE US!*
BEGGING YOUR PARDON, CAPTAIN, BUT IF YOU'RE PLANNING OUR DARING ESCAPE, NOW MIGHT BE A GOOD TIME.
WHAT—?
KOOOMMM
IF THAT IS WHAT I THINK IT IS, IT MIGHT BE A GOOD IDEA TO *NOT* BE STANDING IN THE CENTER OF THE ROOM...
KOOOOMMMM
WHAT IS THAT NOISE?!
THAT?
THAT'S THE BEGINNING OF YOUR END.
KOOOOMMM
IMPOSSIB—

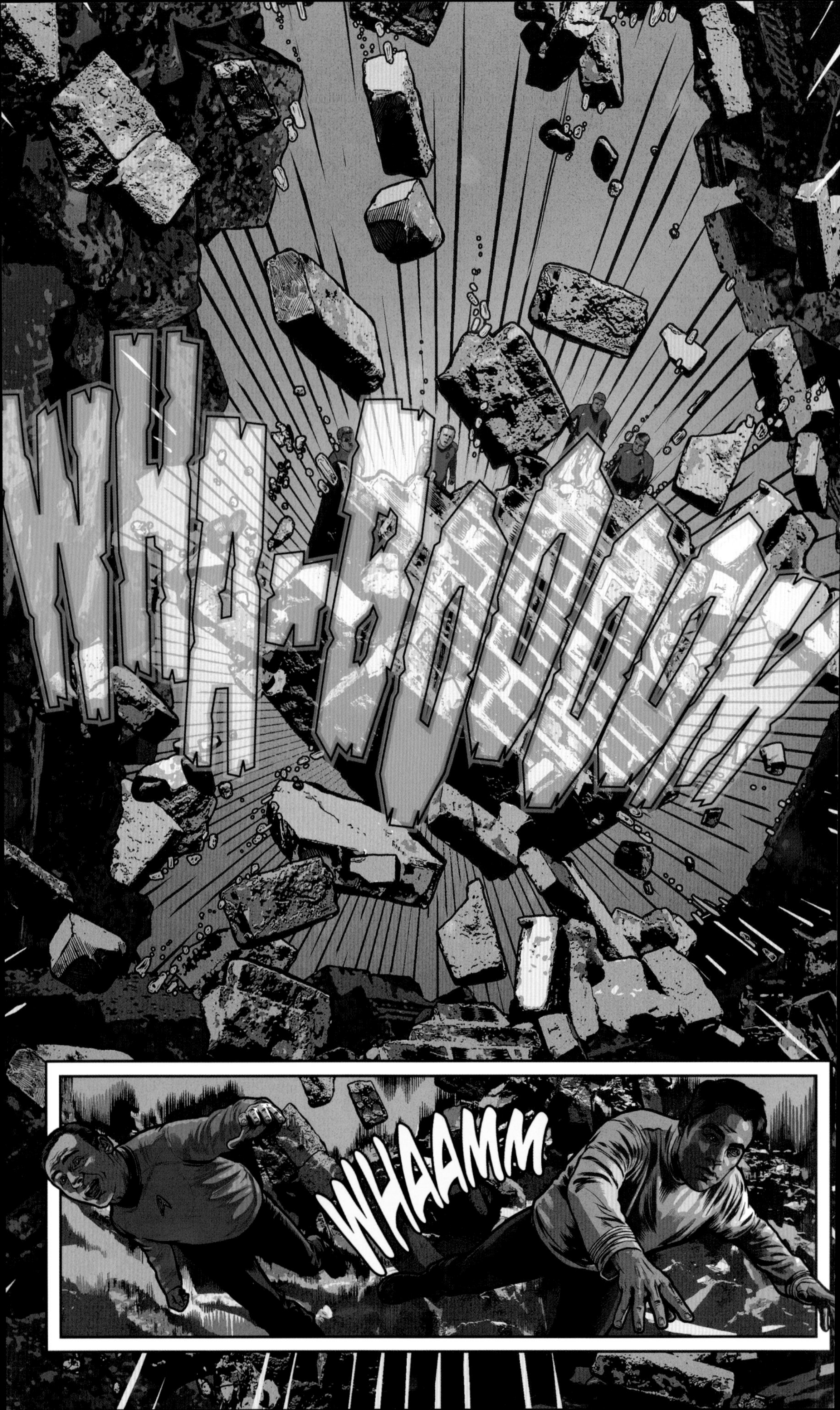
WHA-BOOOOM
WHAAMM

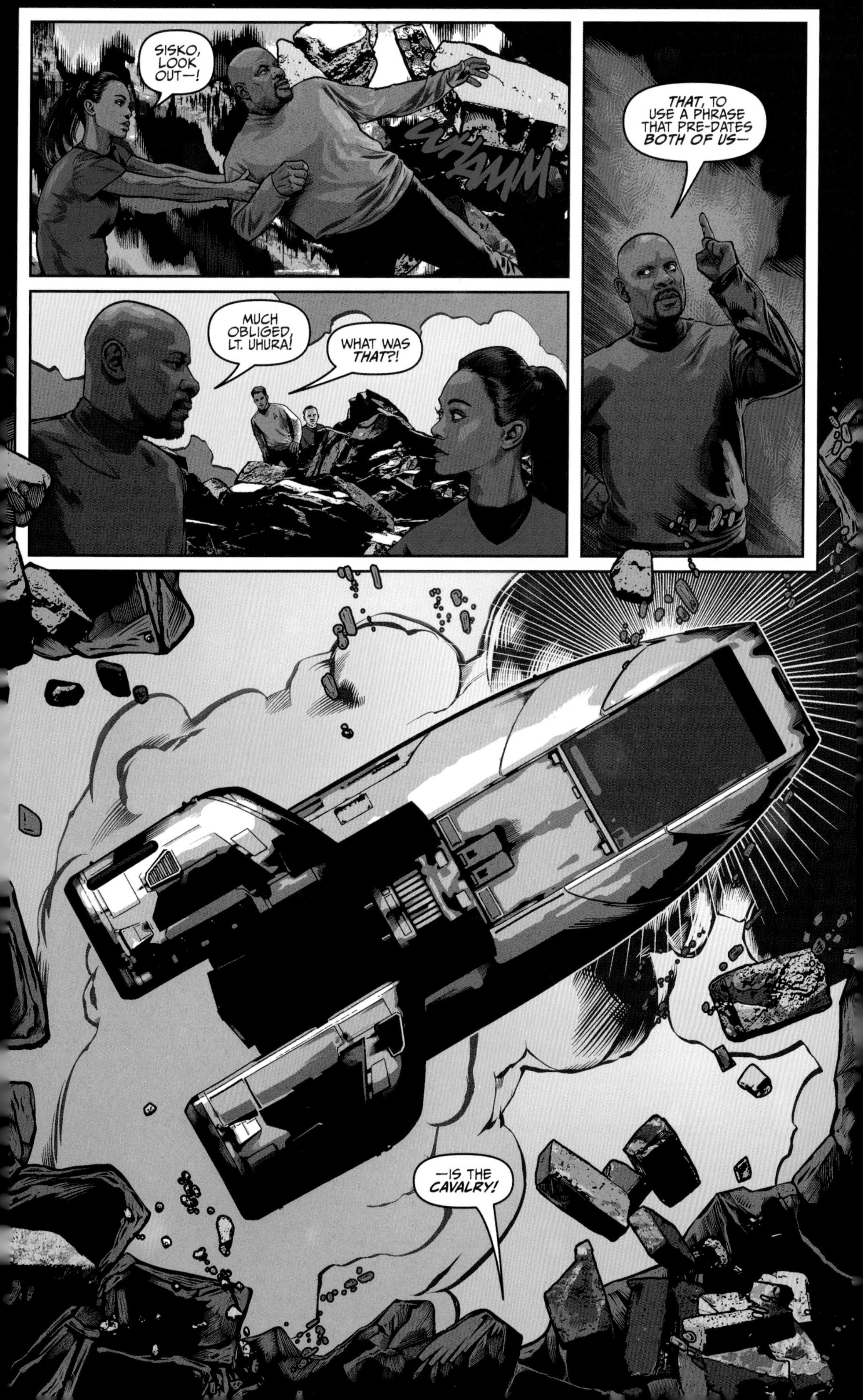
SISKO, LOOK OUT—!
WHAMM
MUCH OBLIGED, LT. UHURA!
WHAT WAS THAT?!
THAT, TO USE A PHRASE THAT PRE-DATES BOTH OF US—
—IS THE CAVALRY!

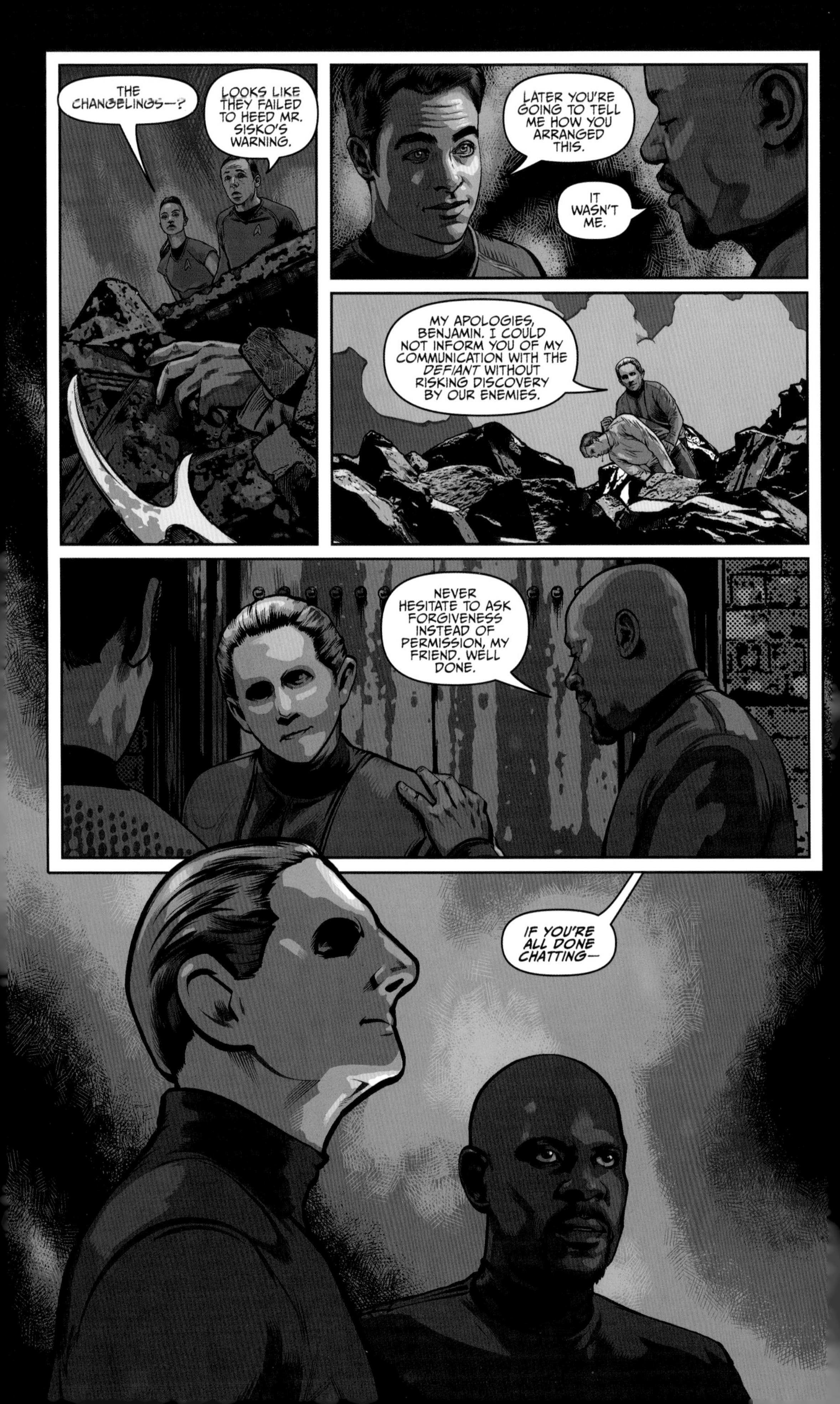
THE CHANGELINGS--?
LOOKS LIKE THEY FAILED TO HEED MR. SISKO'S WARNING.
LATER YOU'RE GOING TO TELL ME HOW YOU ARRANGED THIS.
IT WASN'T ME.
MY APOLOGIES, BENJAMIN. I COULD NOT INFORM YOU OF MY COMMUNICATION WITH THE DEFIANT WITHOUT RISKING DISCOVERY BY OUR ENEMIES.
NEVER HESITATE TO ASK FORGIVENESS INSTEAD OF PERMISSION, MY FRIEND. WELL DONE.
IF YOU'RE ALL DONE CHATTING--

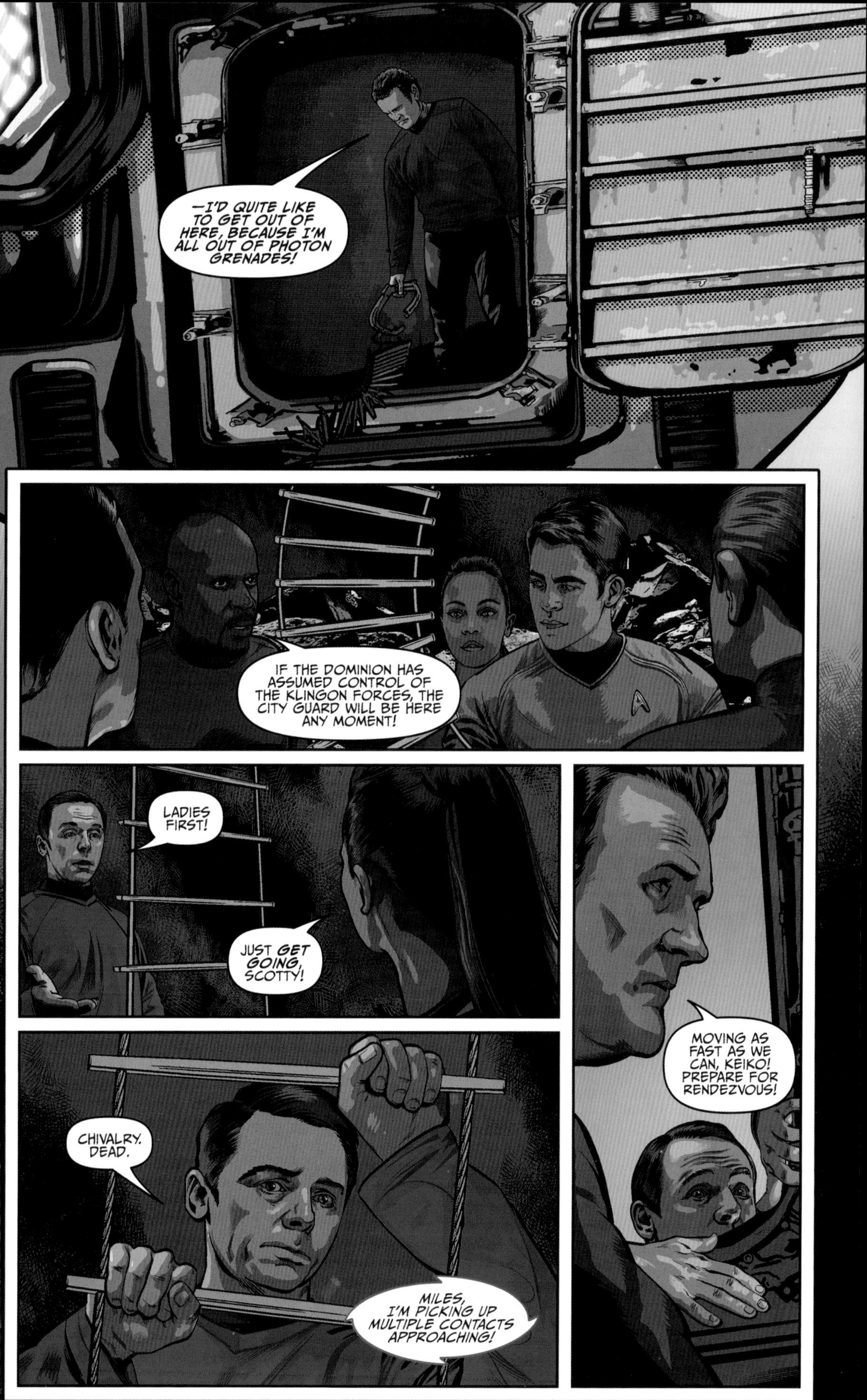
—I'D QUITE LIKE TO GET OUT OF HERE, BECAUSE I'M ALL OUT OF PHOTON GRENADES!
IF THE DOMINION HAS ASSUMED CONTROL OF THE KLINGON FORCES, THE CITY GUARD WILL BE HERE ANY MOMENT!
LADIES FIRST!
JUST GET GOING, SCOTTY!
CHIVALRY. DEAD.
MILES, I'M PICKING UP MULTIPLE CONTACTS APPROACHING!
MOVING AS FAST AS WE CAN, KEIKO! PREPARE FOR RENDEZVOUS!

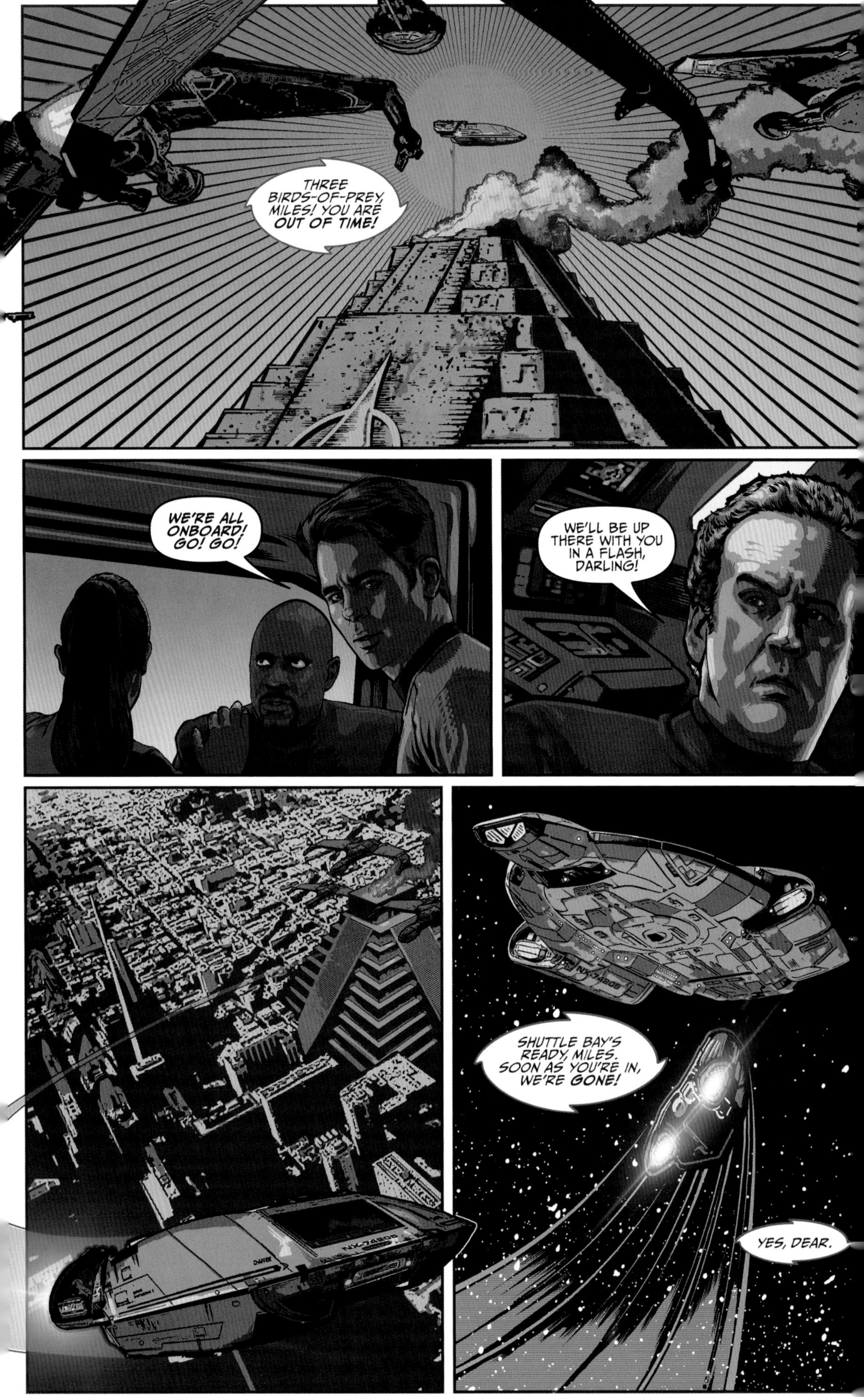

THREE BIRDS-OF-PREY, MILES! YOU ARE OUT OF TIME!
WE'RE ALL ONBOARD! GO! GO!
WE'LL BE UP THERE WITH YOU IN A FLASH, DARLING!
SHUTTLE BAY'S READY, MILES. SOON AS YOU'RE IN, WE'RE GONE!
YES, DEAR.

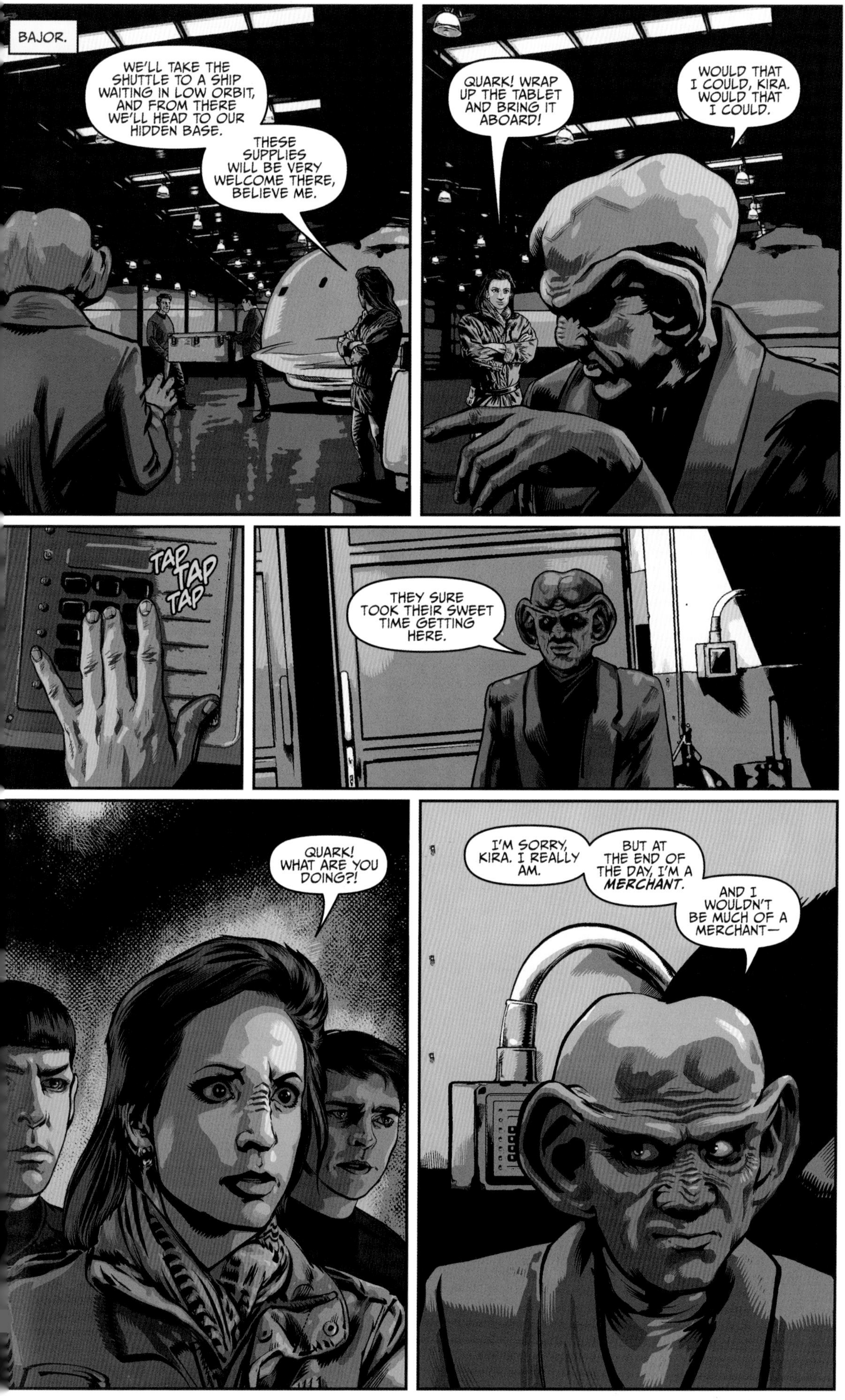
BAJOR.
WE'LL TAKE THE SHUTTLE TO A SHIP WAITING IN LOW ORBIT, AND FROM THERE WE'LL HEAD TO OUR HIDDEN BASE.
THESE SUPPLIES WILL BE VERY WELCOME THERE, BELIEVE ME.
QUARK! WRAP UP THE TABLET AND BRING IT ABOARD!
WOULD THAT I COULD, KIRA. WOULD THAT I COULD.
TAP TAP TAP
THEY SURE TOOK THEIR SWEET TIME GETTING HERE.
QUARK! WHAT ARE YOU DOING?!
I'M SORRY, KIRA. I REALLY AM.
BUT AT THE END OF THE DAY, I'M A *MERCHANT*.
AND I WOULDN'T BE MUCH OF A MERCHANT—

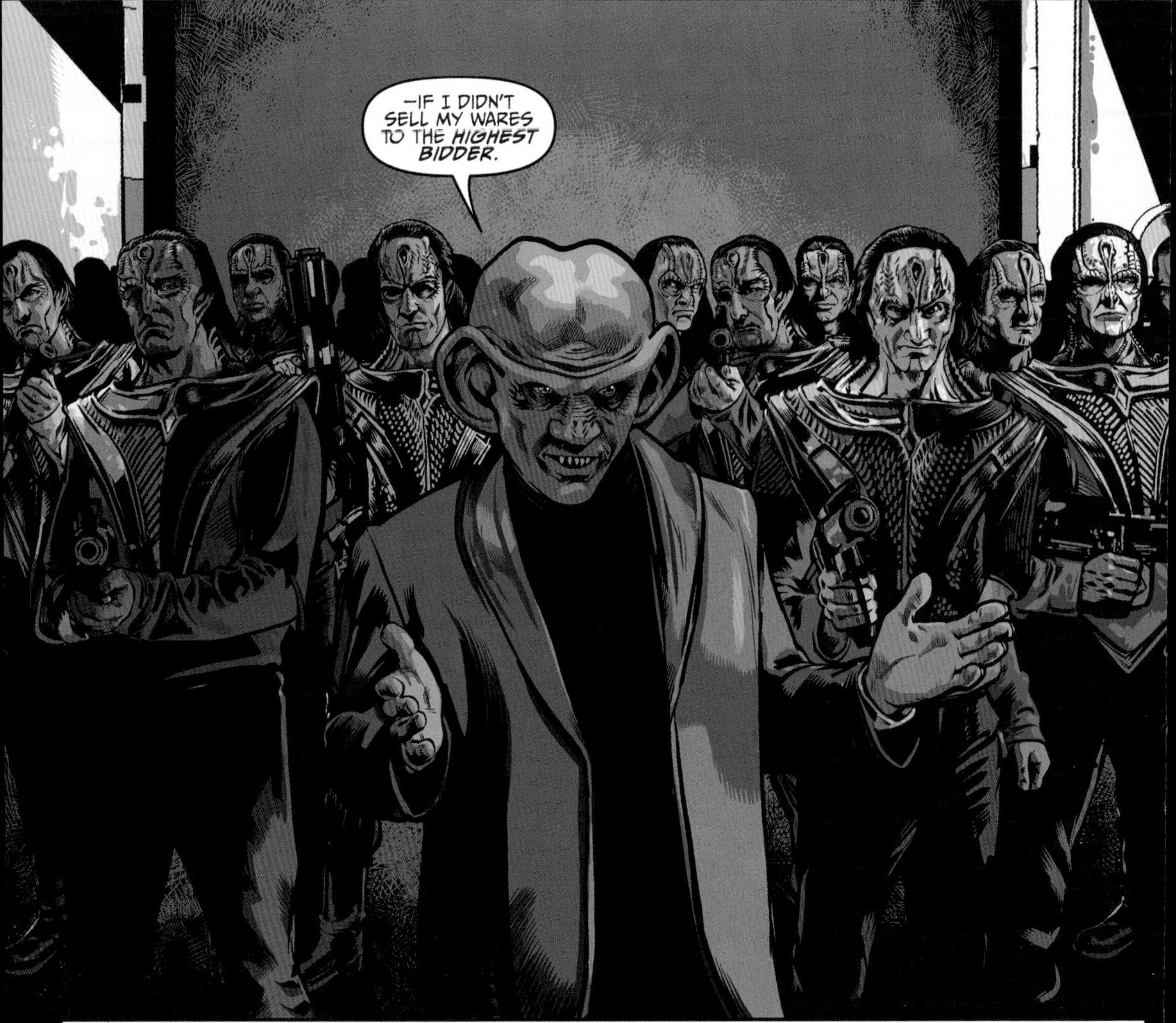
—IF I DIDN'T SELL MY WARES TO THE *HIGHEST BIDDER*.

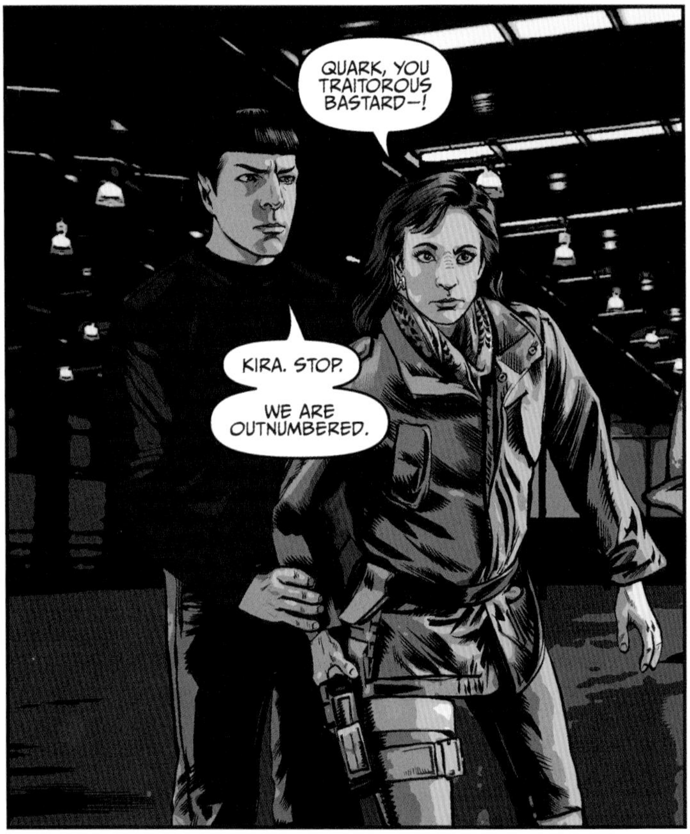
QUARK, YOU TRAITOROUS BASTARD—!
KIRA. STOP.
WE ARE OUTNUMBERED.

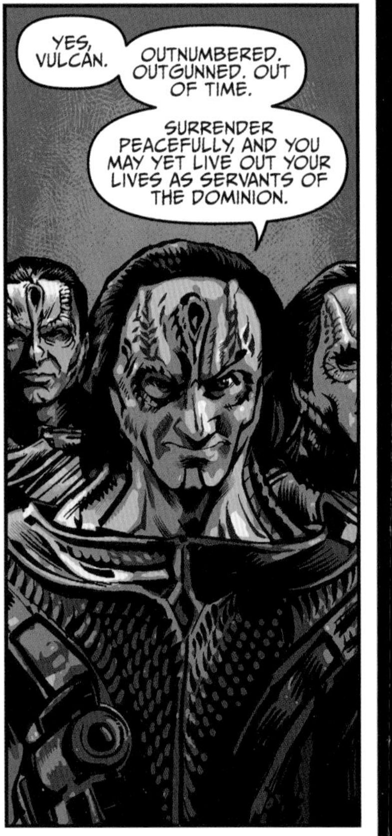
YES, VULCAN.
OUTNUMBERED. OUTGUNNED. OUT OF TIME.
SURRENDER PEACEFULLY, AND YOU MAY YET LIVE OUT YOUR LIVES AS SERVANTS OF THE DOMINION.

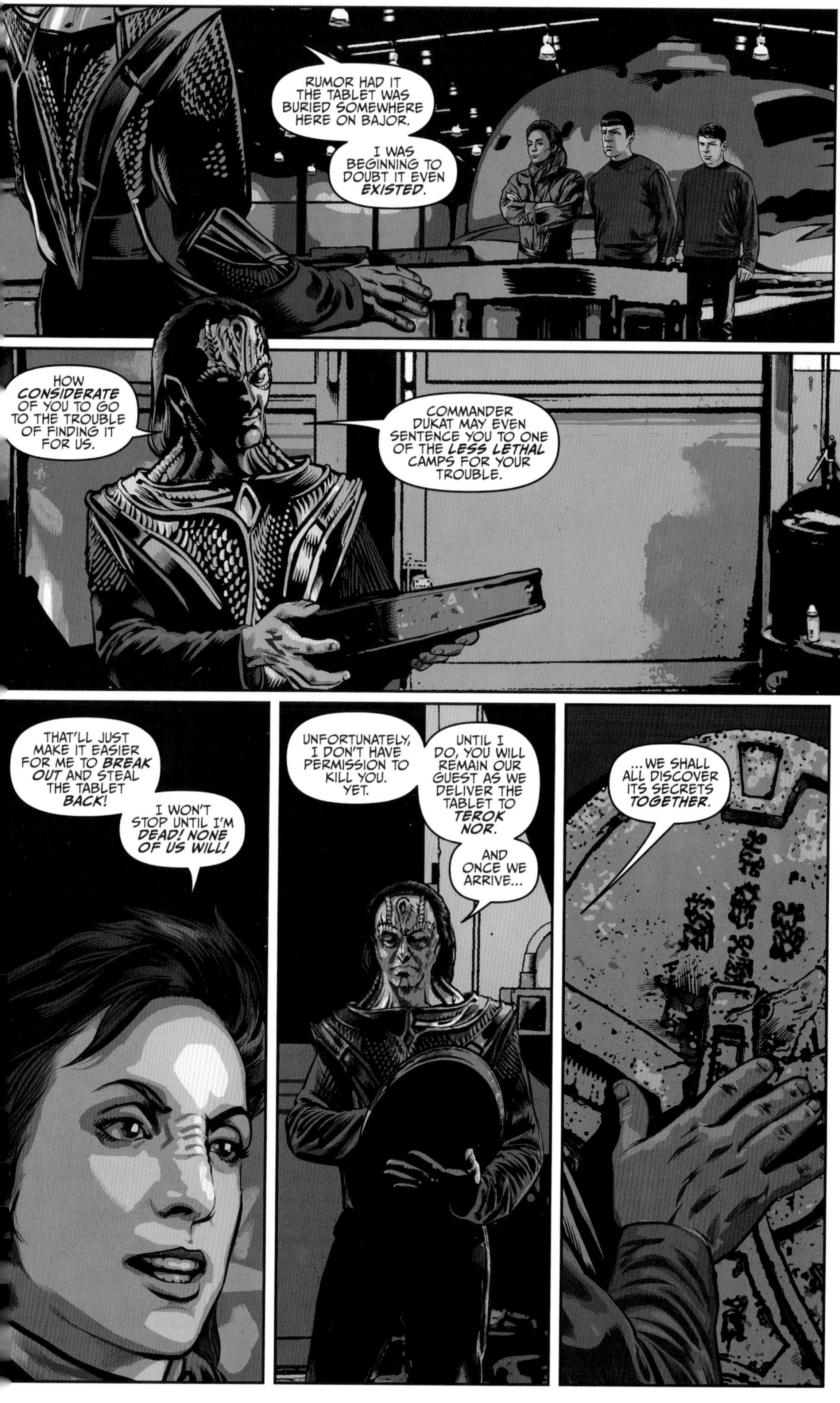
RUMOR HAD IT THE TABLET WAS BURIED SOMEWHERE HERE ON BAJOR.
I WAS BEGINNING TO DOUBT IT EVEN EXISTED.
HOW CONSIDERATE OF YOU TO GO TO THE TROUBLE OF FINDING IT FOR US.
COMMANDER DUKAT MAY EVEN SENTENCE YOU TO ONE OF THE LESS LETHAL CAMPS FOR YOUR TROUBLE.
THAT'LL JUST MAKE IT EASIER FOR ME TO BREAK OUT AND STEAL THE TABLET BACK!
I WON'T STOP UNTIL I'M DEAD! NONE OF US WILL!
UNFORTUNATELY, I DON'T HAVE PERMISSION TO KILL YOU. YET.
UNTIL I DO, YOU WILL REMAIN OUR GUEST AS WE DELIVER THE TABLET TO TEROK NOR.
AND ONCE WE ARRIVE...
...WE SHALL ALL DISCOVER ITS SECRETS TOGETHER.

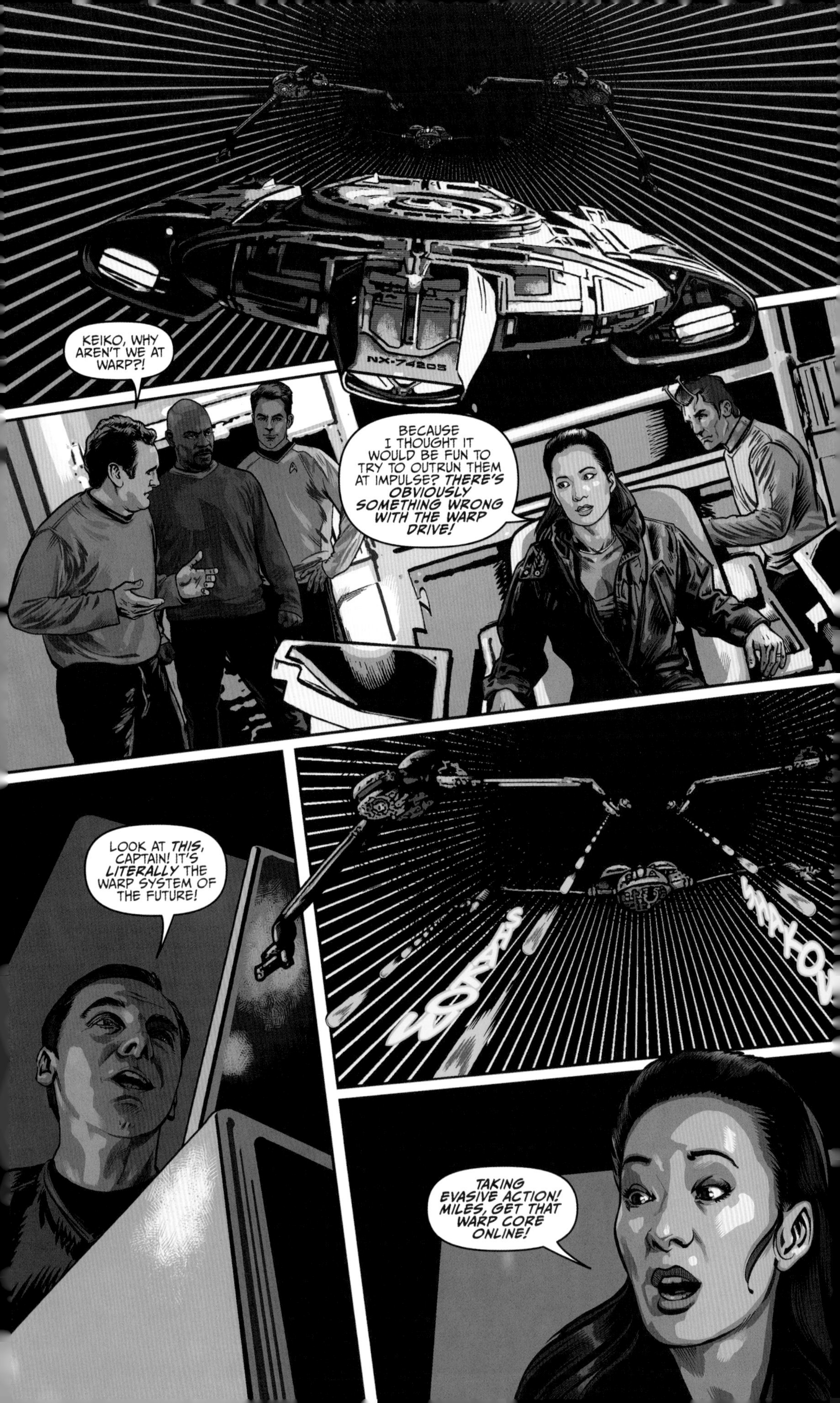

NX-74205
KEIKO, WHY AREN'T WE AT WARP?!
BECAUSE I THOUGHT IT WOULD BE FUN TO TRY TO OUTRUN THEM AT IMPULSE? *THERE'S OBVIOUSLY SOMETHING WRONG WITH THE WARP DRIVE!*
LOOK AT *THIS*, CAPTAIN! IT'S *LITERALLY* THE WARP SYSTEM OF THE FUTURE!
TAKING EVASIVE ACTION! MILES, GET THAT WARP CORE ONLINE!

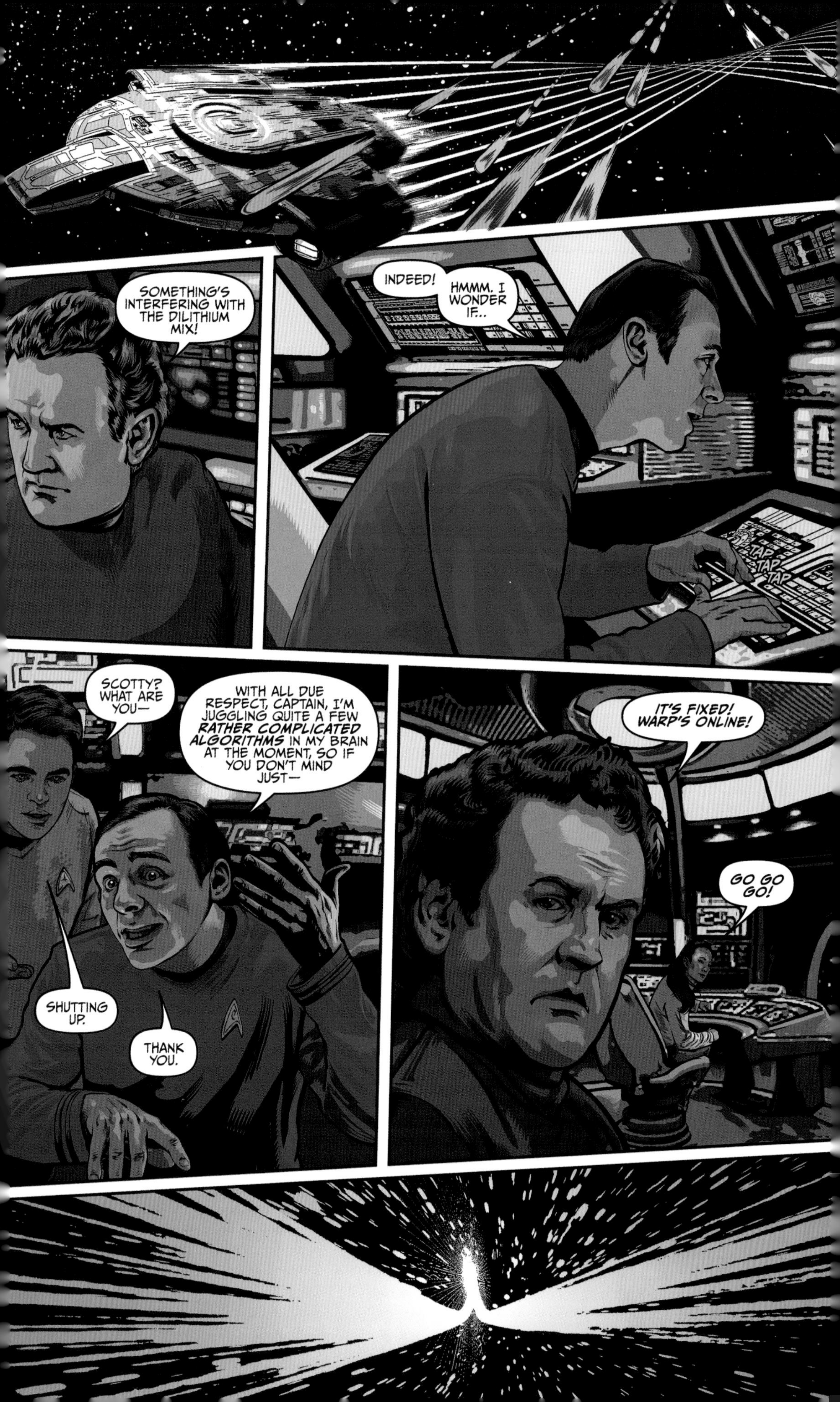
SOMETHING'S INTERFERING WITH THE DILITHIUM MIX!
INDEED!
HMMM. I WONDER IF...
TAP TAP TAP
SCOTTY? WHAT ARE YOU—
WITH ALL DUE RESPECT, CAPTAIN, I'M JUGGLING QUITE A FEW RATHER COMPLICATED ALGORITHMS IN MY BRAIN AT THE MOMENT, SO IF YOU DON'T MIND JUST—
SHUTTING UP.
THANK YOU.
IT'S FIXED! WARP'S ONLINE!
GO GO GO!

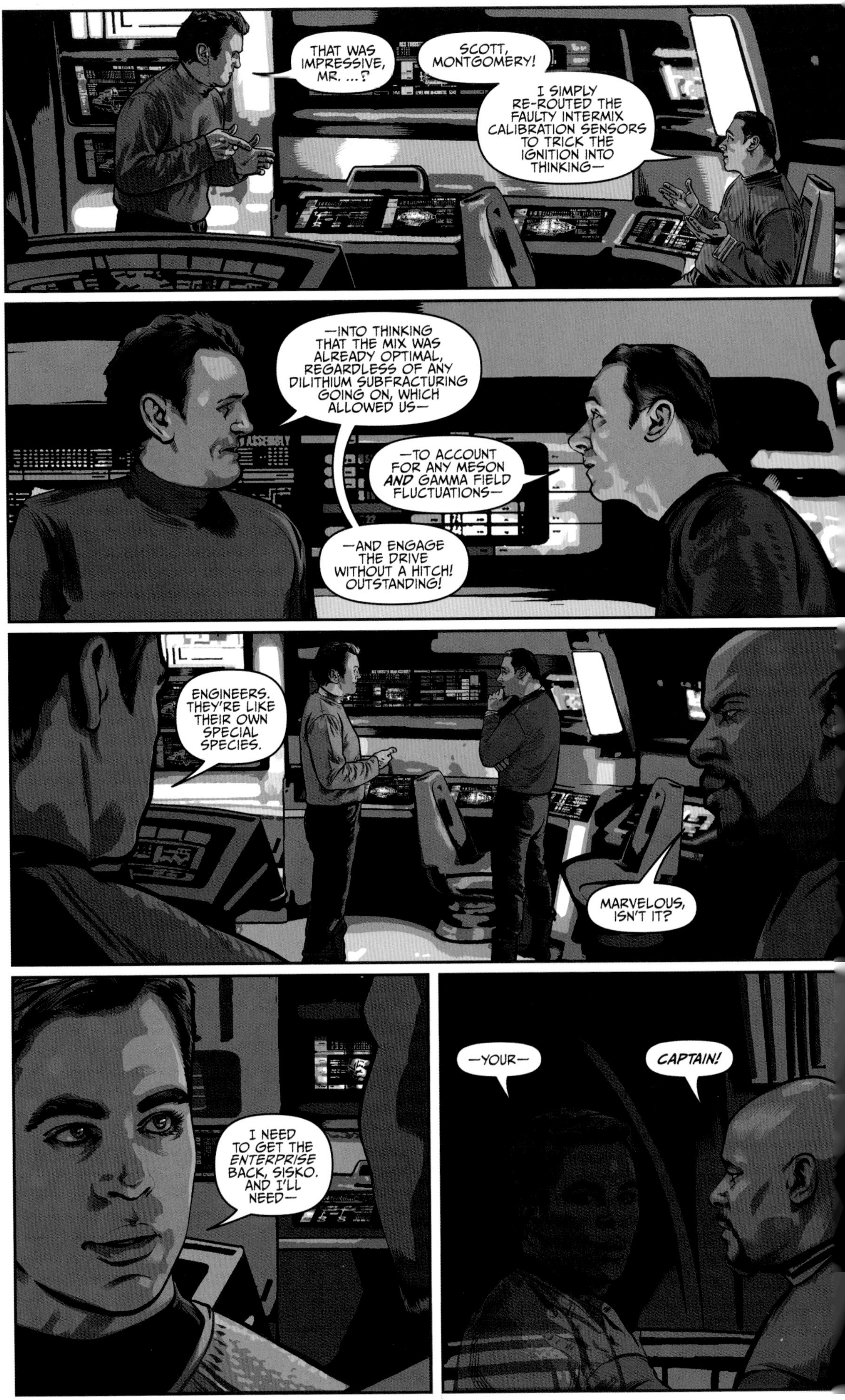
THAT WAS IMPRESSIVE, MR. ...?
SCOTT, MONTGOMERY!
I SIMPLY RE-ROUTED THE FAULTY INTERMIX CALIBRATION SENSORS TO TRICK THE IGNITION INTO THINKING—
—INTO THINKING THAT THE MIX WAS ALREADY OPTIMAL, REGARDLESS OF ANY DILITHIUM SUBFRACTURING GOING ON, WHICH ALLOWED US—
—TO ACCOUNT FOR ANY MESON *AND* GAMMA FIELD FLUCTUATIONS—
—AND ENGAGE THE DRIVE WITHOUT A HITCH! OUTSTANDING!
ENGINEERS. THEY'RE LIKE THEIR OWN SPECIAL SPECIES.
MARVELOUS, ISN'T IT?
I NEED TO GET THE *ENTERPRISE* BACK, SISKO. AND I'LL NEED—
—YOUR—
CAPTAIN!

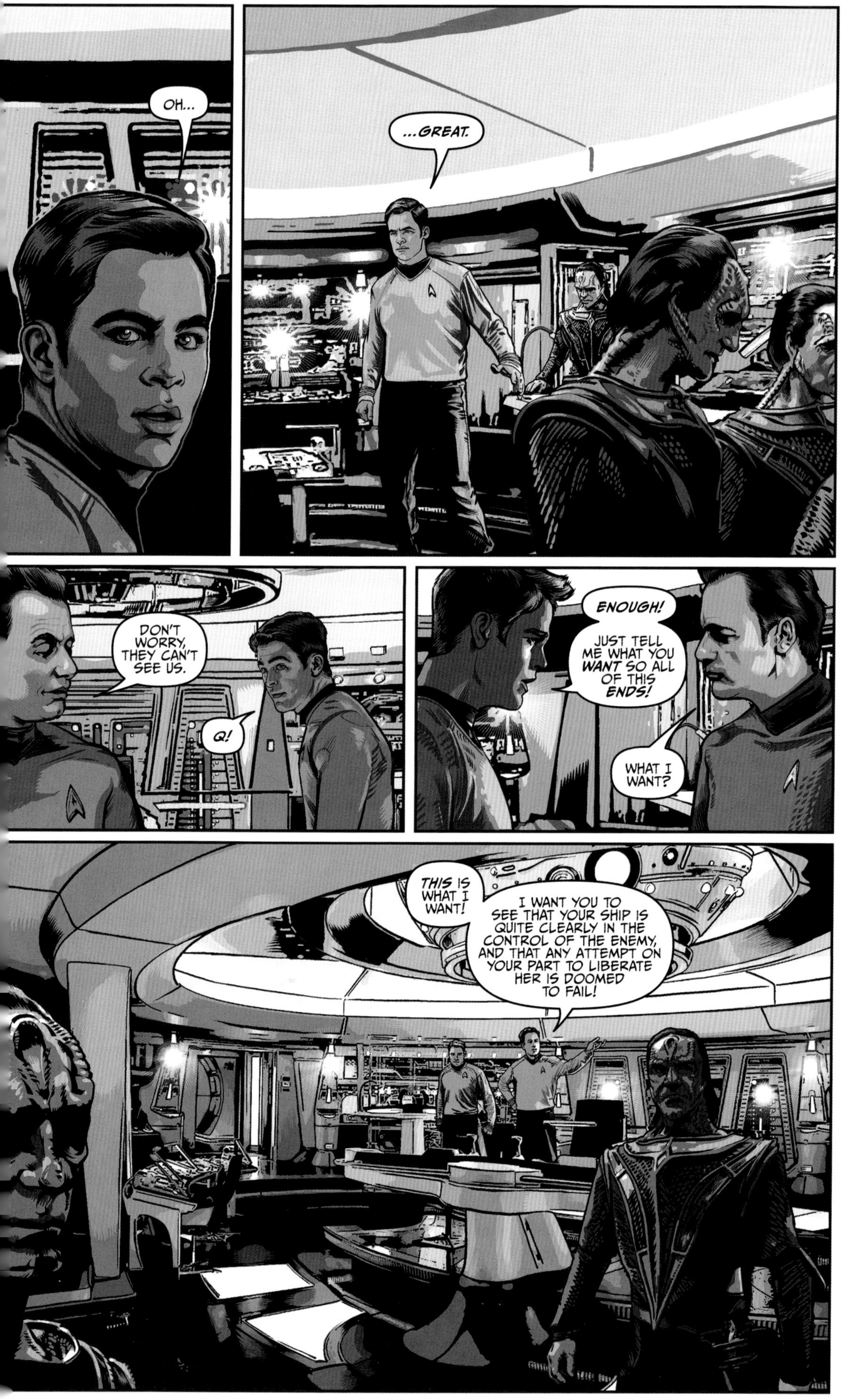
OH...
...GREAT.
DON'T WORRY, THEY CAN'T SEE US.
Q!
ENOUGH!
JUST TELL ME WHAT YOU WANT SO ALL OF THIS ENDS!
WHAT I WANT?
THIS IS WHAT I WANT!
I WANT YOU TO SEE THAT YOUR SHIP IS QUITE CLEARLY IN THE CONTROL OF THE ENEMY, AND THAT ANY ATTEMPT ON YOUR PART TO LIBERATE HER IS DOOMED TO FAIL!

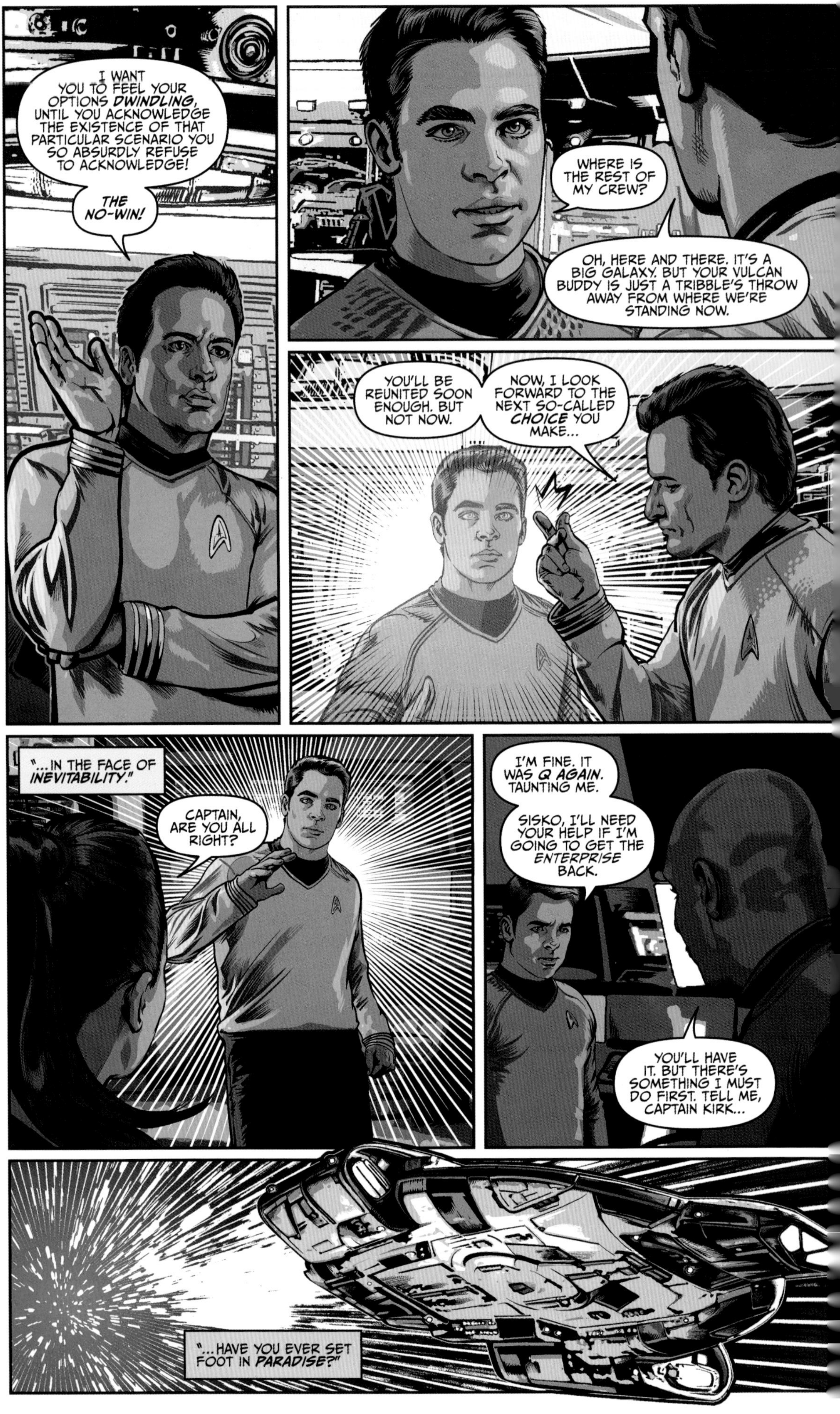
I WANT YOU TO FEEL YOUR OPTIONS *DWINDLING*, UNTIL YOU ACKNOWLEDGE THE EXISTENCE OF THAT PARTICULAR SCENARIO YOU SO ABSURDLY REFUSE TO ACKNOWLEDGE!
THE NO-WIN!
WHERE IS THE REST OF MY CREW?
OH, HERE AND THERE. IT'S A BIG GALAXY. BUT YOUR VULCAN BUDDY IS JUST A TRIBBLE'S THROW AWAY FROM WHERE WE'RE STANDING NOW.
YOU'LL BE REUNITED SOON ENOUGH. BUT NOT NOW.
NOW, I LOOK FORWARD TO THE NEXT SO-CALLED *CHOICE* YOU MAKE...
"...IN THE FACE OF *INEVITABILITY*."
CAPTAIN, ARE YOU ALL RIGHT?
I'M FINE. IT WAS *Q AGAIN*. TAUNTING ME.
SISKO, I'LL NEED YOUR HELP IF I'M GOING TO GET THE *ENTERPRISE* BACK.
YOU'LL HAVE IT, BUT THERE'S SOMETHING I MUST DO FIRST. TELL ME, CAPTAIN KIRK...
"...HAVE YOU EVER SET FOOT IN *PARADISE*?"

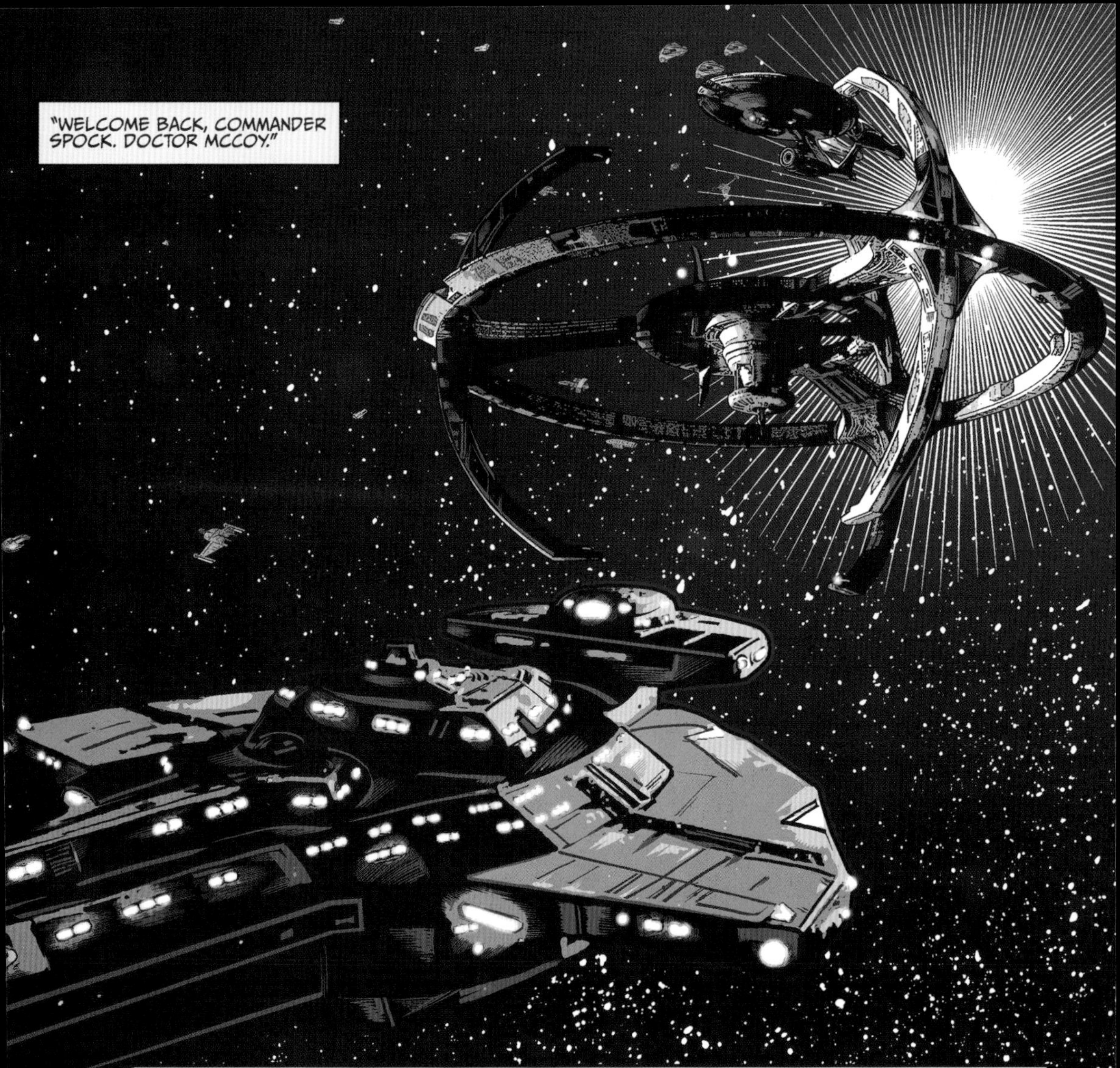
"WELCOME BACK, COMMANDER SPOCK. DOCTOR MCCOY."

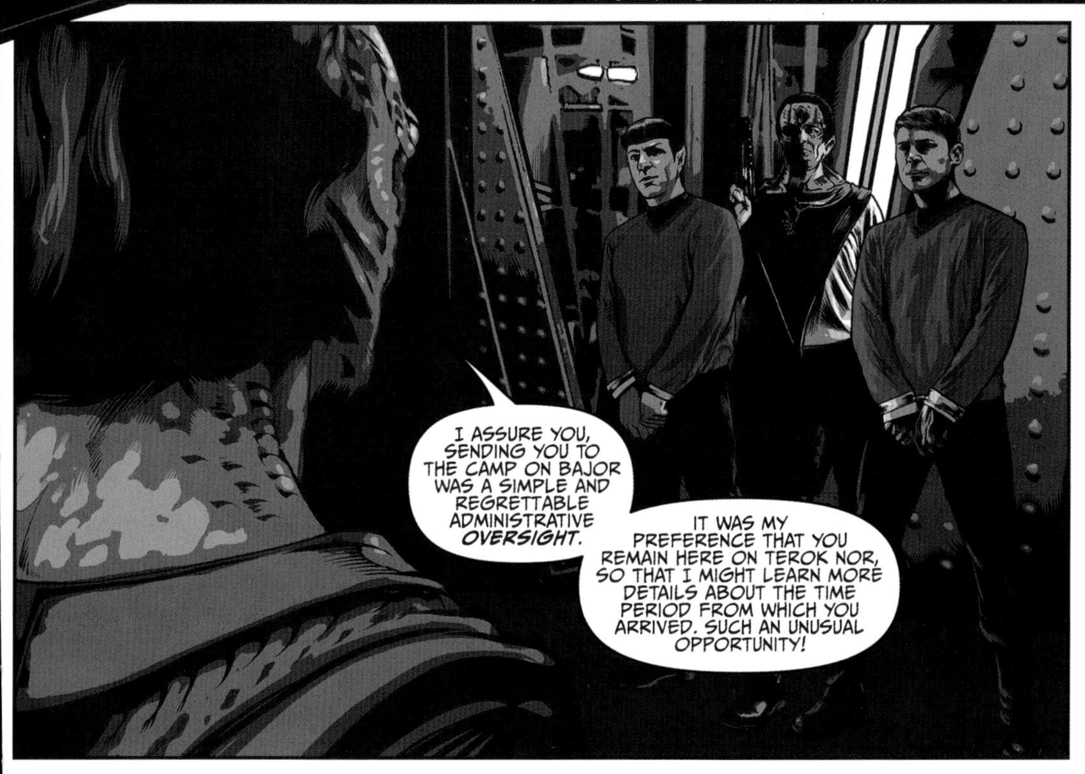
I ASSURE YOU, SENDING YOU TO THE CAMP ON BAJOR WAS A SIMPLE AND REGRETTABLE ADMINISTRATIVE *OVERSIGHT*.
IT WAS MY PREFERENCE THAT YOU REMAIN HERE ON TEROK NOR, SO THAT I MIGHT LEARN MORE DETAILS ABOUT THE TIME PERIOD FROM WHICH YOU ARRIVED. SUCH AN UNUSUAL OPPORTUNITY!

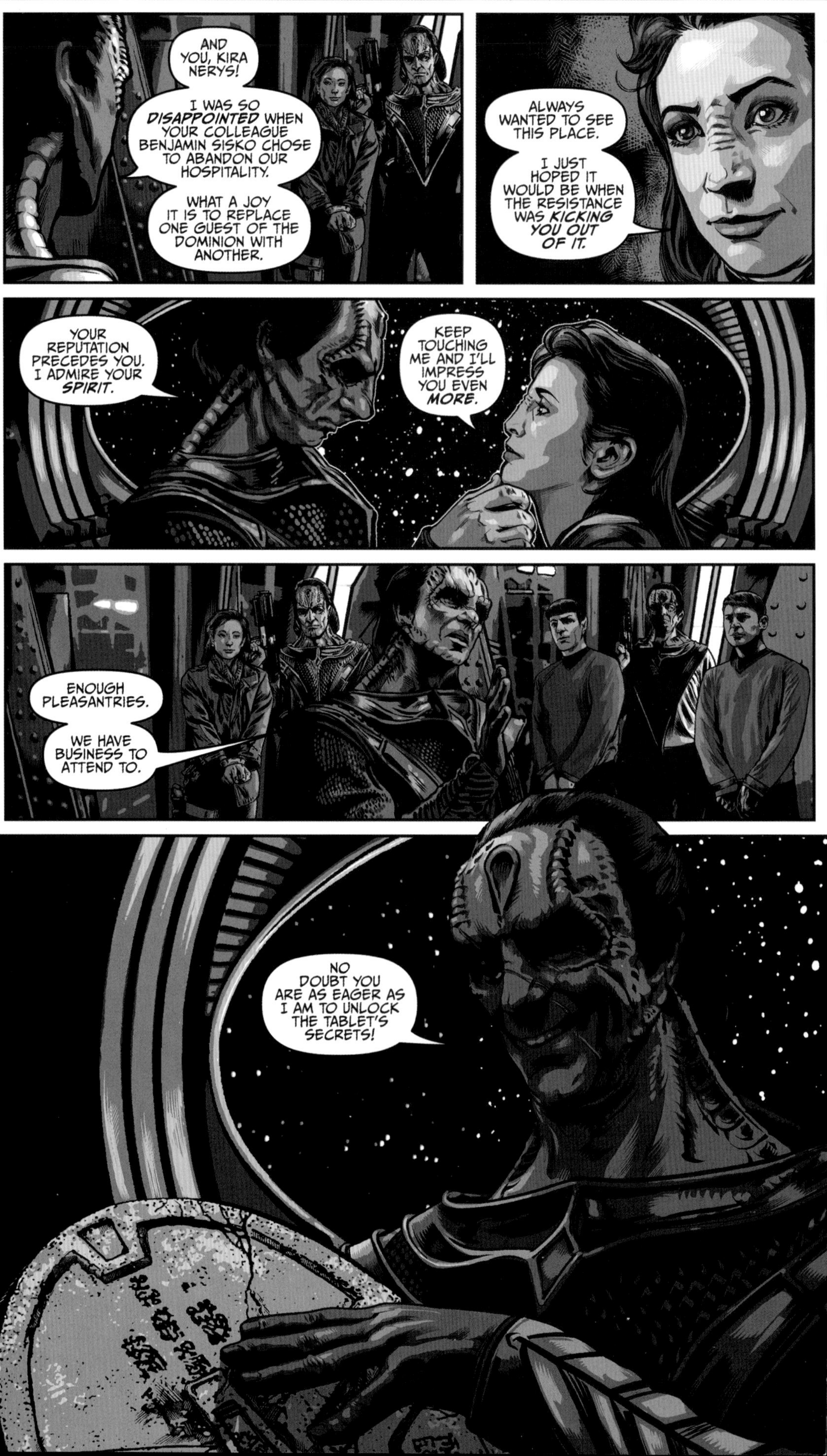
AND YOU, KIRA NERYS!
I WAS SO DISAPPOINTED WHEN YOUR COLLEAGUE BENJAMIN SISKO CHOSE TO ABANDON OUR HOSPITALITY.
WHAT A JOY IT IS TO REPLACE ONE GUEST OF THE DOMINION WITH ANOTHER.
ALWAYS WANTED TO SEE THIS PLACE.
I JUST HOPED IT WOULD BE WHEN THE RESISTANCE WAS KICKING YOU OUT OF IT.
YOUR REPUTATION PRECEDES YOU. I ADMIRE YOUR SPIRIT.
KEEP TOUCHING ME AND I'LL IMPRESS YOU EVEN MORE.
ENOUGH PLEASANTRIES.
WE HAVE BUSINESS TO ATTEND TO.
NO DOUBT YOU ARE AS EAGER AS I AM TO UNLOCK THE TABLET'S SECRETS!

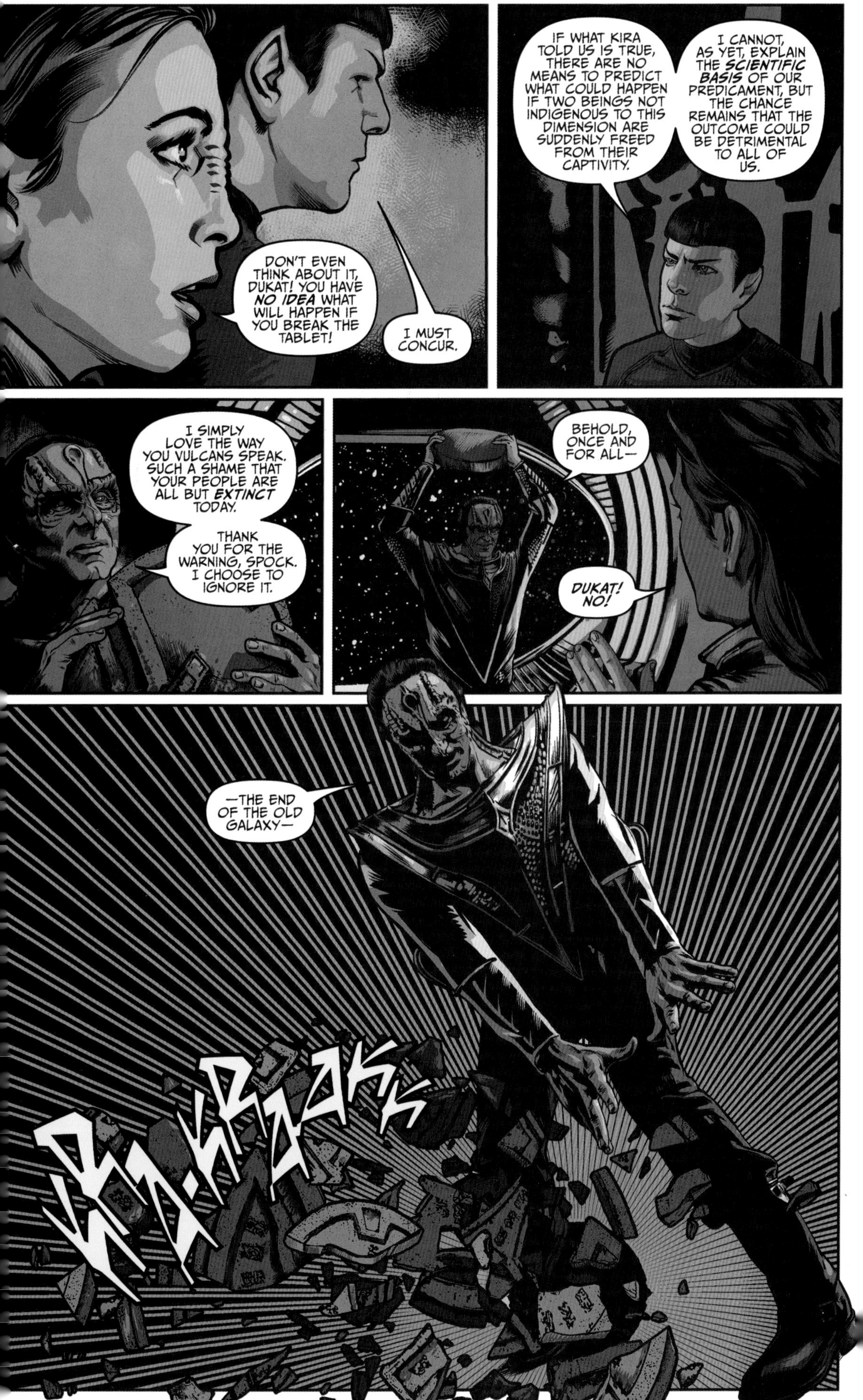
DON'T EVEN THINK ABOUT IT, DUKAT! YOU HAVE ***NO IDEA*** WHAT WILL HAPPEN IF YOU BREAK THE TABLET!
I MUST CONCUR.
IF WHAT KIRA TOLD US IS TRUE, THERE ARE NO MEANS TO PREDICT WHAT COULD HAPPEN IF TWO BEINGS NOT INDIGENOUS TO THIS DIMENSION ARE SUDDENLY FREED FROM THEIR CAPTIVITY.
I CANNOT, AS YET, EXPLAIN THE ***SCIENTIFIC BASIS*** OF OUR PREDICAMENT, BUT THE CHANCE REMAINS THAT THE OUTCOME COULD BE DETRIMENTAL TO ALL OF US.
I SIMPLY LOVE THE WAY YOU VULCANS SPEAK. SUCH A SHAME THAT YOUR PEOPLE ARE ALL BUT ***EXTINCT*** TODAY.
THANK YOU FOR THE WARNING, SPOCK. I CHOOSE TO IGNORE IT.
BEHOLD, ONCE AND FOR ALL—
DUKAT! NO!
—THE END OF THE OLD GALAXY—
BA-KRAAKK

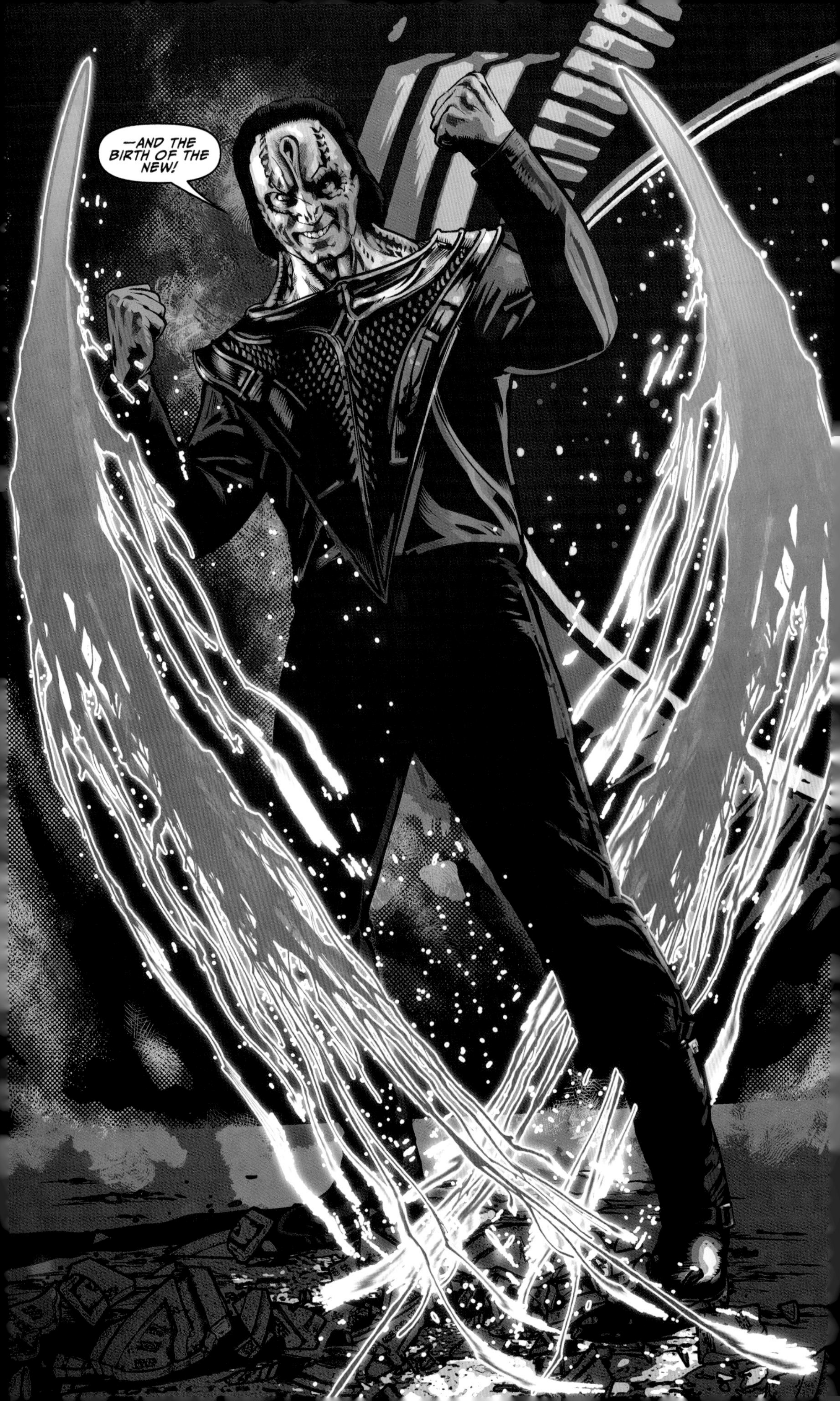
—AND THE BIRTH OF THE NEW!

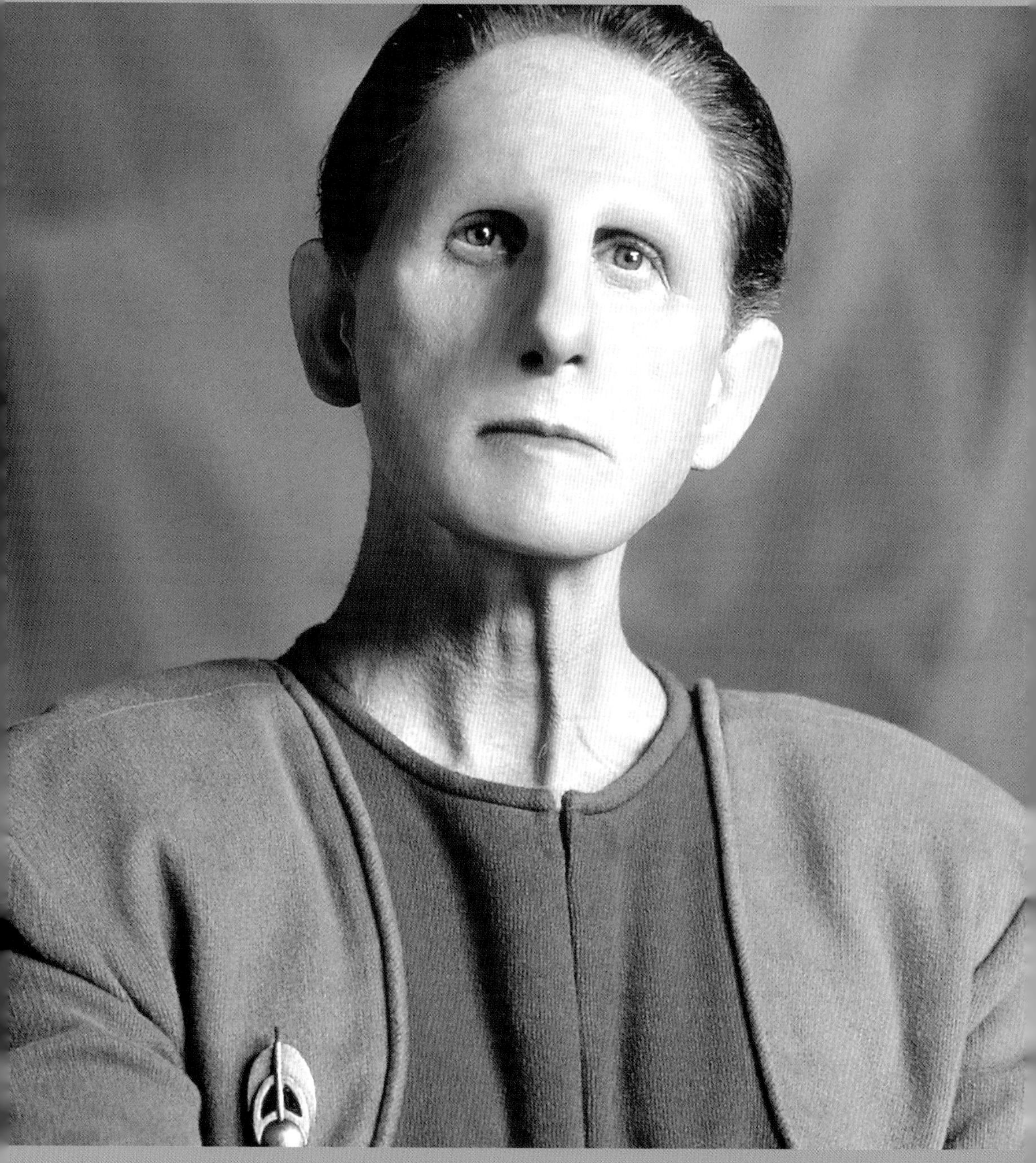

CHAPTER 5

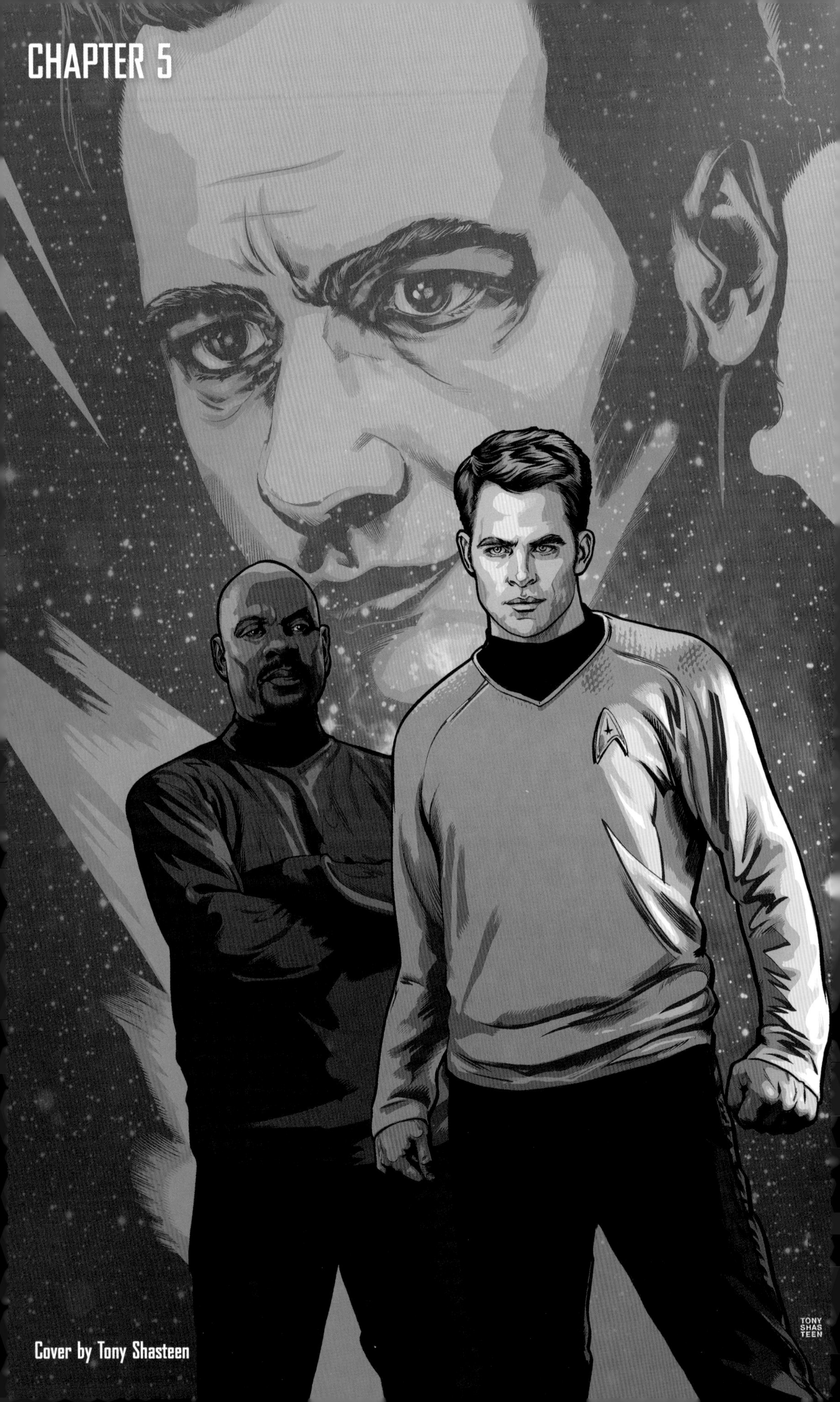
TONY
SHAS
TEEN

Cover by Tony Shasteen

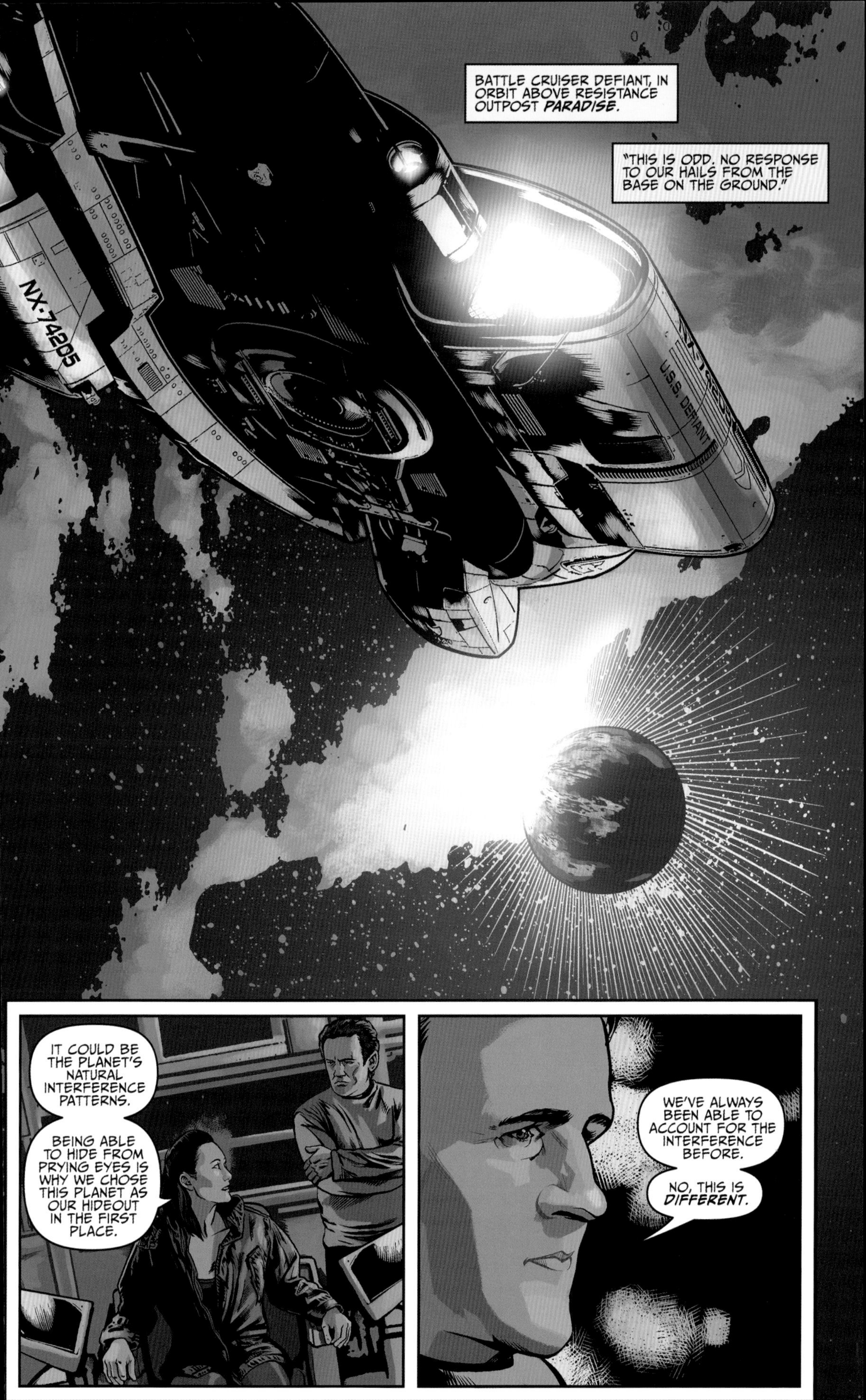
BATTLE CRUISER DEFIANT, IN ORBIT ABOVE RESISTANCE OUTPOST *PARADISE*.
"THIS IS ODD. NO RESPONSE TO OUR HAILS FROM THE BASE ON THE GROUND."
NX-74205
U.S.S. DEFIANT
IT COULD BE THE PLANET'S NATURAL INTERFERENCE PATTERNS.
BEING ABLE TO HIDE FROM PRYING EYES IS WHY WE CHOSE THIS PLANET AS OUR HIDEOUT IN THE FIRST PLACE.
WE'VE ALWAYS BEEN ABLE TO ACCOUNT FOR THE INTERFERENCE BEFORE.
NO, THIS IS *DIFFERENT*.

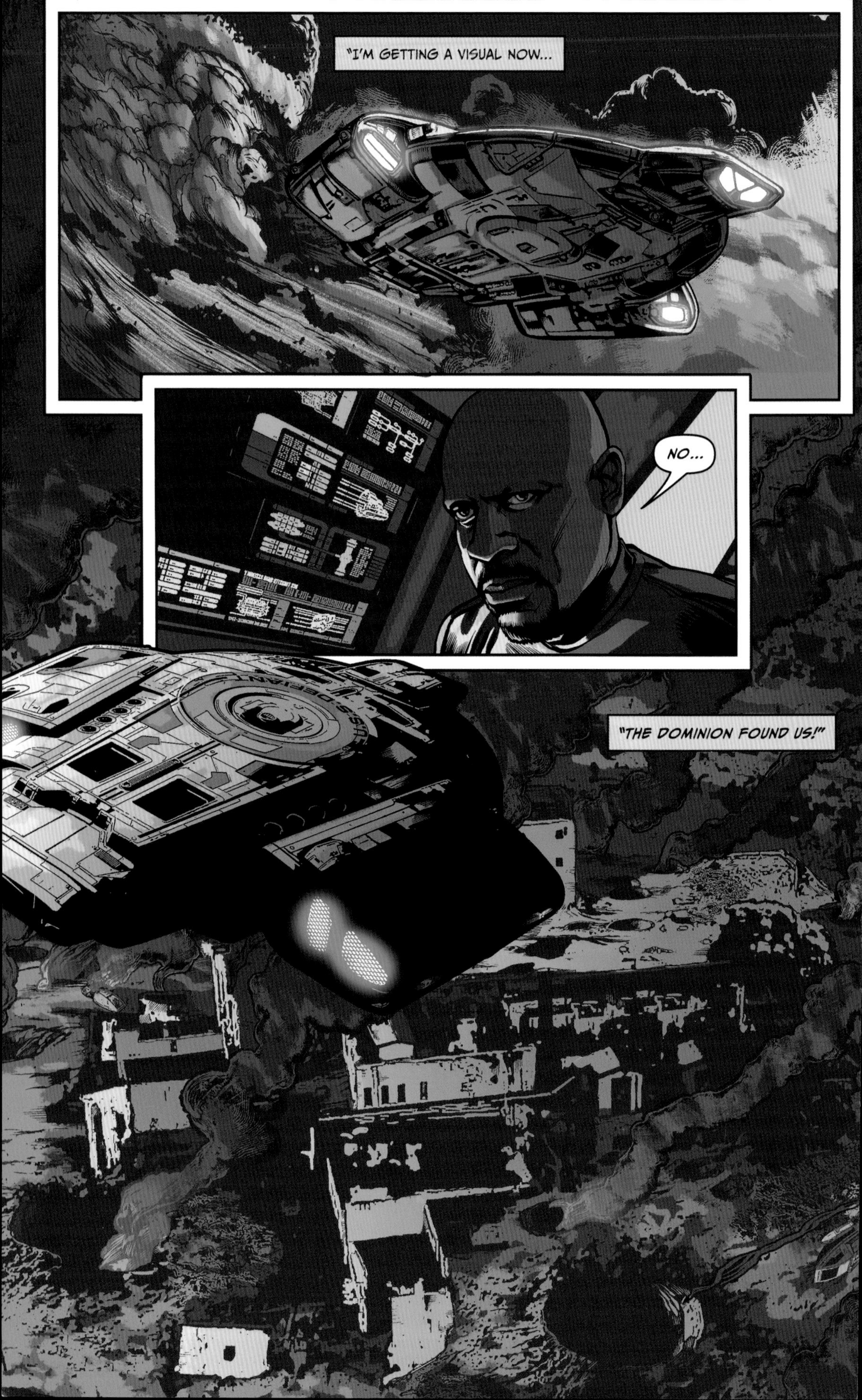
"I'M GETTING A VISUAL NOW...
NO...
"THE DOMINION FOUND US!"

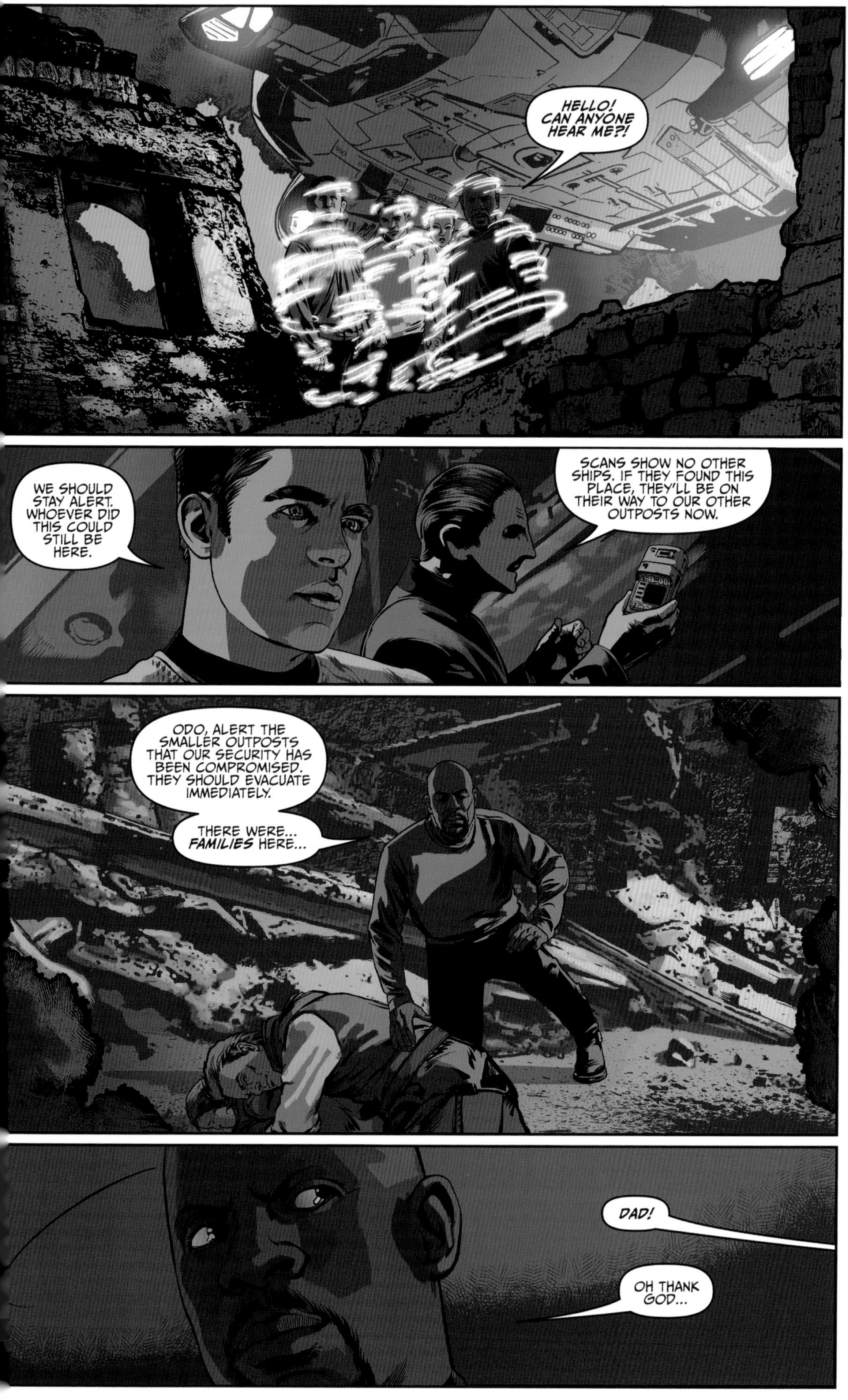

HELLO! CAN ANYONE HEAR ME?!
WE SHOULD STAY ALERT. WHOEVER DID THIS COULD STILL BE HERE.
SCANS SHOW NO OTHER SHIPS. IF THEY FOUND THIS PLACE, THEY'LL BE ON THEIR WAY TO OUR OTHER OUTPOSTS NOW.
ODO, ALERT THE SMALLER OUTPOSTS THAT OUR SECURITY HAS BEEN COMPROMISED. THEY SHOULD EVACUATE IMMEDIATELY.
THERE WERE... *FAMILIES* HERE...
DAD!
OH THANK GOD...

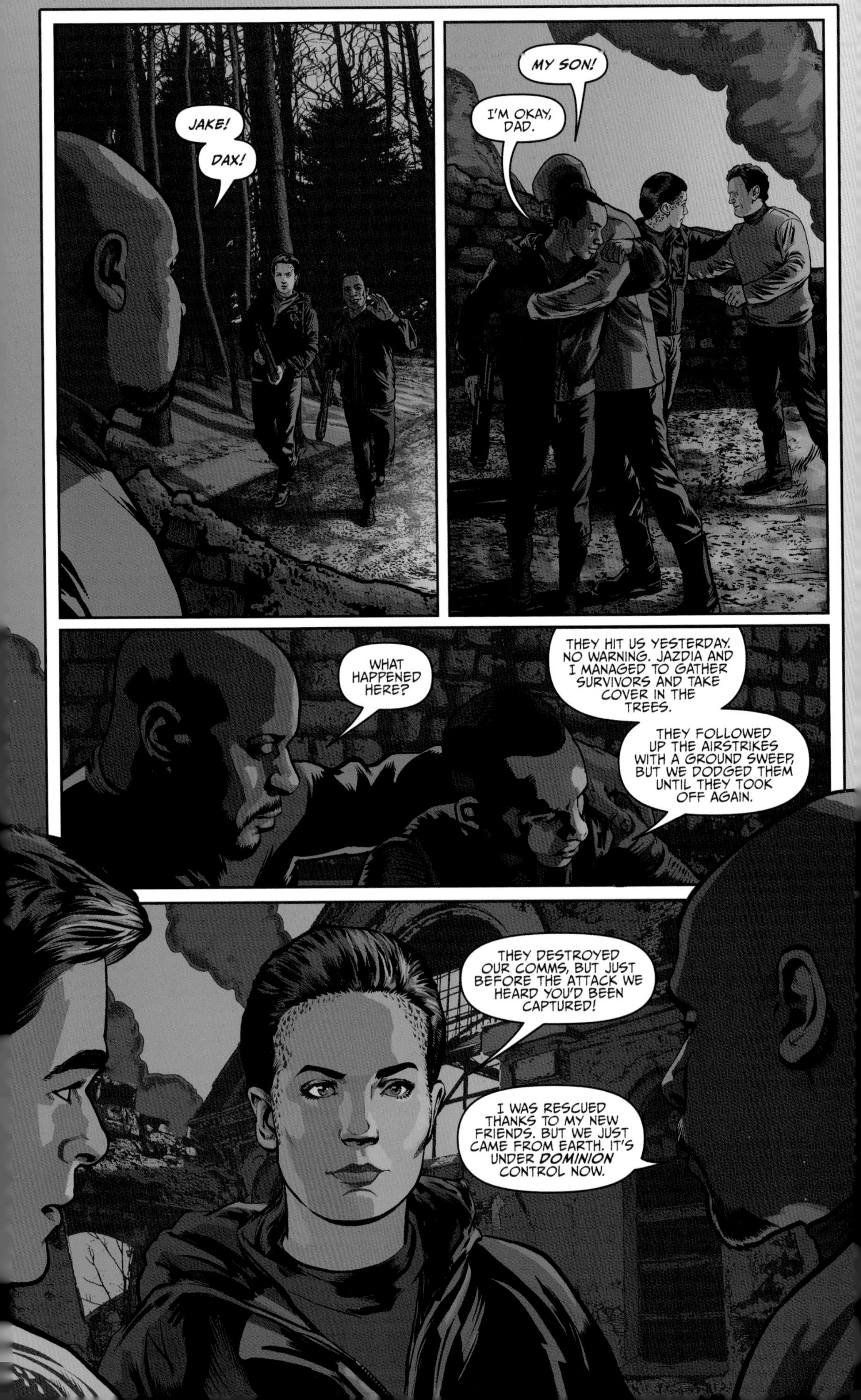

JAKE!
DAX!
MY SON!
I'M OKAY, DAD.
WHAT HAPPENED HERE?
THEY HIT US YESTERDAY. NO WARNING. JAZDIA AND I MANAGED TO GATHER SURVIVORS AND TAKE COVER IN THE TREES.
THEY FOLLOWED UP THE AIRSTRIKES WITH A GROUND SWEEP, BUT WE DODGED THEM UNTIL THEY TOOK OFF AGAIN.
THEY DESTROYED OUR COMMS, BUT JUST BEFORE THE ATTACK WE HEARD YOU'D BEEN CAPTURED!
I WAS RESCUED THANKS TO MY NEW FRIENDS. BUT WE JUST CAME FROM EARTH. IT'S UNDER *DOMINION* CONTROL NOW.

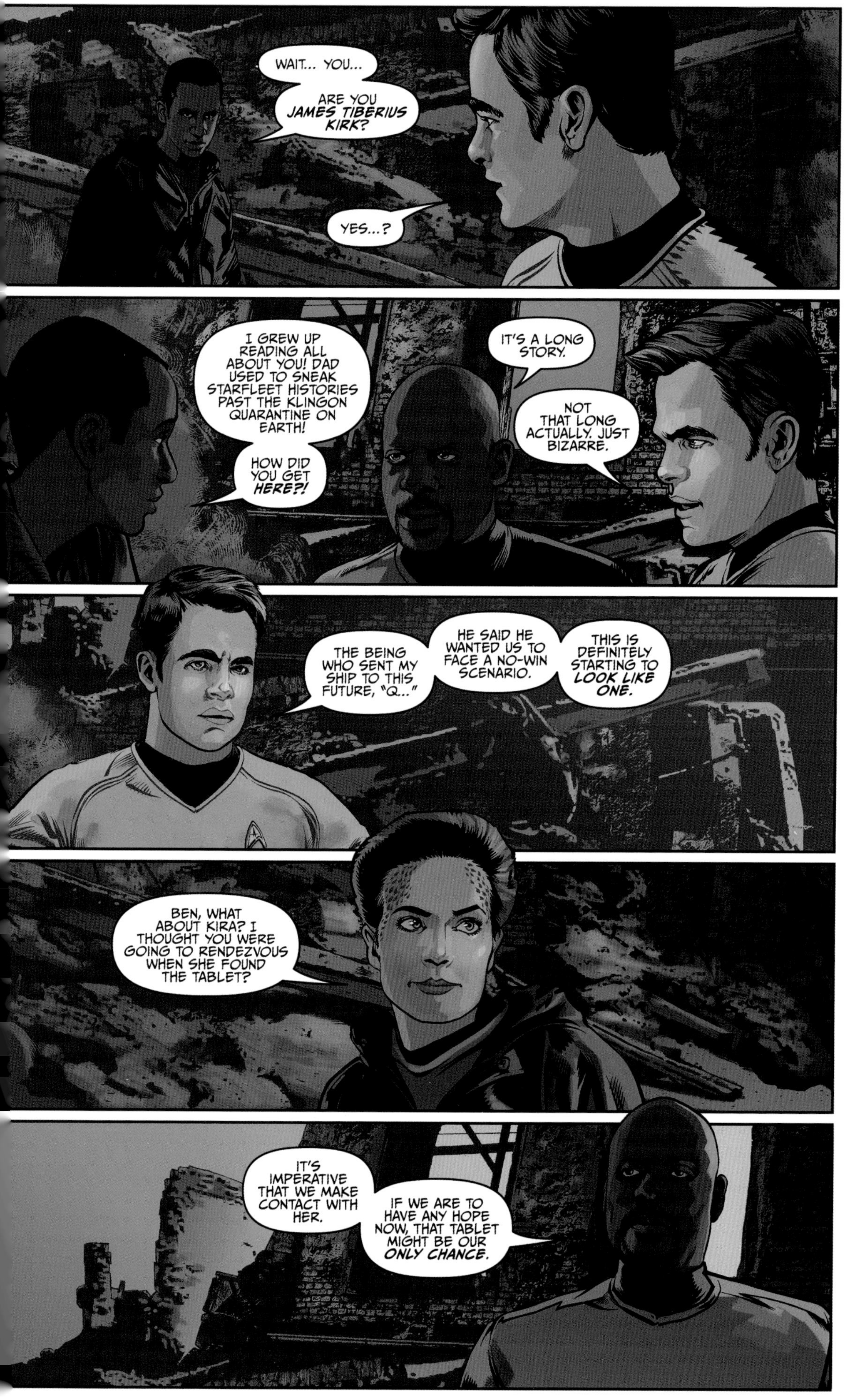
WAIT... YOU...
ARE YOU JAMES TIBERIUS KIRK?
YES...?
I GREW UP READING ALL ABOUT YOU! DAD USED TO SNEAK STARFLEET HISTORIES PAST THE KLINGON QUARANTINE ON EARTH!
HOW DID YOU GET HERE?!
IT'S A LONG STORY.
NOT THAT LONG ACTUALLY. JUST BIZARRE.
THE BEING WHO SENT MY SHIP TO THIS FUTURE, "Q..."
HE SAID HE WANTED US TO FACE A NO-WIN SCENARIO.
THIS IS DEFINITELY STARTING TO LOOK LIKE ONE.
BEN, WHAT ABOUT KIRA? I THOUGHT YOU WERE GOING TO RENDEZVOUS WHEN SHE FOUND THE TABLET?
IT'S IMPERATIVE THAT WE MAKE CONTACT WITH HER.
IF WE ARE TO HAVE ANY HOPE NOW, THAT TABLET MIGHT BE OUR ONLY CHANCE.

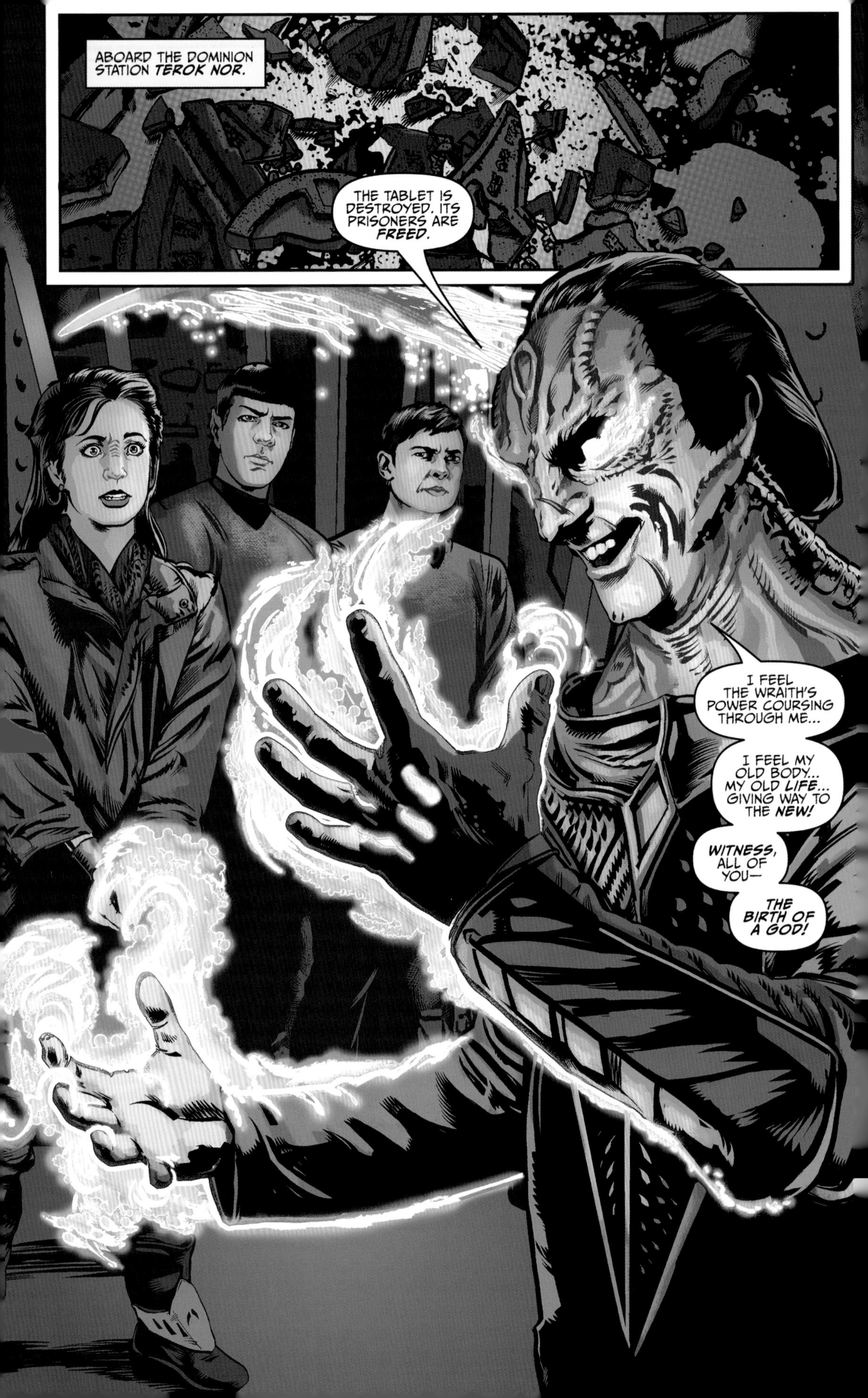
ABOARD THE DOMINION STATION TEROK NOR.
THE TABLET IS DESTROYED. ITS PRISONERS ARE FREED.
I FEEL THE WRAITH'S POWER COURSING THROUGH ME...
I FEEL MY OLD BODY... MY OLD LIFE... GIVING WAY TO THE NEW!
WITNESS, ALL OF YOU—
THE BIRTH OF A GOD!

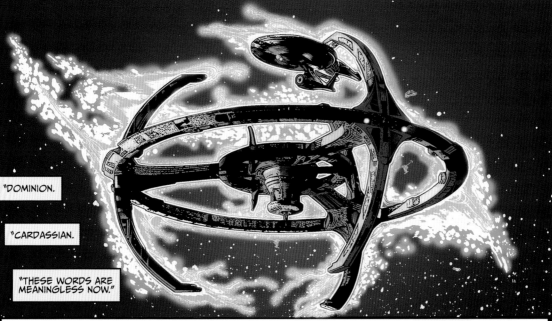

"DOMINION.

"CARDASSIAN.

"THESE WORDS ARE MEANINGLESS NOW."

NOW THERE IS ONLY *DUKAT*.

THE LAST PROPHET—!

IT SENSES A WILLING VESSEL TO POSSESS.

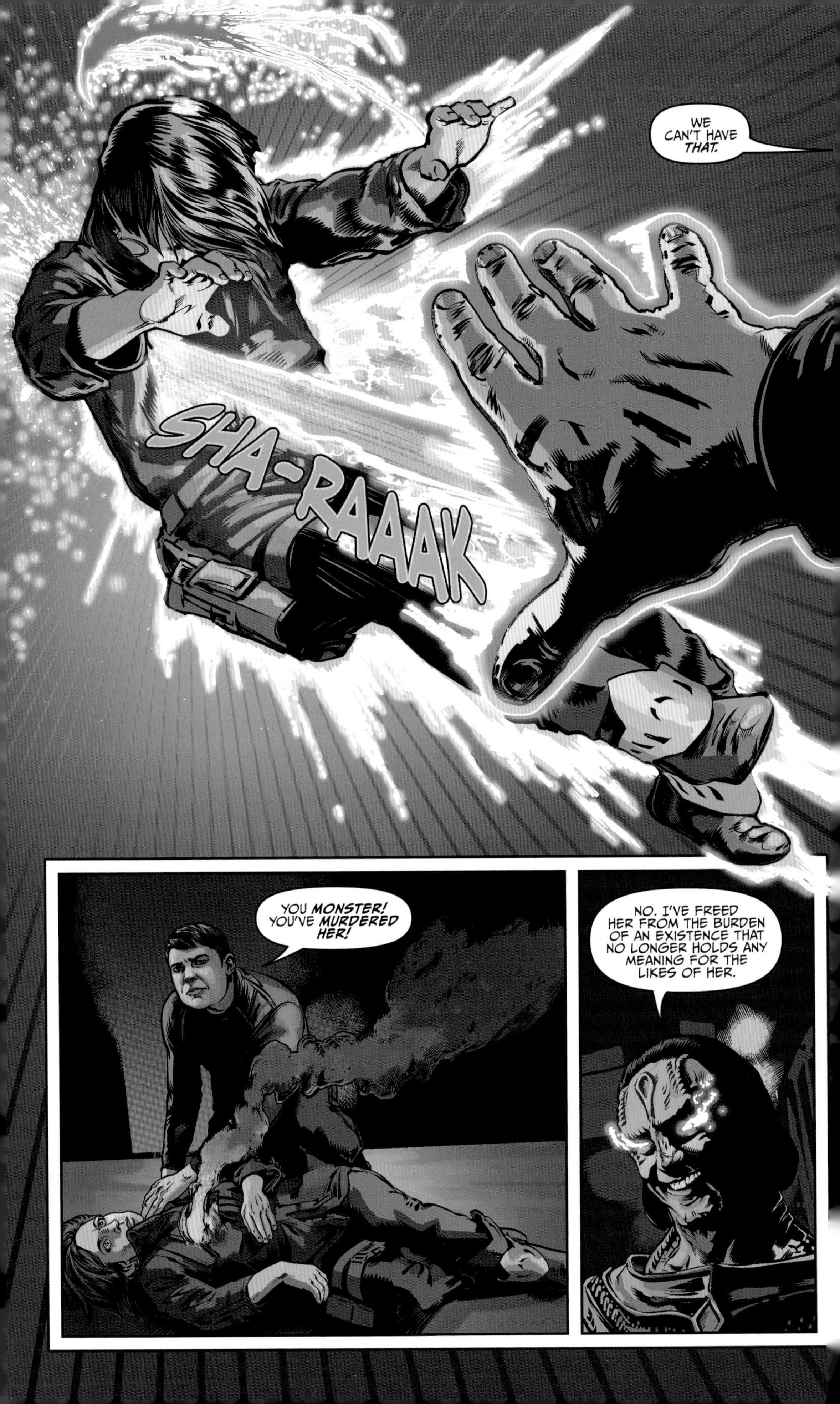
WE CAN'T HAVE *THAT.*
SHA-RAAAK
YOU **MONSTER!** YOU'VE **MURDERED** HER!
NO. I'VE FREED HER FROM THE BURDEN OF AN EXISTENCE THAT NO LONGER HOLDS ANY MEANING FOR THE LIKES OF HER.

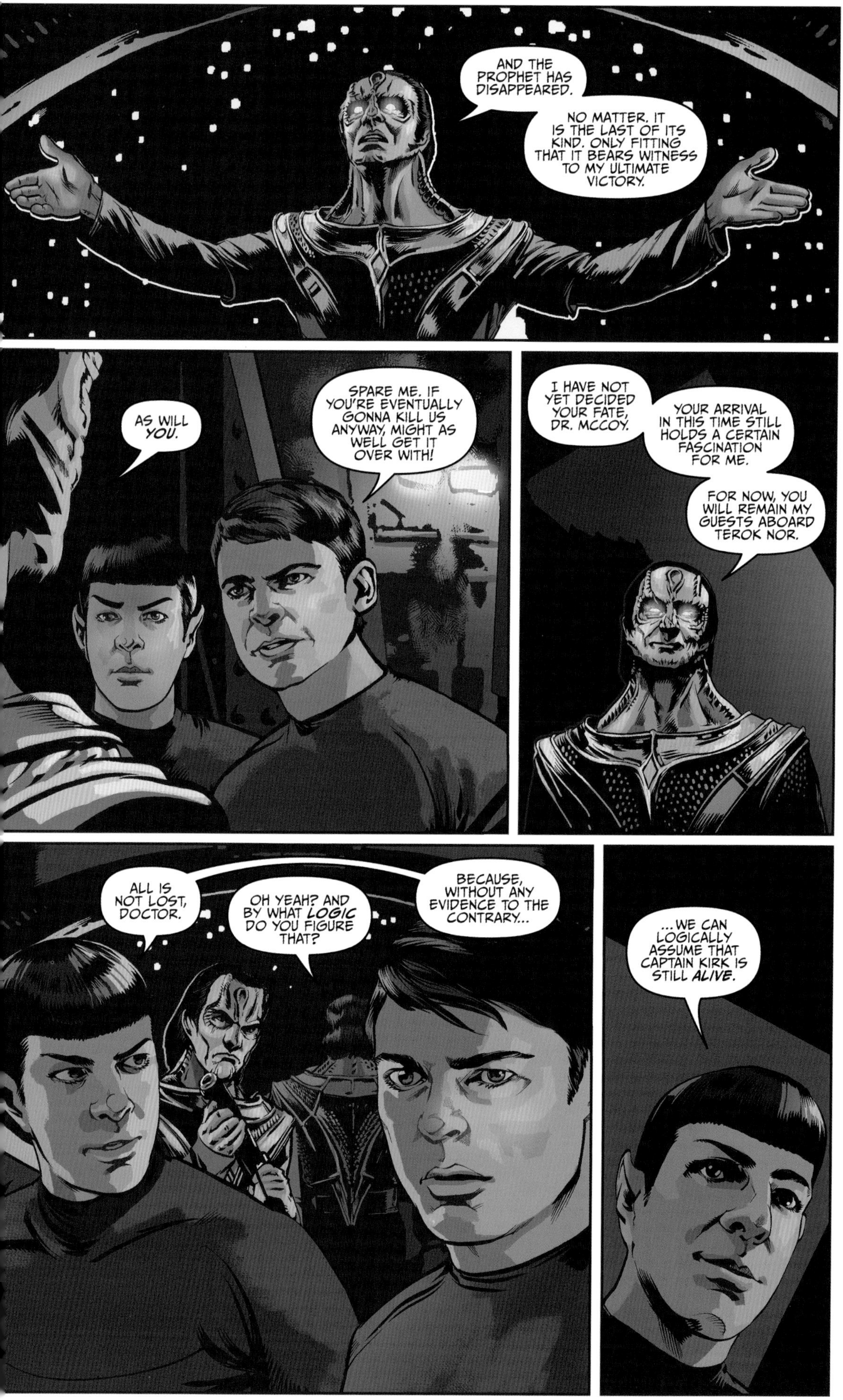
AND THE PROPHET HAS DISAPPEARED.
NO MATTER. IT IS THE LAST OF ITS KIND. ONLY FITTING THAT IT BEARS WITNESS TO MY ULTIMATE VICTORY.
AS WILL *YOU*.
SPARE ME. IF YOU'RE EVENTUALLY GONNA KILL US ANYWAY, MIGHT AS WELL GET IT OVER WITH!
I HAVE NOT YET DECIDED YOUR FATE, DR. MCCOY.
YOUR ARRIVAL IN THIS TIME STILL HOLDS A CERTAIN FASCINATION FOR ME.
FOR NOW, YOU WILL REMAIN MY GUESTS ABOARD TEROK NOR.
ALL IS NOT LOST, DOCTOR.
OH YEAH? AND BY WHAT *LOGIC* DO YOU FIGURE THAT?
BECAUSE, WITHOUT ANY EVIDENCE TO THE CONTRARY...
...WE CAN LOGICALLY ASSUME THAT CAPTAIN KIRK IS STILL *ALIVE*.

PARADISE.

Q!

I KNOW YOU CAN HEAR ME!

I WANT TO TALK, Q!

O CAPTAIN, MY CAPTAIN... NO NEED TO *SHOUT*.

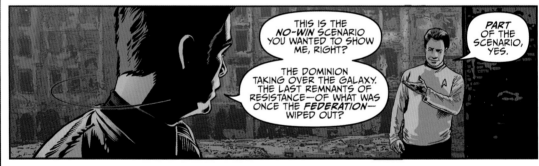

THIS IS THE *NO-WIN* SCENARIO YOU WANTED TO SHOW ME, RIGHT?

THE DOMINION TAKING OVER THE GALAXY. THE LAST REMNANTS OF RESISTANCE—OF WHAT WAS ONCE THE *FEDERATION*—WIPED OUT?

PART OF THE SCENARIO, YES.

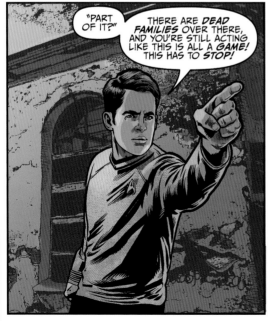

"PART OF IT?" THERE ARE *DEAD FAMILIES* OVER THERE, AND YOU'RE STILL ACTING LIKE THIS IS ALL A *GAME!* THIS HAS TO *STOP!*

OH, IT WILL STOP, JAMES. SOON.

BUT IT'S A GAME YOU HAVE TO PLAY TO THE *END*. NOW IF YOU'RE DONE WHINING ABOUT THE *RULES*...

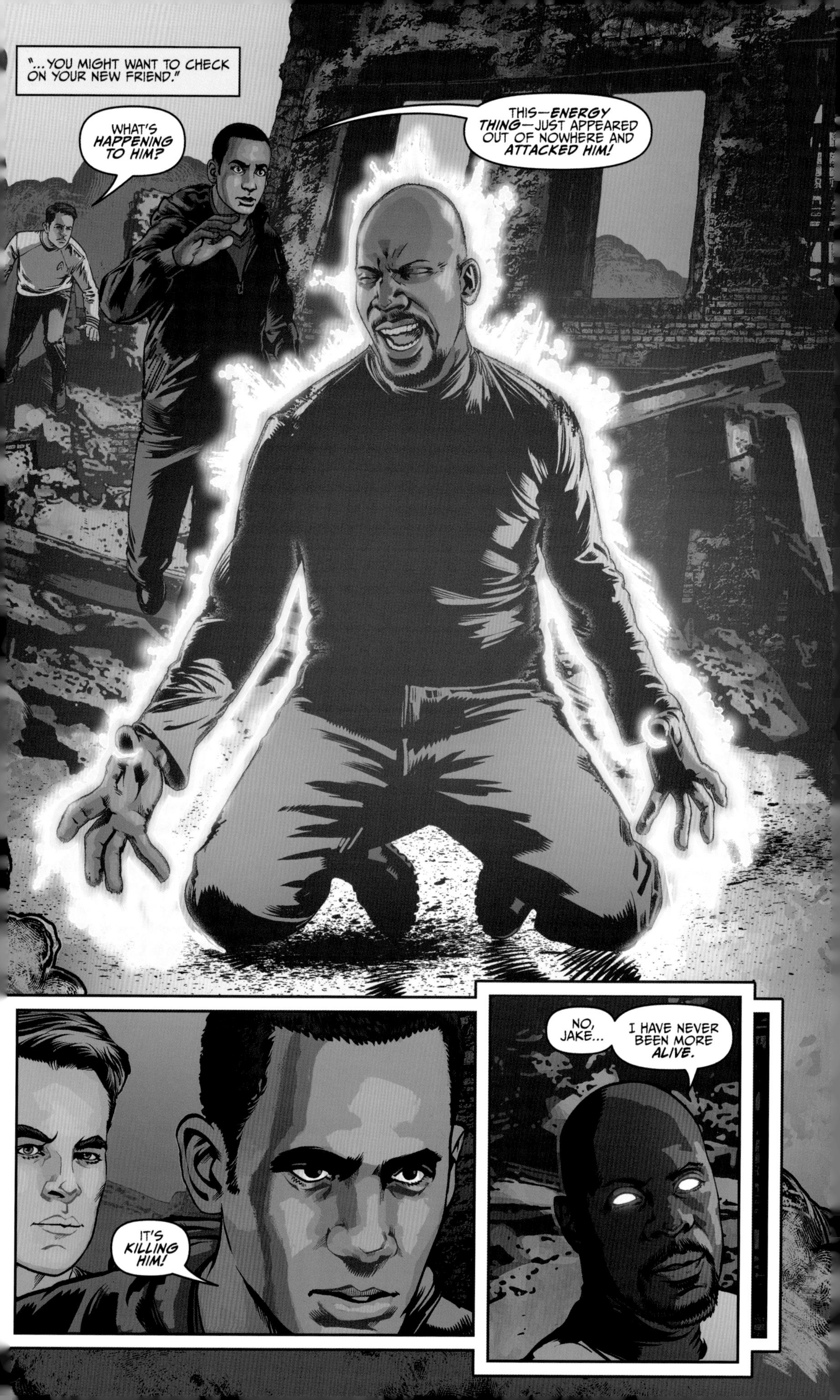
"...YOU MIGHT WANT TO CHECK ON YOUR NEW FRIEND."
WHAT'S HAPPENING TO HIM?
THIS—ENERGY THING—JUST APPEARED OUT OF NOWHERE AND ATTACKED HIM!
IT'S KILLING HIM!
NO, JAKE...
I HAVE NEVER BEEN MORE ALIVE.

I AM BENJAMIN SISKO.

BUT I AM NOW ALSO... SOMETHING... *ELSE.*

IT'S THE *PROPHET!* IT HAS CHOSEN *BEN* AS ITS VESSEL!

WHAT "PROPHET"?

A RACE OF EXTRA-DIMENSIONAL BEINGS. *PEACEFUL* BEINGS. WE THOUGHT THEM ALL WIPED OUT BY THEIR ENEMY, THE PAH-WRAITHS.

THERE WERE RUMORS THAT ONE PROPHET REMAINED TRAPPED IN A LEGENDARY TABLET. OUR PLAN WAS TO FREE IT IN THE HOPES IT COULD HELP US FIGHT BACK AGAINST THE DOMINION.

IF THIS *IS* THAT PROPHET, IT MEANS THE TABLET WAS SHATTERED. BUT WHO SHATTERED IT? AND WHERE'S *KIRA?*

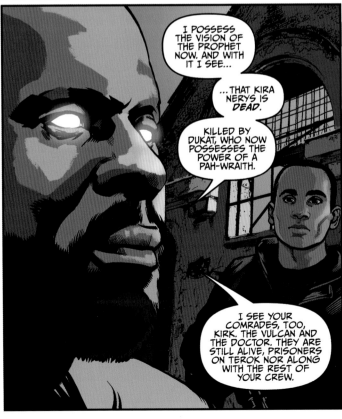

I POSSESS THE VISION OF THE PROPHET NOW. AND WITH IT I SEE...

...THAT KIRA NERYS IS *DEAD.*

KILLED BY DUKAT, WHO NOW POSSESSES THE POWER OF A PAH-WRAITH.

I SEE YOUR COMRADES, TOO, KIRK. THE VULCAN AND THE DOCTOR. THEY ARE STILL ALIVE, PRISONERS ON TEROK NOR ALONG WITH THE REST OF YOUR CREW.

THEN TEROK NOR IS *WHERE WE'RE GOING.*

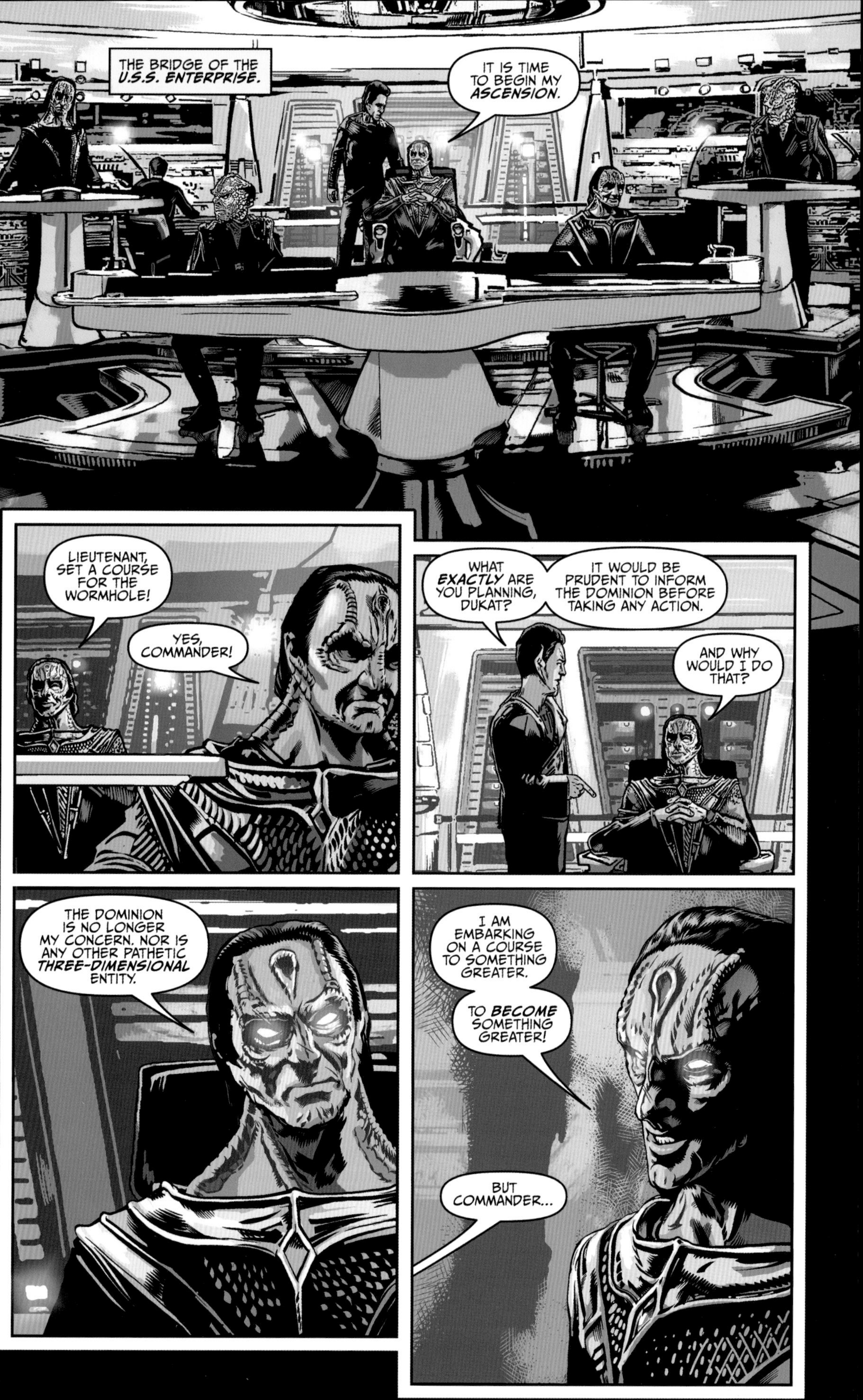
THE BRIDGE OF THE U.S.S. ENTERPRISE.
IT IS TIME TO BEGIN MY ASCENSION.
LIEUTENANT, SET A COURSE FOR THE WORMHOLE!
YES, COMMANDER!
WHAT EXACTLY ARE YOU PLANNING, DUKAT?
IT WOULD BE PRUDENT TO INFORM THE DOMINION BEFORE TAKING ANY ACTION.
AND WHY WOULD I DO THAT?
THE DOMINION IS NO LONGER MY CONCERN. NOR IS ANY OTHER PATHETIC THREE-DIMENSIONAL ENTITY.
I AM EMBARKING ON A COURSE TO SOMETHING GREATER.
TO BECOME SOMETHING GREATER!
BUT COMMANDER...

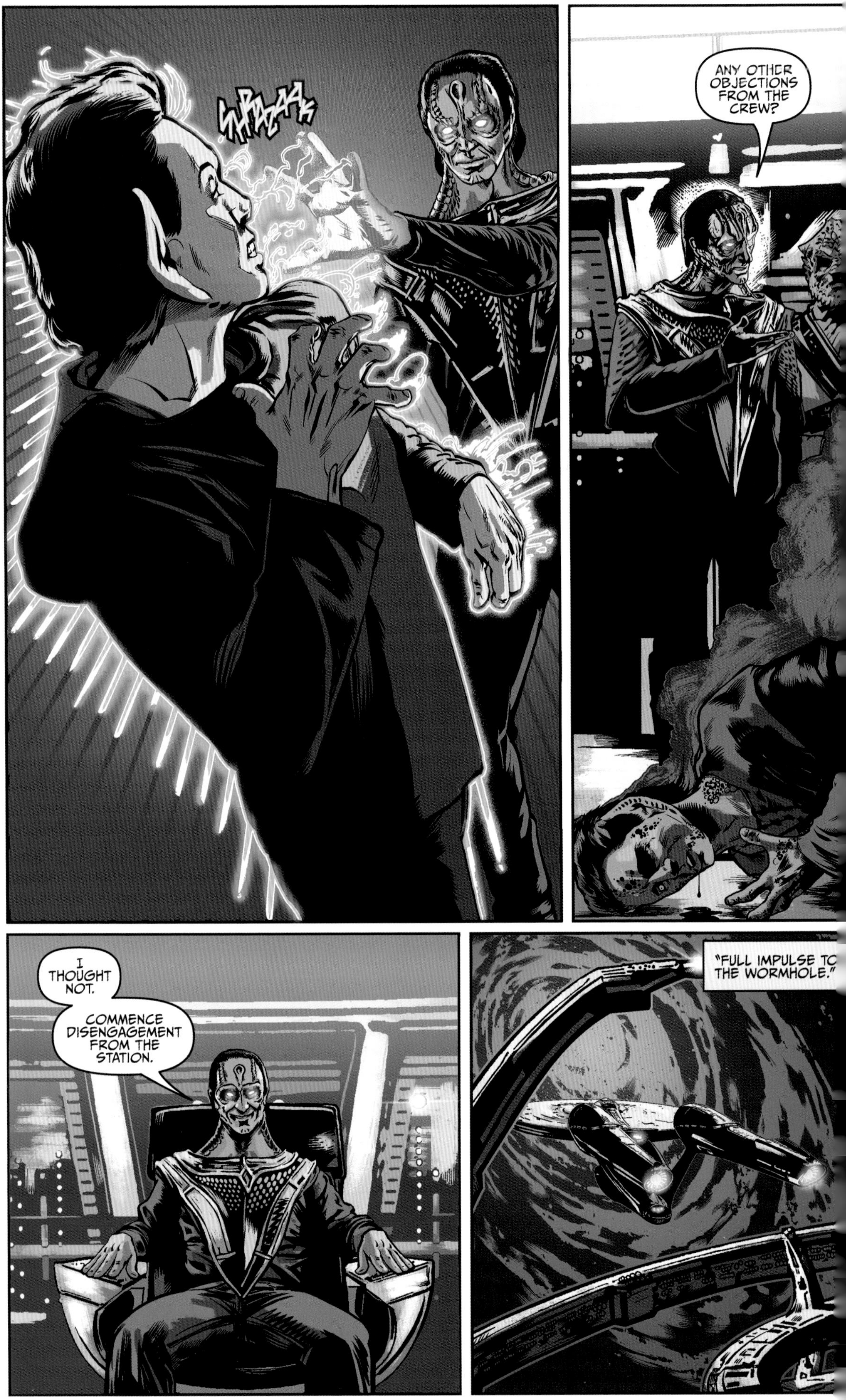
SKRAZAAK
ANY OTHER OBJECTIONS FROM THE CREW?
I THOUGHT NOT.
COMMENCE DISENGAGEMENT FROM THE STATION.
"FULL IMPULSE TO THE WORMHOLE."

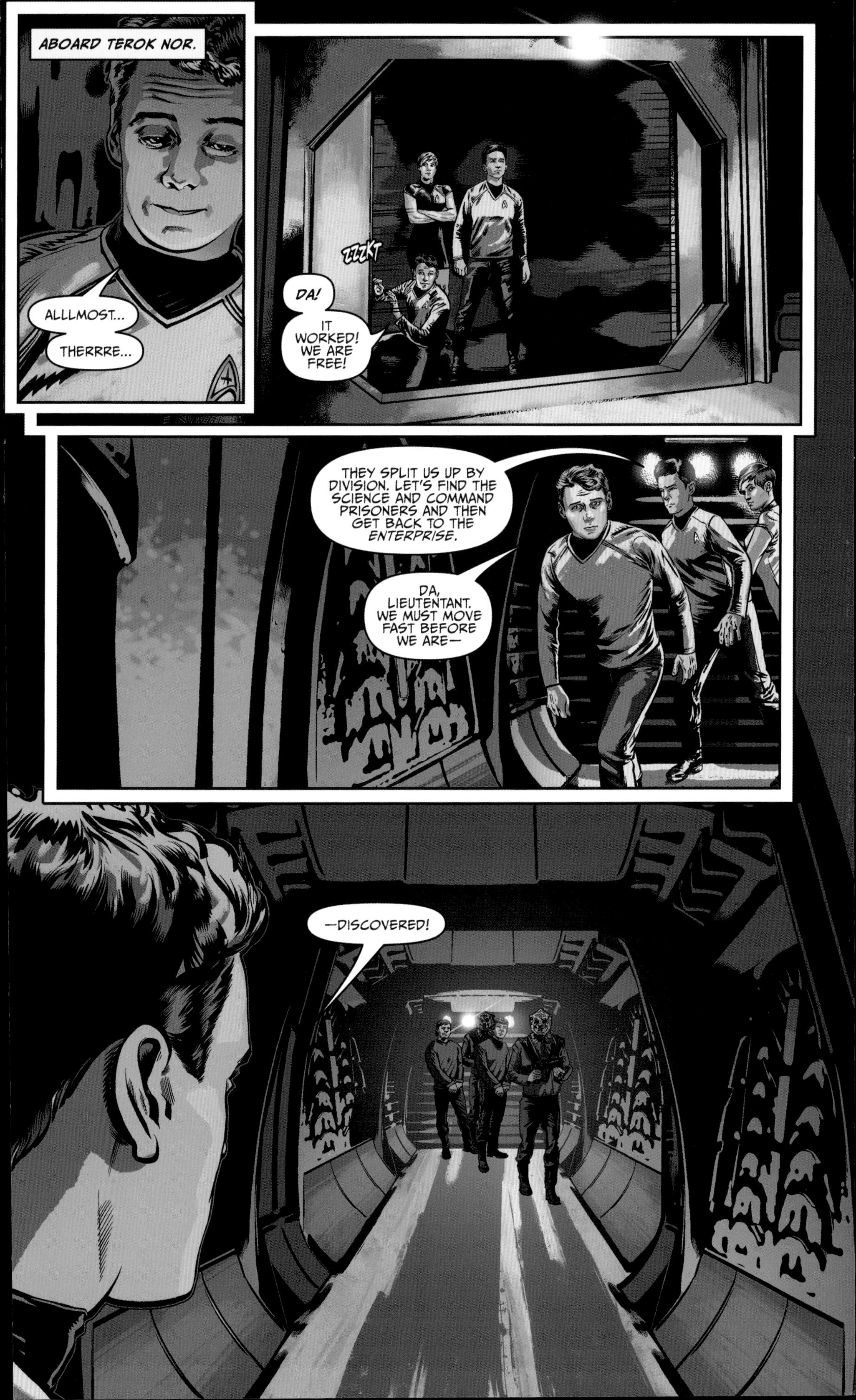
ABOARD TEROK NOR.
ALLLMOST...
THERRRE...
ZZZKT
DA!
IT WORKED! WE ARE FREE!
THEY SPLIT US UP BY DIVISION. LET'S FIND THE SCIENCE AND COMMAND PRISONERS AND THEN GET BACK TO THE *ENTERPRISE.*
DA, LIEUTENTANT. WE MUST MOVE FAST BEFORE WE ARE—
—DISCOVERED!

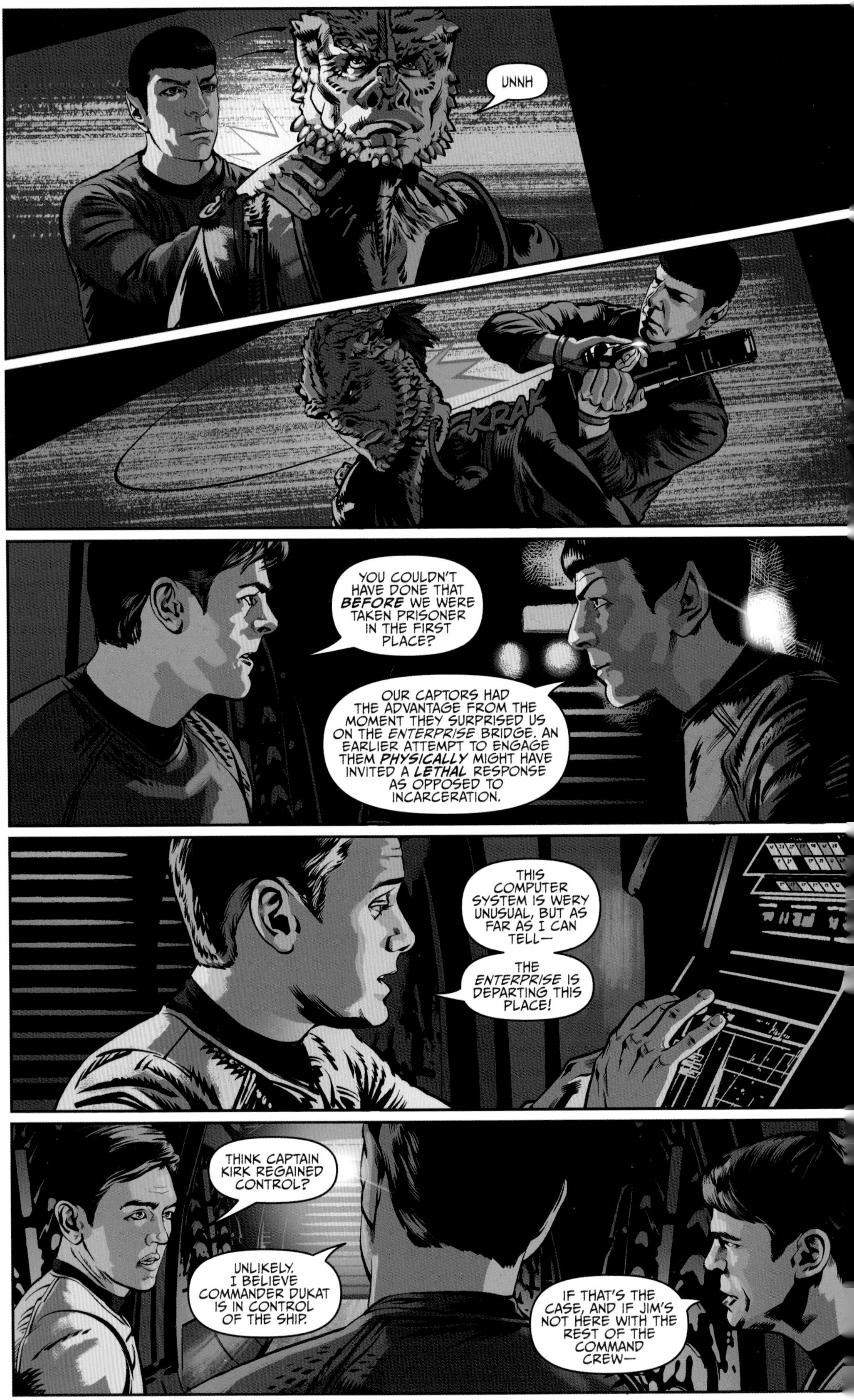
UNNH
KRAK
YOU COULDN'T HAVE DONE THAT BEFORE WE WERE TAKEN PRISONER IN THE FIRST PLACE?
OUR CAPTORS HAD THE ADVANTAGE FROM THE MOMENT THEY SURPRISED US ON THE ENTERPRISE BRIDGE. AN EARLIER ATTEMPT TO ENGAGE THEM PHYSICALLY MIGHT HAVE INVITED A LETHAL RESPONSE AS OPPOSED TO INCARCERATION.
THIS COMPUTER SYSTEM IS WERY UNUSUAL, BUT AS FAR AS I CAN TELL—
THE ENTERPRISE IS DEPARTING THIS PLACE!
THINK CAPTAIN KIRK REGAINED CONTROL?
UNLIKELY. I BELIEVE COMMANDER DUKAT IS IN CONTROL OF THE SHIP.
IF THAT'S THE CASE, AND IF JIM'S NOT HERE WITH THE REST OF THE COMMAND CREW—

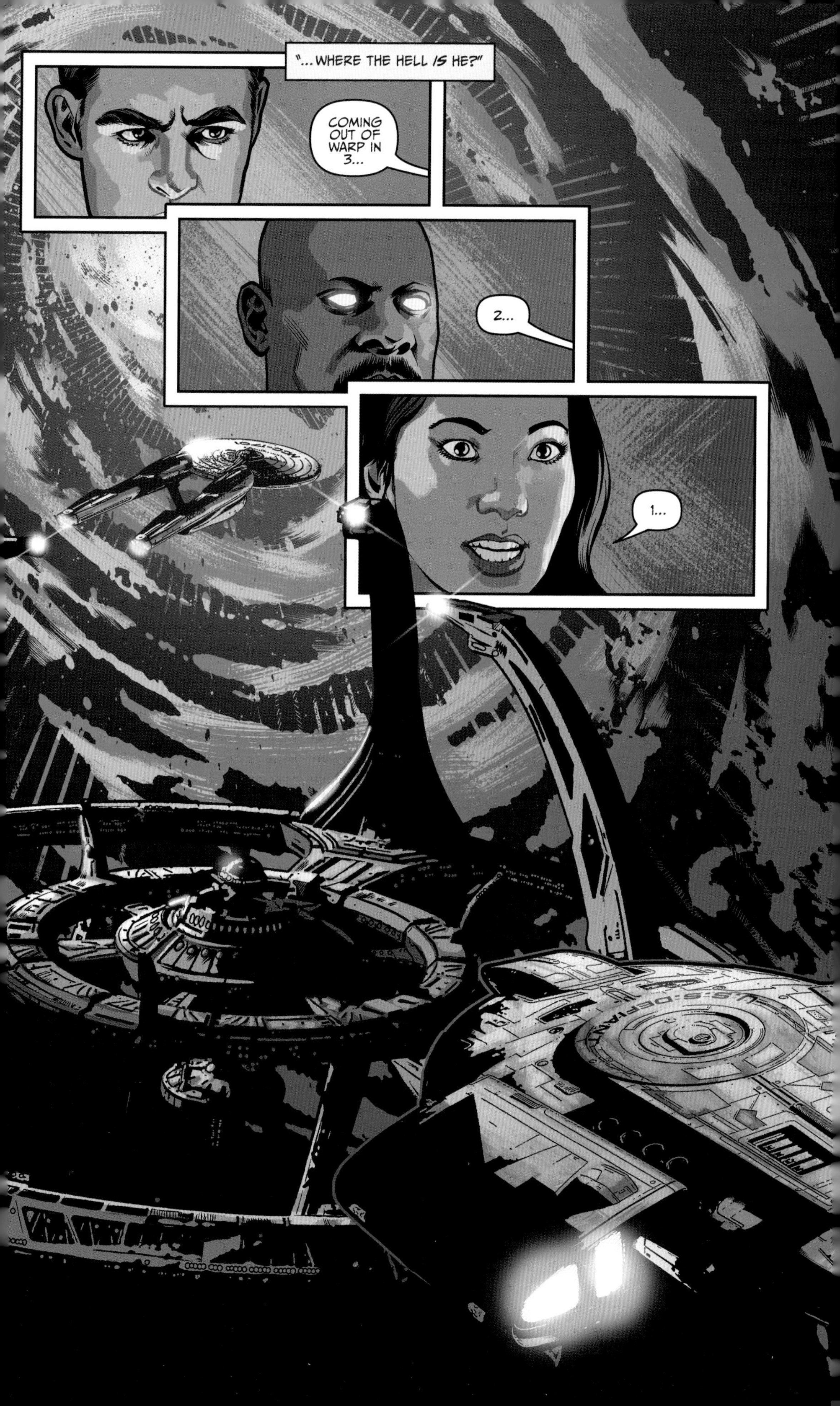
"...WHERE THE HELL *IS* HE?"
COMING OUT OF WARP IN 3...
2...
1...
U.S.S. DEFIANT

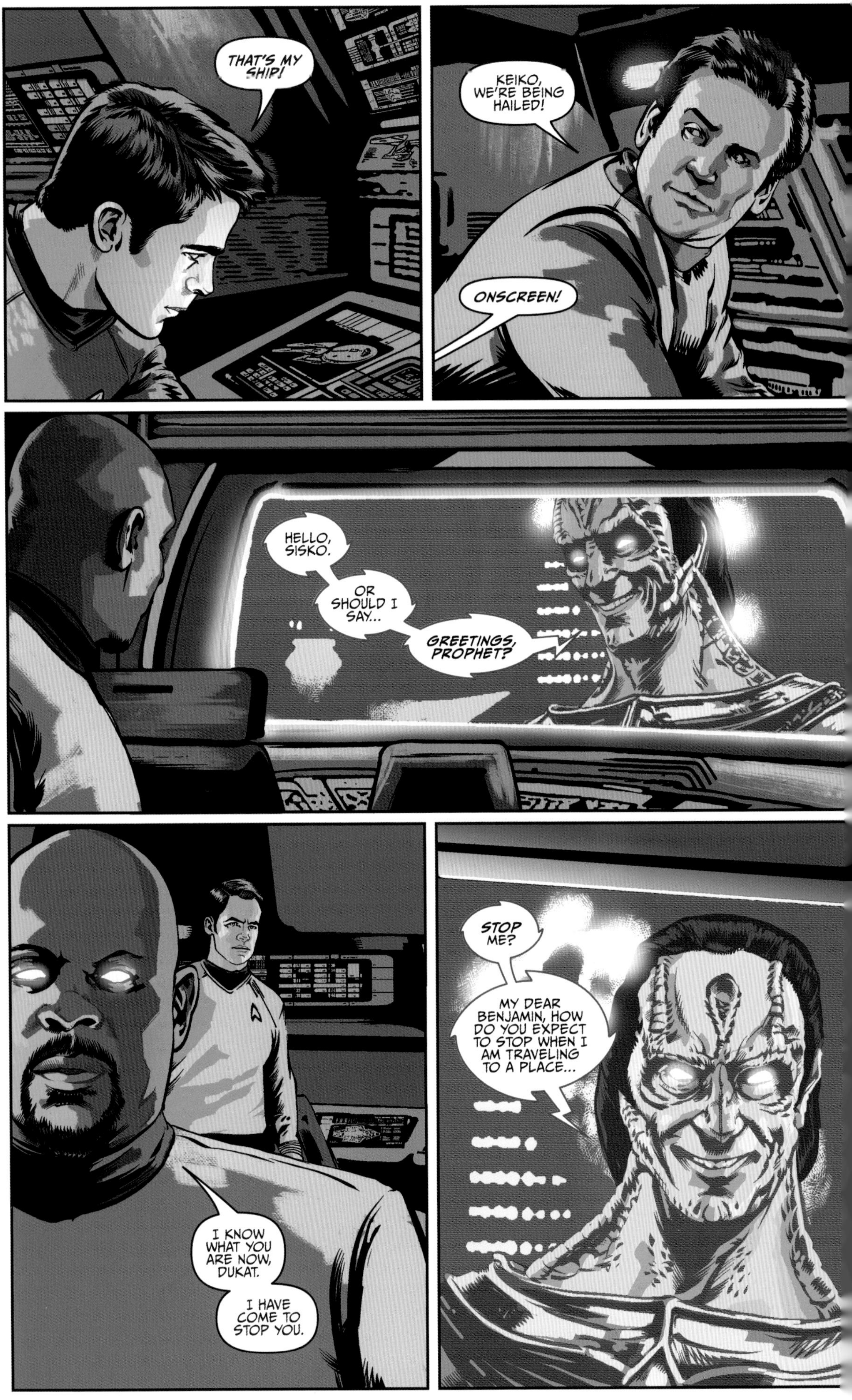
THAT'S MY SHIP!
KEIKO, WE'RE BEING HAILED!
ONSCREEN!
HELLO, SISKO.
OR SHOULD I SAY...
GREETINGS, PROPHET?
I KNOW WHAT YOU ARE NOW, DUKAT.
I HAVE COME TO STOP YOU.
STOP ME?
MY DEAR BENJAMIN, HOW DO YOU EXPECT TO STOP WHEN I AM TRAVELING TO A PLACE...

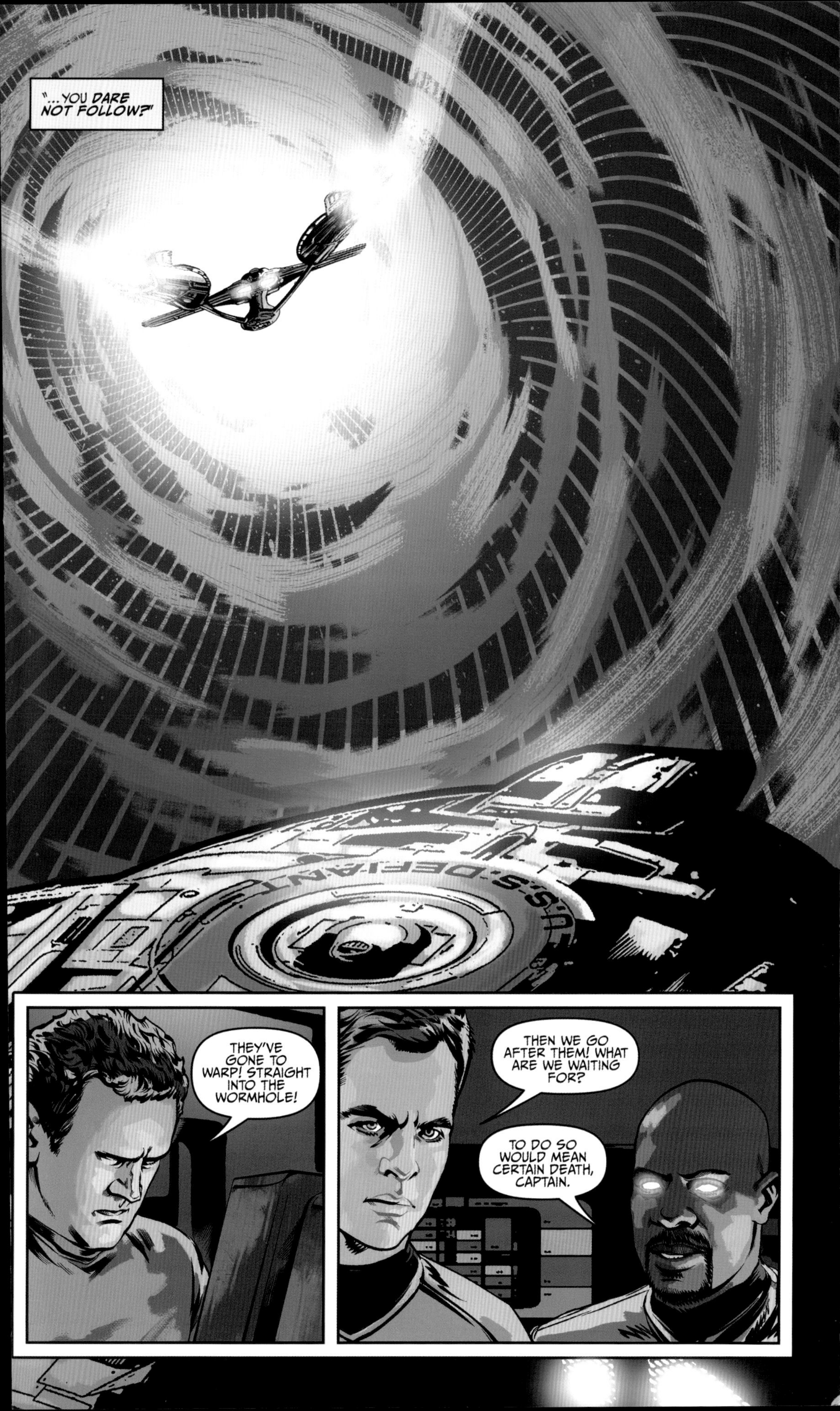
"...YOU DARE NOT FOLLOW?"
U.S.S. DEFIANT
THEY'VE GONE TO WARP! STRAIGHT INTO THE WORMHOLE!
THEN WE GO AFTER THEM! WHAT ARE WE WAITING FOR?
TO DO SO WOULD MEAN CERTAIN DEATH, CAPTAIN.

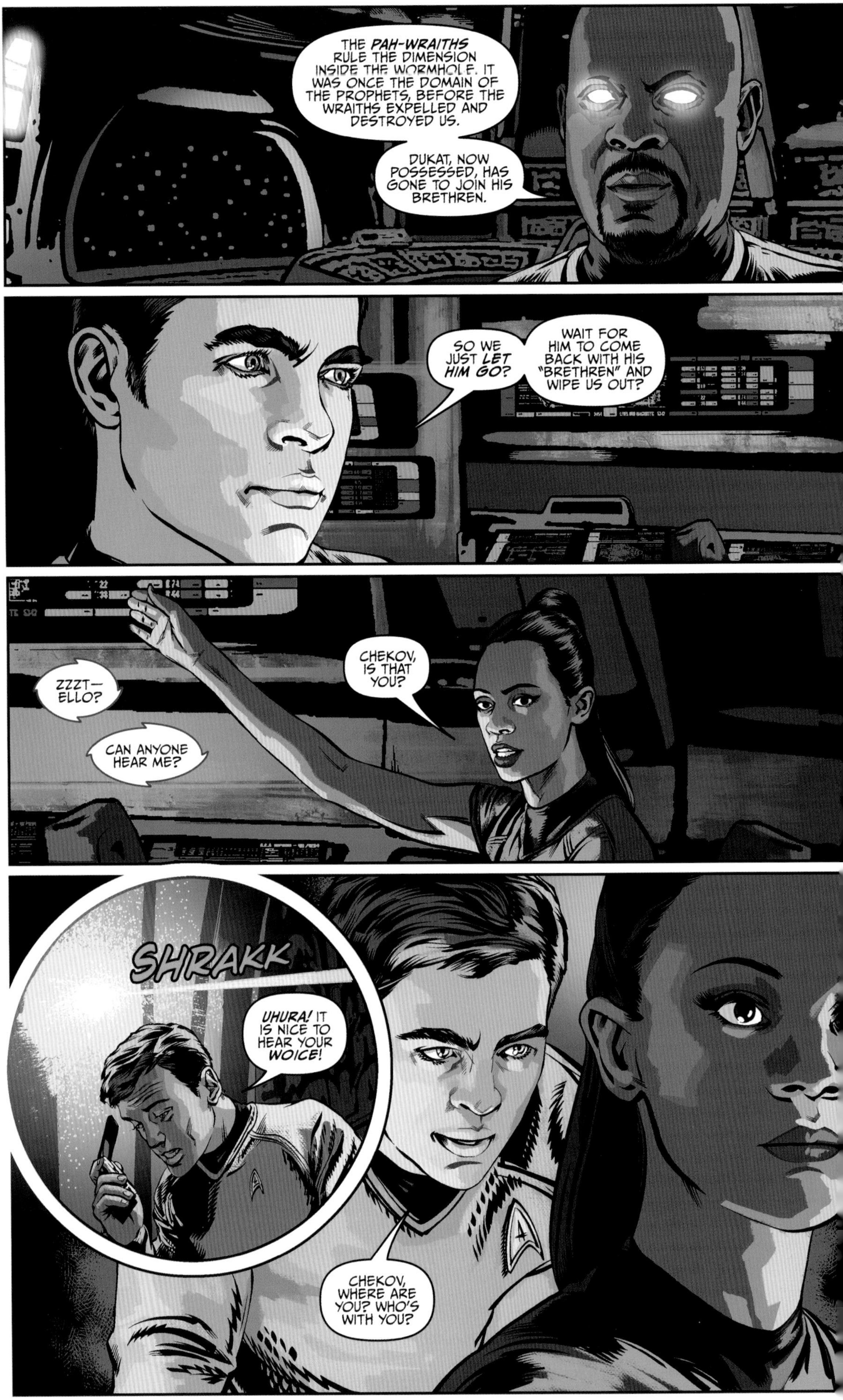
THE PAH-WRAITHS RULE THE DIMENSION INSIDE THE WORMHOLE. IT WAS ONCE THE DOMAIN OF THE PROPHETS, BEFORE THE WRAITHS EXPELLED AND DESTROYED US.
DUKAT, NOW POSSESSED, HAS GONE TO JOIN HIS BRETHREN.
SO WE JUST LET HIM GO?
WAIT FOR HIM TO COME BACK WITH HIS "BRETHREN" AND WIPE US OUT?
CHEKOV, IS THAT YOU?
ZZZT—ELLO?
CAN ANYONE HEAR ME?
SHRAKK
UHURA! IT IS NICE TO HEAR YOUR WOICE!
CHEKOV, WHERE ARE YOU? WHO'S WITH YOU?

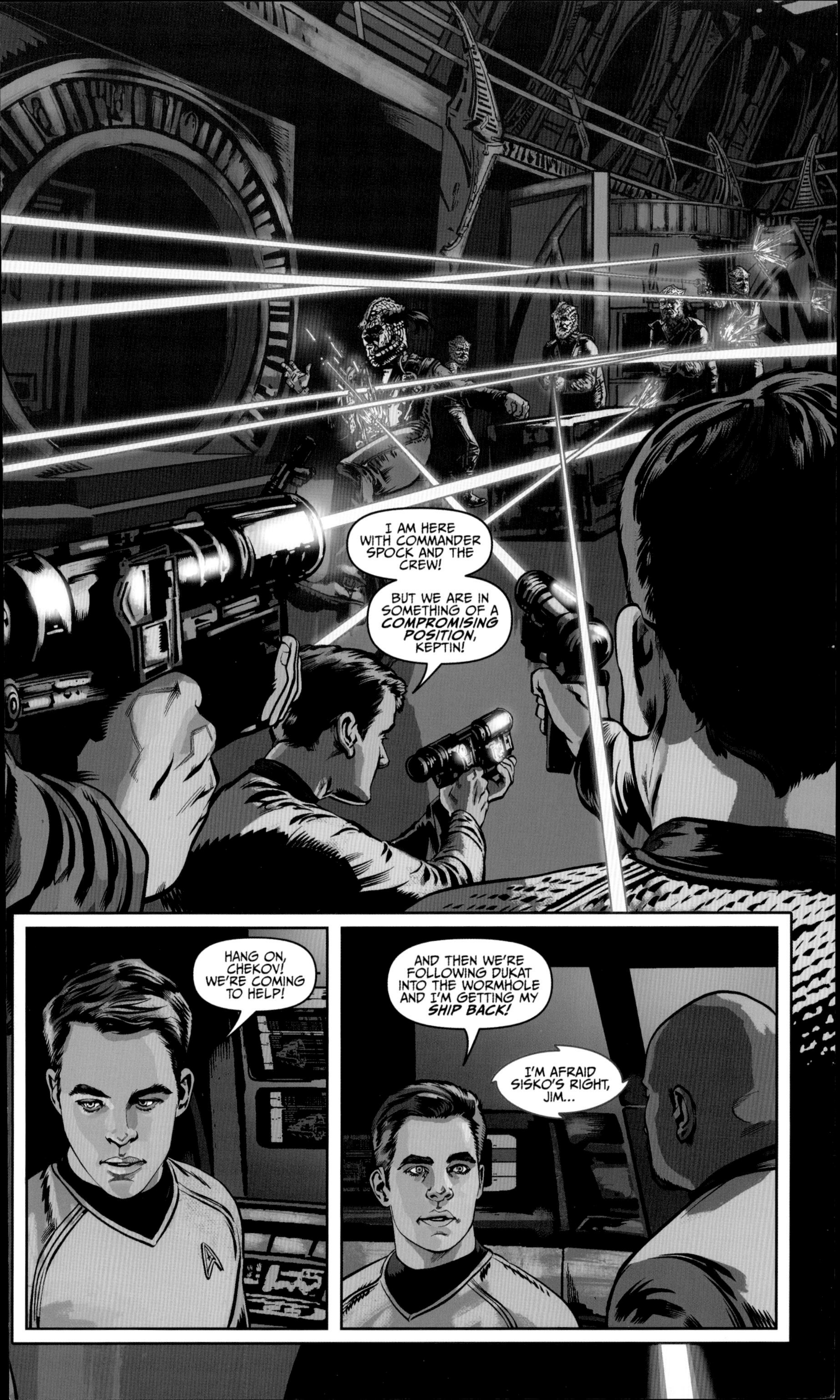
I AM HERE WITH COMMANDER SPOCK AND THE CREW!
BUT WE ARE IN SOMETHING OF A *COMPROMISING POSITION*, KEPTIN!
HANG ON, CHEKOV! WE'RE COMING TO HELP!
AND THEN WE'RE FOLLOWING DUKAT INTO THE WORMHOLE AND I'M GETTING MY *SHIP BACK!*
I'M AFRAID SISKO'S RIGHT, JIM...

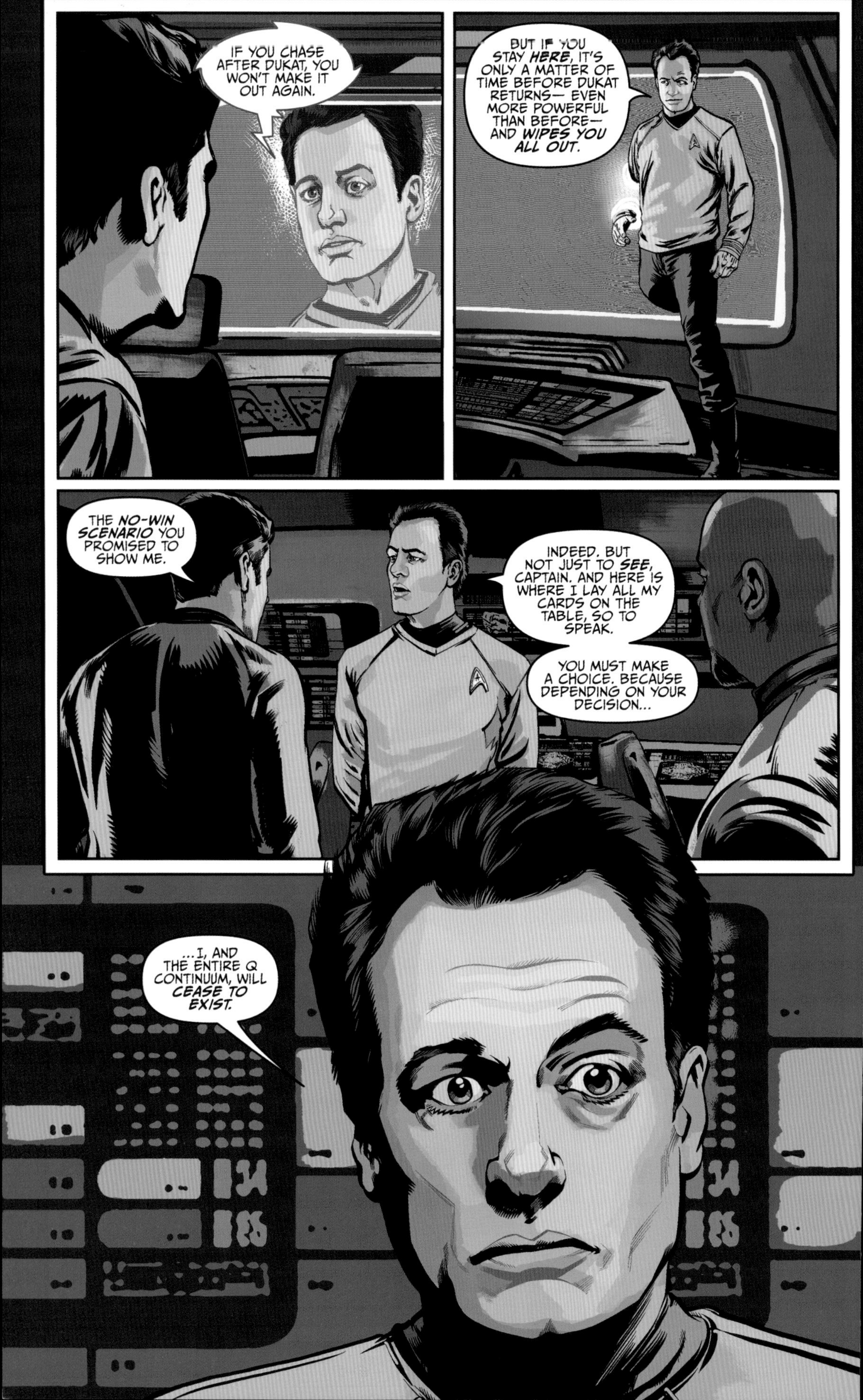
IF YOU CHASE AFTER DUKAT, YOU WON'T MAKE IT OUT AGAIN.
BUT IF YOU STAY HERE, IT'S ONLY A MATTER OF TIME BEFORE DUKAT RETURNS— EVEN MORE POWERFUL THAN BEFORE— AND WIPES YOU ALL OUT.
THE NO-WIN SCENARIO YOU PROMISED TO SHOW ME.
INDEED. BUT NOT JUST TO SEE, CAPTAIN. AND HERE IS WHERE I LAY ALL MY CARDS ON THE TABLE, SO TO SPEAK.
YOU MUST MAKE A CHOICE. BECAUSE DEPENDING ON YOUR DECISION...
...I, AND THE ENTIRE Q CONTINUUM, WILL CEASE TO EXIST.

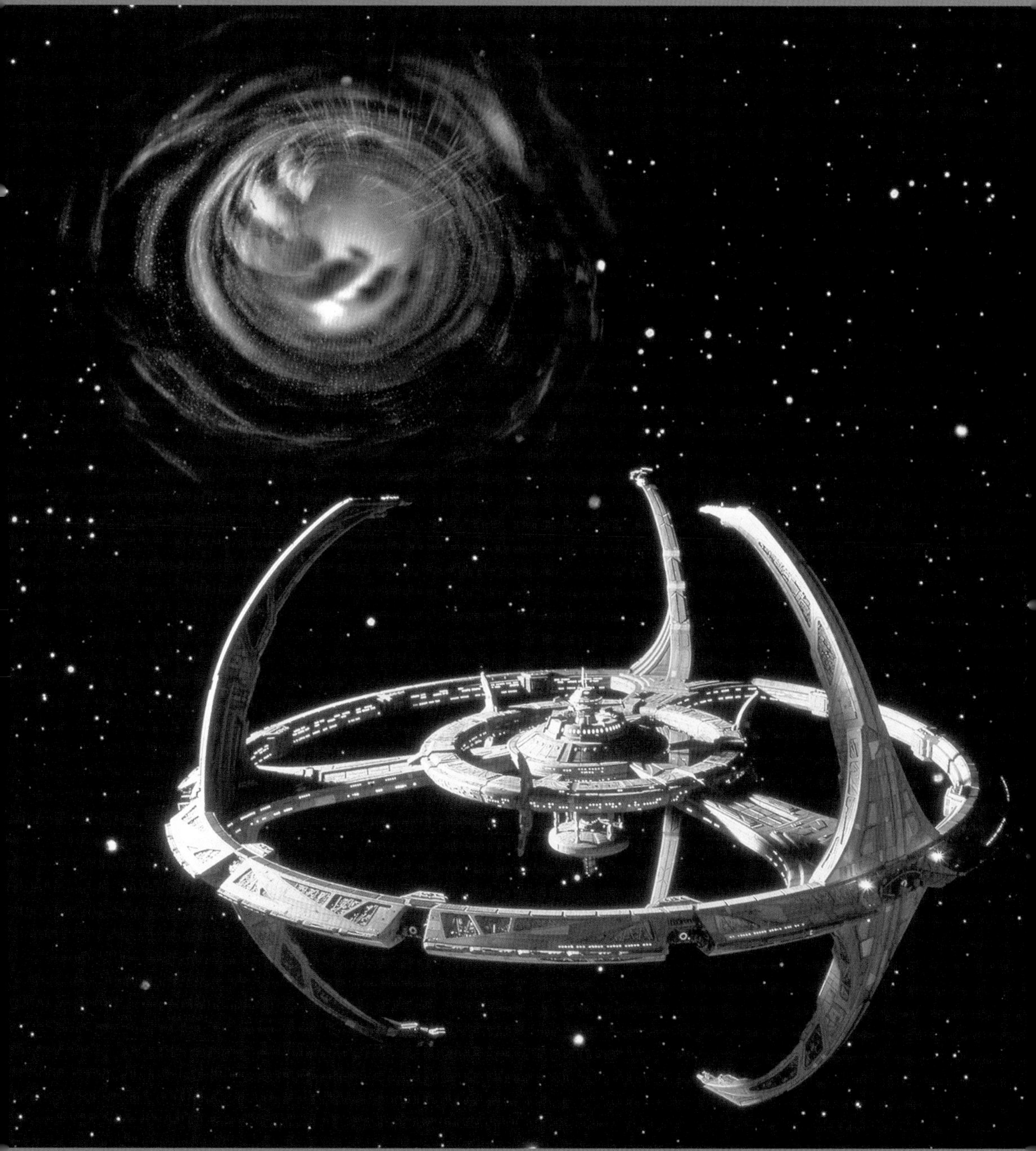

CHAPTER 6

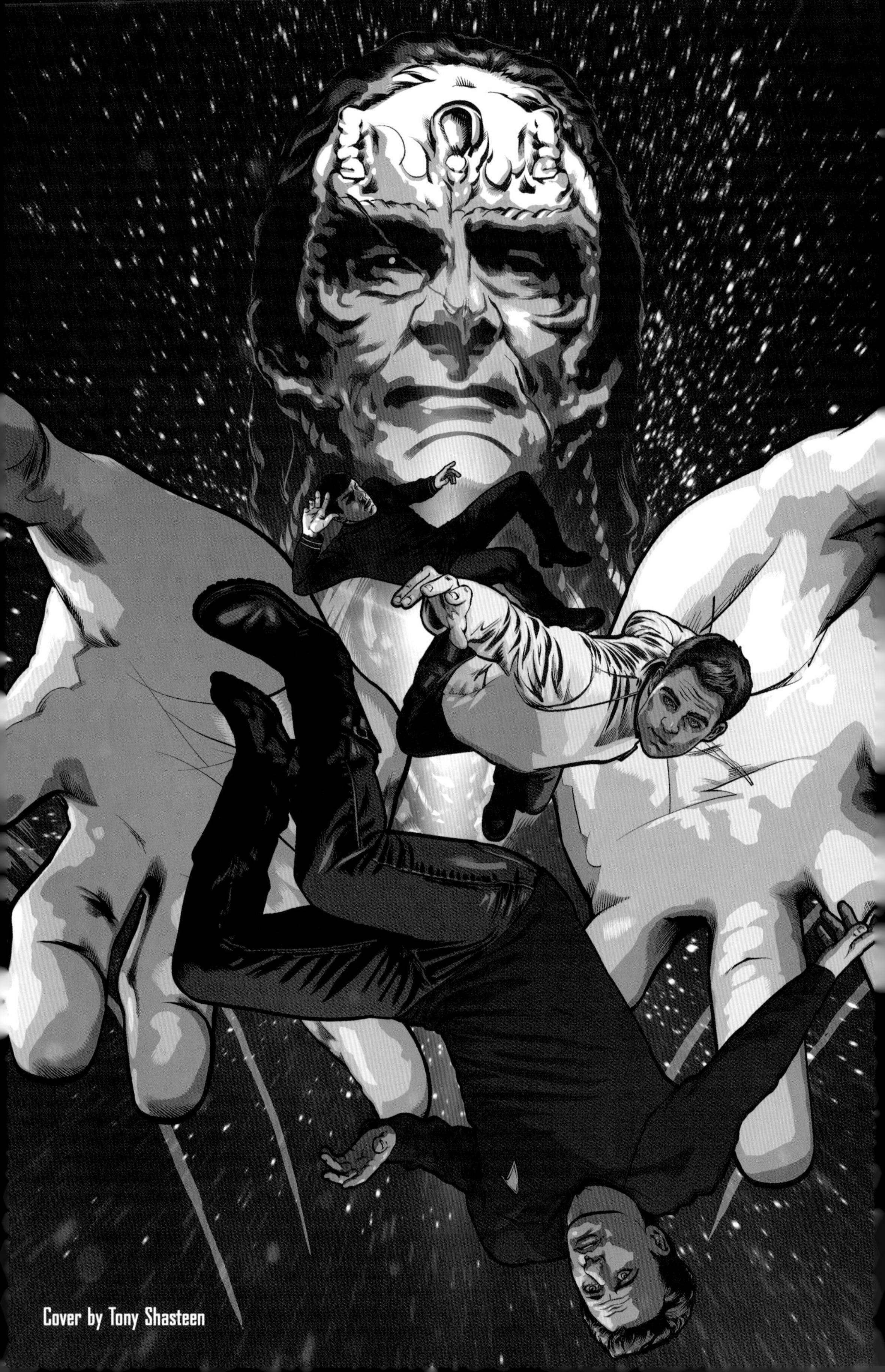

Cover by Tony Shasteen

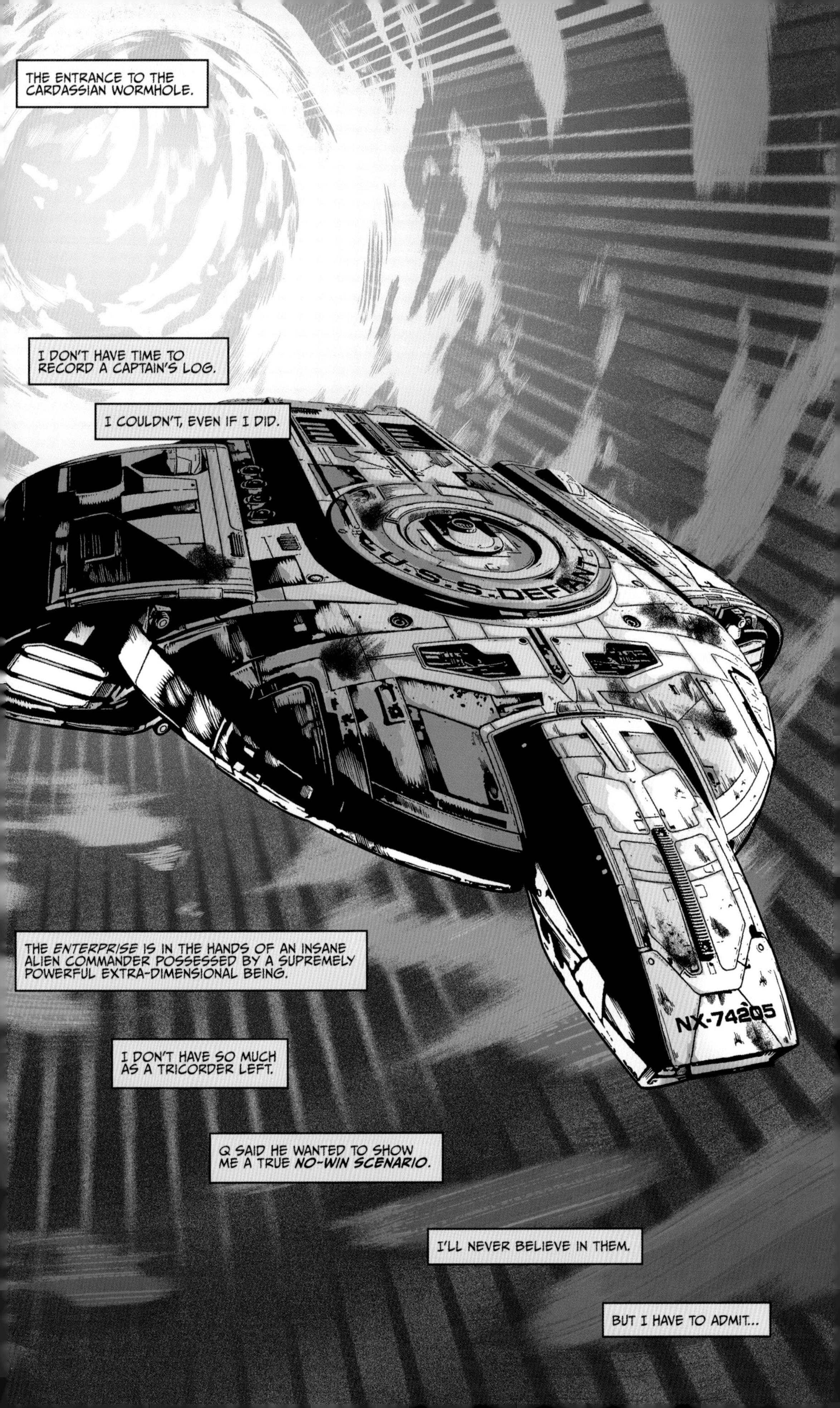
THE ENTRANCE TO THE CARDASSIAN WORMHOLE.
I DON'T HAVE TIME TO RECORD A CAPTAIN'S LOG.
I COULDN'T, EVEN IF I DID.
U.S.S. DEFIANT
THE *ENTERPRISE* IS IN THE HANDS OF AN INSANE ALIEN COMMANDER POSSESSED BY A SUPREMELY POWERFUL EXTRA-DIMENSIONAL BEING.
NX-74205
I DON'T HAVE SO MUCH AS A TRICORDER LEFT.
Q SAID HE WANTED TO SHOW ME A TRUE ***NO-WIN SCENARIO***.
I'LL NEVER BELIEVE IN THEM.
BUT I HAVE TO ADMIT...

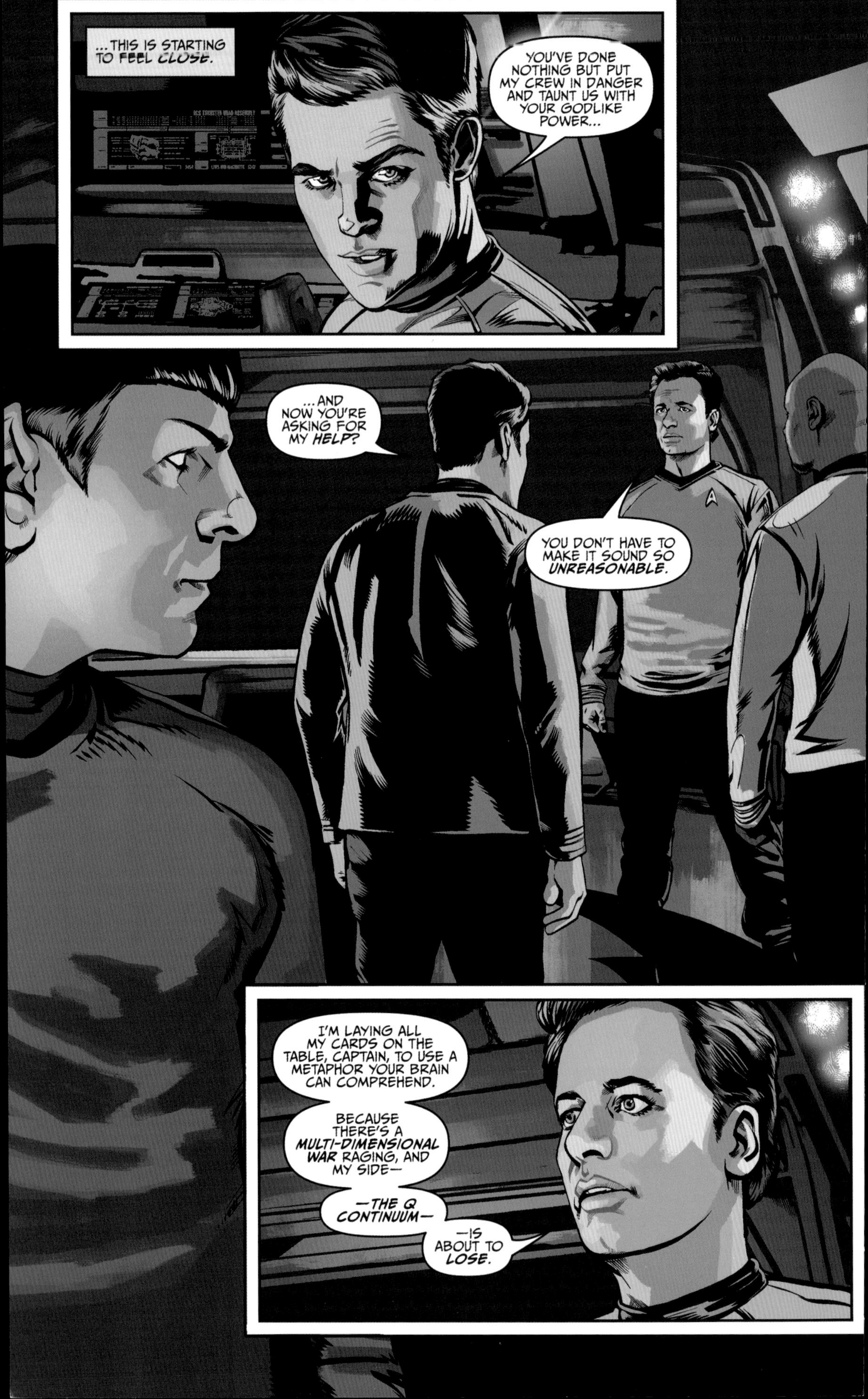
...THIS IS STARTING TO FEEL CLOSE.
YOU'VE DONE NOTHING BUT PUT MY CREW IN DANGER AND TAUNT US WITH YOUR GODLIKE POWER...
...AND NOW YOU'RE ASKING FOR MY HELP?
YOU DON'T HAVE TO MAKE IT SOUND SO UNREASONABLE.
I'M LAYING ALL MY CARDS ON THE TABLE, CAPTAIN, TO USE A METAPHOR YOUR BRAIN CAN COMPREHEND.
BECAUSE THERE'S A MULTI-DIMENSIONAL WAR RAGING, AND MY SIDE—
—THE Q CONTINUUM—
—IS ABOUT TO LOSE.

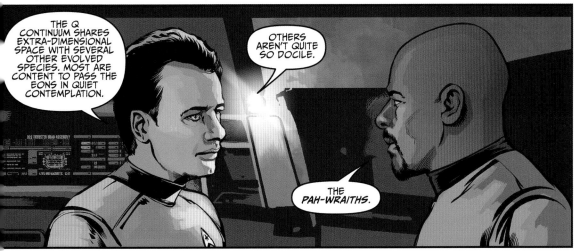

THE Q CONTINUUM SHARES EXTRA-DIMENSIONAL SPACE WITH SEVERAL OTHER EVOLVED SPECIES. MOST ARE CONTENT TO PASS THE EONS IN QUIET CONTEMPLATION.

OTHERS AREN'T QUITE SO DOCILE.

THE *PAH-WRAITHS.*

PRECISELY. THEY'RE OUT TO DESTROY THEIR MULTI-DIMENSIONAL NEIGHBORS.

NOT JUST THE PROPHETS WITH WHOM YOU ARE SO CLOSELY BONDED, SISKO, BUT AGAINST THE CONTINUUM AS WELL.

AND FOR ALL OF THE POWER WE Q CAN WIELD IN THREE DIMENSIONS, WE HAVEN'T BEEN ABLE TO STOP THE WRAITHS.

BUT YOU'RE OMNISCIENT, AREN'T YOU? AT LEAST YOU ENJOY MAKING US THINK YOU ARE.

YOU MUST ALREADY KNOW HOW THIS PLAYS OUT.

NOT WHEN IT COMES TO MY OWN EXTRA-DIMENSIONAL HOME. THERE I'M AS CLUELESS TO MY OWN FUTURE, AND THE FUTURE OF MY RACE, AS YOU ARE TO YOUR OWN. THUS MY ATTEMPT TO FIND A *THREE-DIMENSIONAL* SOLUTION.

SO YES, CAPTAIN, THOUGH IT BRINGS ME NO JOY AND NO SMALL AMOUNT OF EMBARRASSMENT...

I NEED YOUR *HELP.*

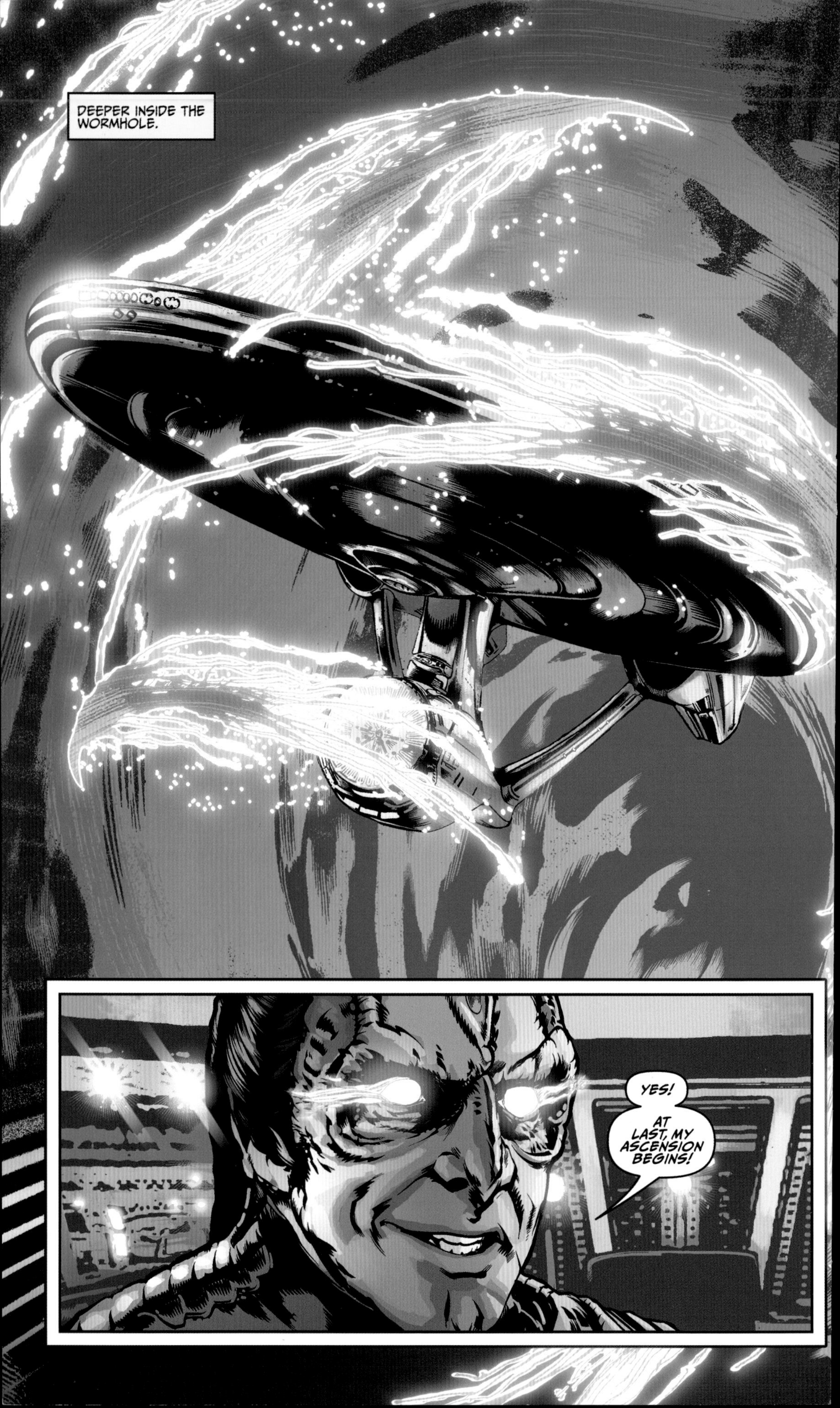
DEEPER INSIDE THE WORMHOLE.
YES!
AT LAST, MY ASCENSION BEGINS!

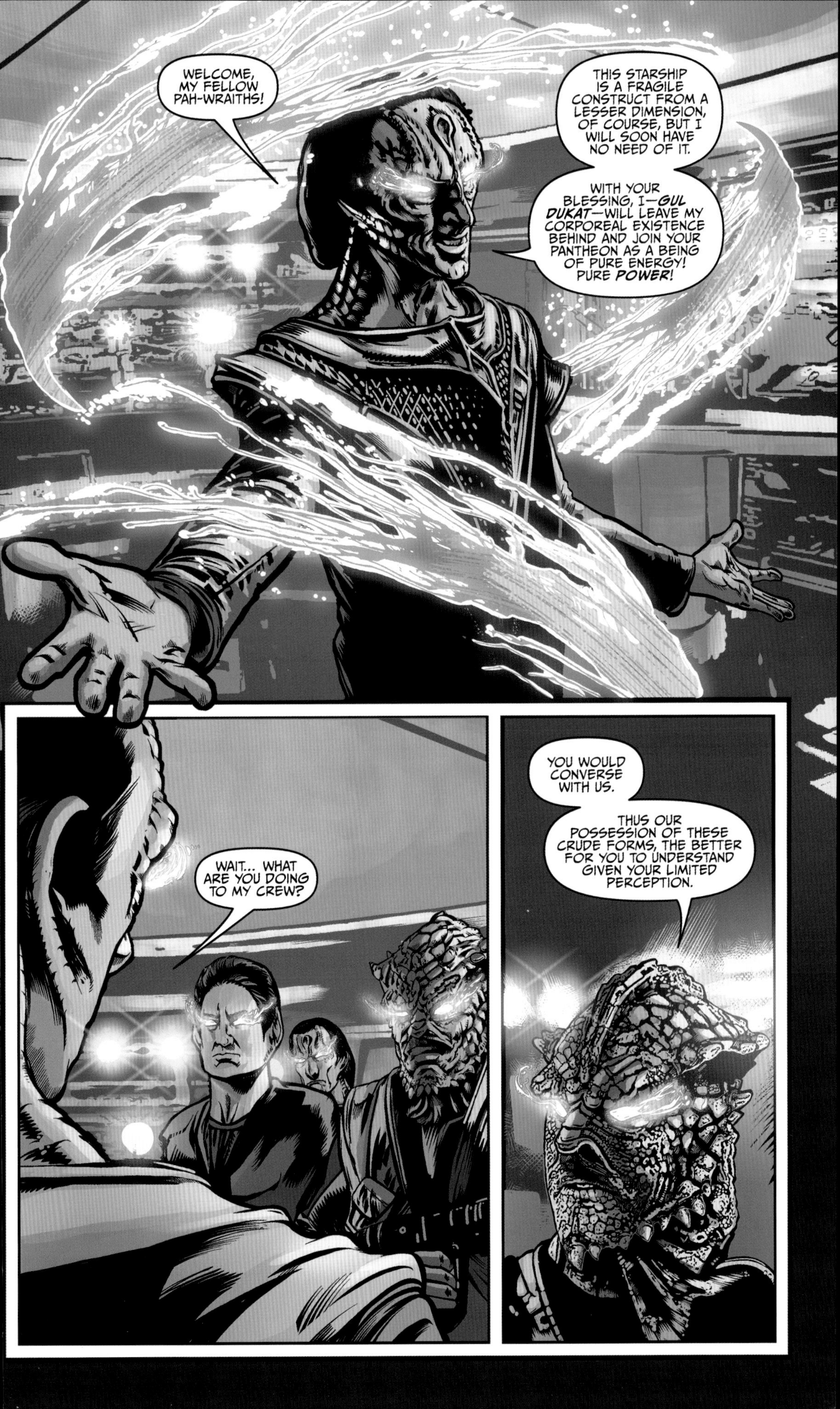
WELCOME, MY FELLOW PAH-WRAITHS!
THIS STARSHIP IS A FRAGILE CONSTRUCT FROM A LESSER DIMENSION, OF COURSE, BUT I WILL SOON HAVE NO NEED OF IT.
WITH YOUR BLESSING, I—GUL DUKAT—WILL LEAVE MY CORPOREAL EXISTENCE BEHIND AND JOIN YOUR PANTHEON AS A BEING OF PURE ENERGY! PURE POWER!
WAIT... WHAT ARE YOU DOING TO MY CREW?
YOU WOULD CONVERSE WITH US.
THUS OUR POSSESSION OF THESE CRUDE FORMS, THE BETTER FOR YOU TO UNDERSTAND GIVEN YOUR LIMITED PERCEPTION.

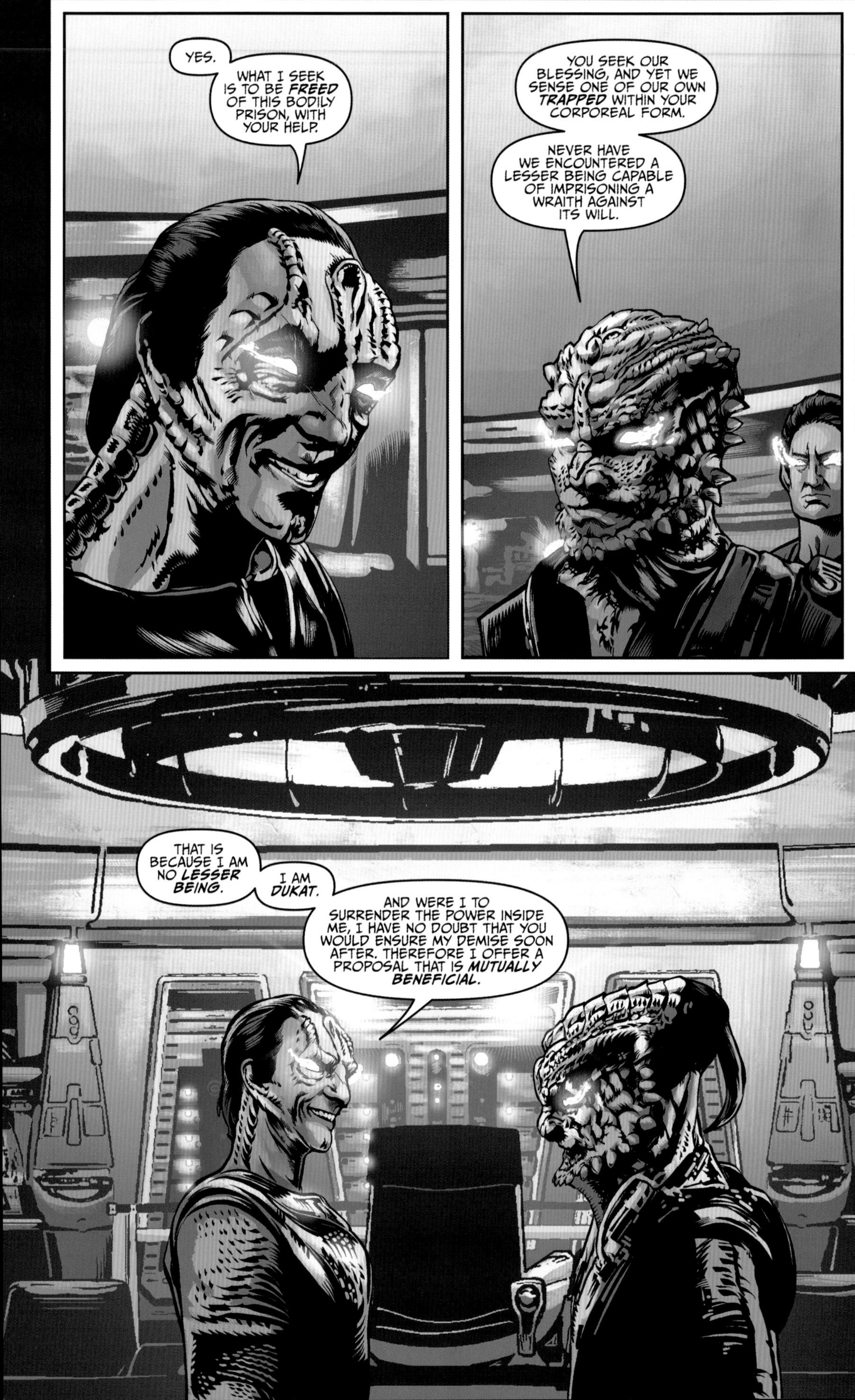
YES.
WHAT I SEEK IS TO BE FREED OF THIS BODILY PRISON, WITH YOUR HELP.
YOU SEEK OUR BLESSING, AND YET WE SENSE ONE OF OUR OWN TRAPPED WITHIN YOUR CORPOREAL FORM.
NEVER HAVE WE ENCOUNTERED A LESSER BEING CAPABLE OF IMPRISONING A WRAITH AGAINST ITS WILL.
THAT IS BECAUSE I AM NO LESSER BEING.
I AM DUKAT.
AND WERE I TO SURRENDER THE POWER INSIDE ME, I HAVE NO DOUBT THAT YOU WOULD ENSURE MY DEMISE SOON AFTER. THEREFORE I OFFER A PROPOSAL THAT IS MUTUALLY BENEFICIAL.

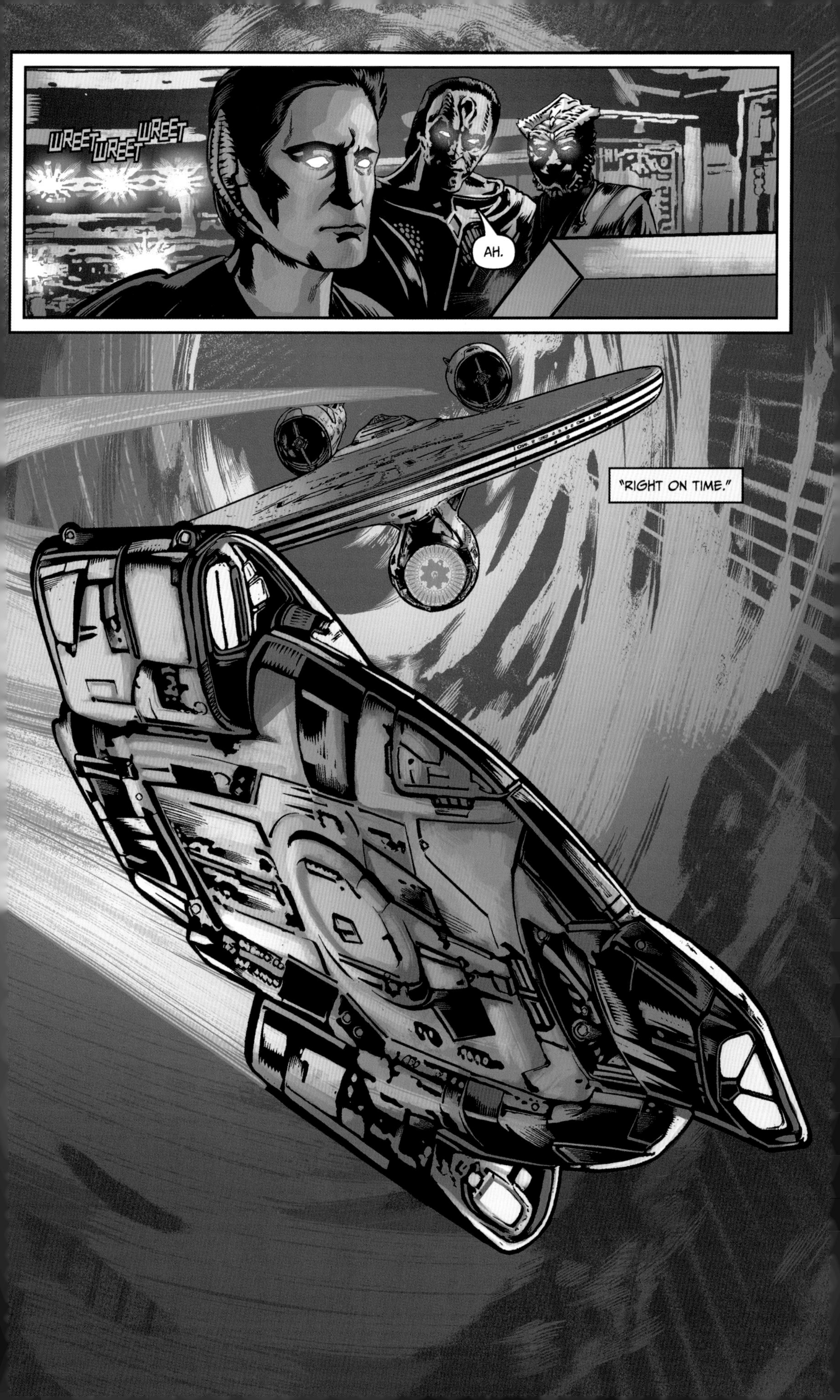
WREET WREET WREET
AH.
"RIGHT ON TIME."

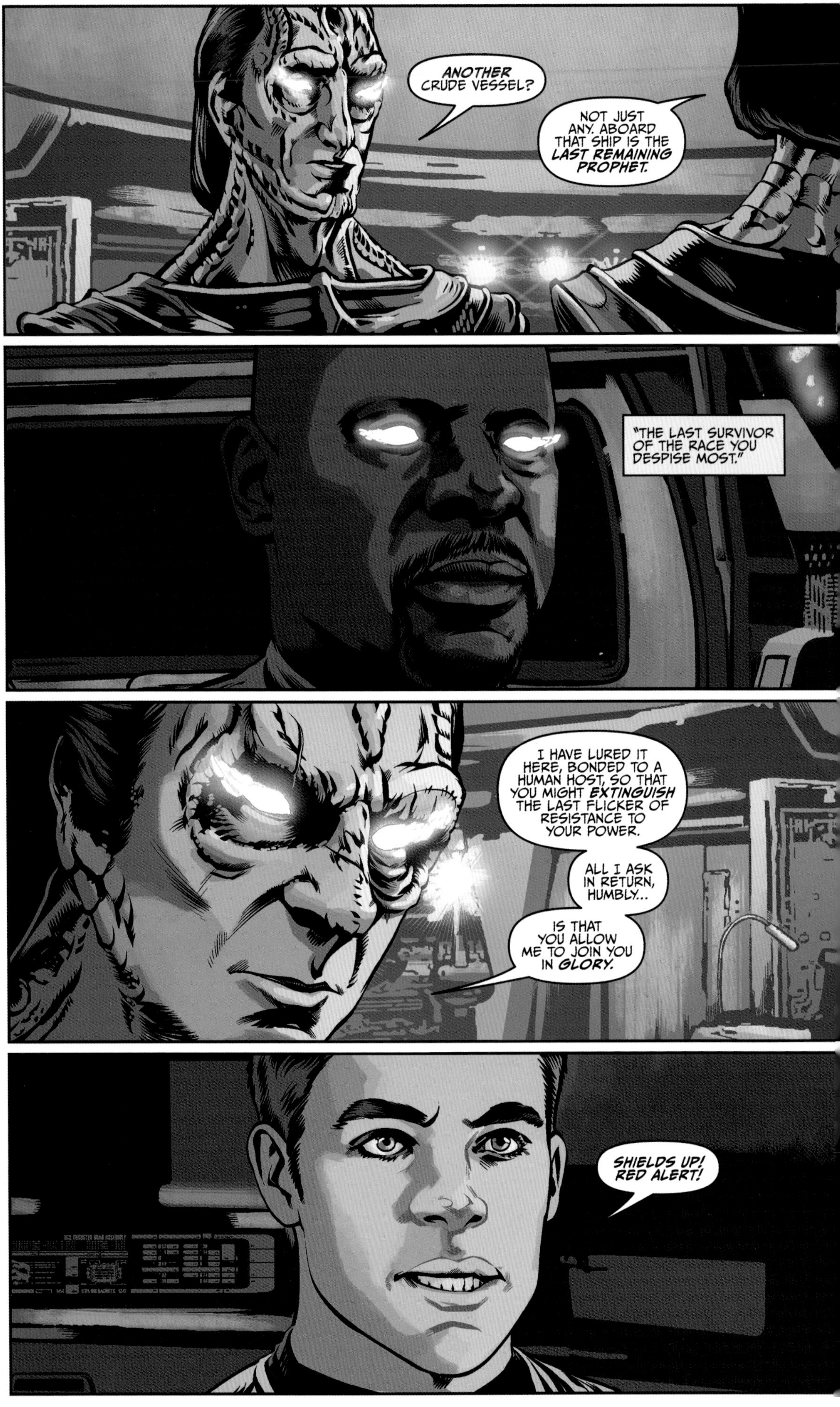
ANOTHER CRUDE VESSEL?
NOT JUST ANY. ABOARD THAT SHIP IS THE LAST REMAINING PROPHET.
"THE LAST SURVIVOR OF THE RACE YOU DESPISE MOST."
I HAVE LURED IT HERE, BONDED TO A HUMAN HOST, SO THAT YOU MIGHT EXTINGUISH THE LAST FLICKER OF RESISTANCE TO YOUR POWER.
ALL I ASK IN RETURN, HUMBLY...
IS THAT YOU ALLOW ME TO JOIN YOU IN GLORY.
SHIELDS UP! RED ALERT!

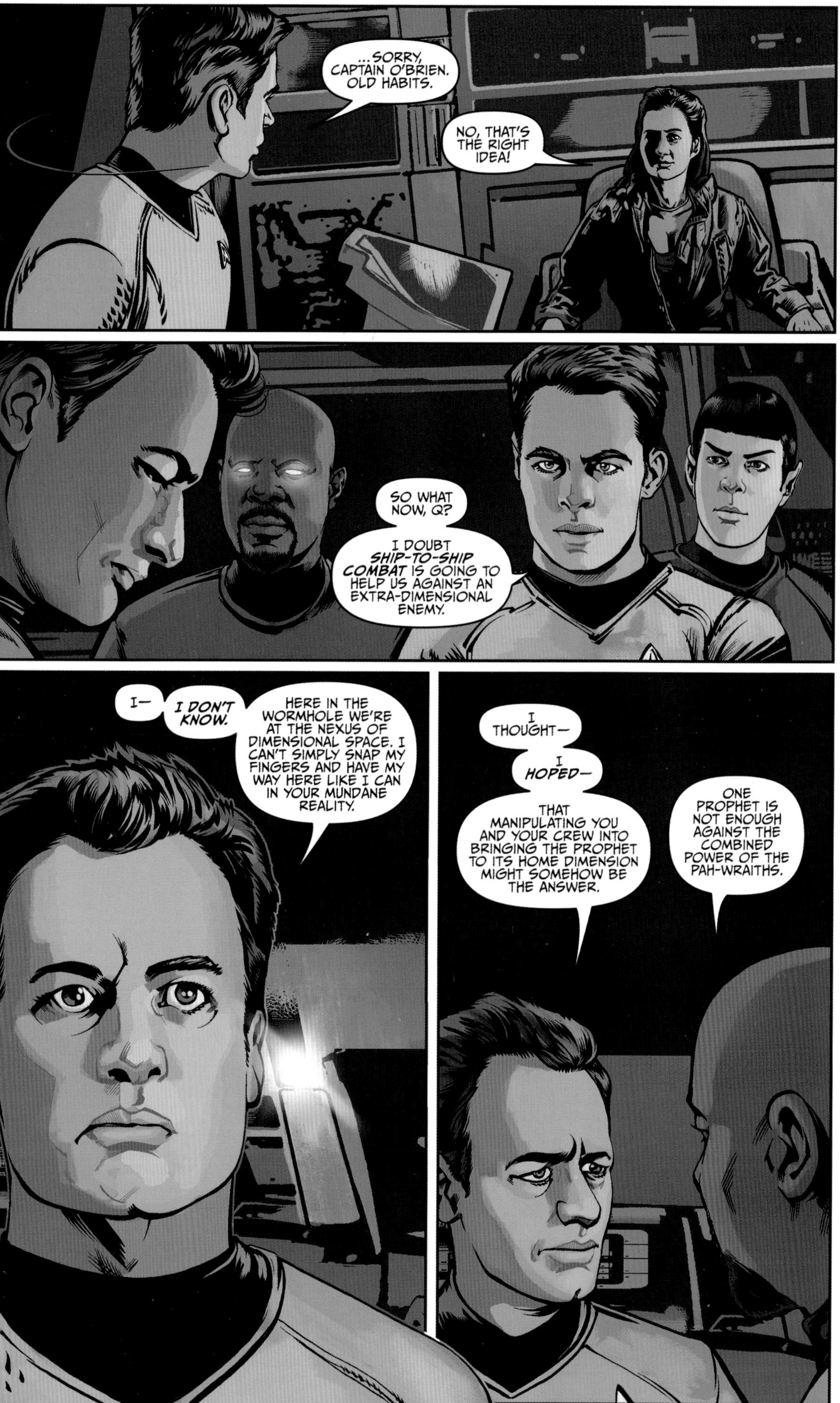

...SORRY, CAPTAIN O'BRIEN. OLD HABITS.
NO, THAT'S THE RIGHT IDEA!
SO WHAT NOW, Q?
I DOUBT *SHIP-TO-SHIP COMBAT* IS GOING TO HELP US AGAINST AN EXTRA-DIMENSIONAL ENEMY.
I—
I DON'T KNOW.
HERE IN THE WORMHOLE WE'RE AT THE NEXUS OF DIMENSIONAL SPACE. I CAN'T SIMPLY SNAP MY FINGERS AND HAVE MY WAY HERE LIKE I CAN IN YOUR MUNDANE REALITY.
I THOUGHT—
I *HOPED*—
THAT MANIPULATING YOU AND YOUR CREW INTO BRINGING THE PROPHET TO ITS HOME DIMENSION MIGHT SOMEHOW BE THE ANSWER.
ONE PROPHET IS NOT ENOUGH AGAINST THE COMBINED POWER OF THE PAH-WRAITHS.

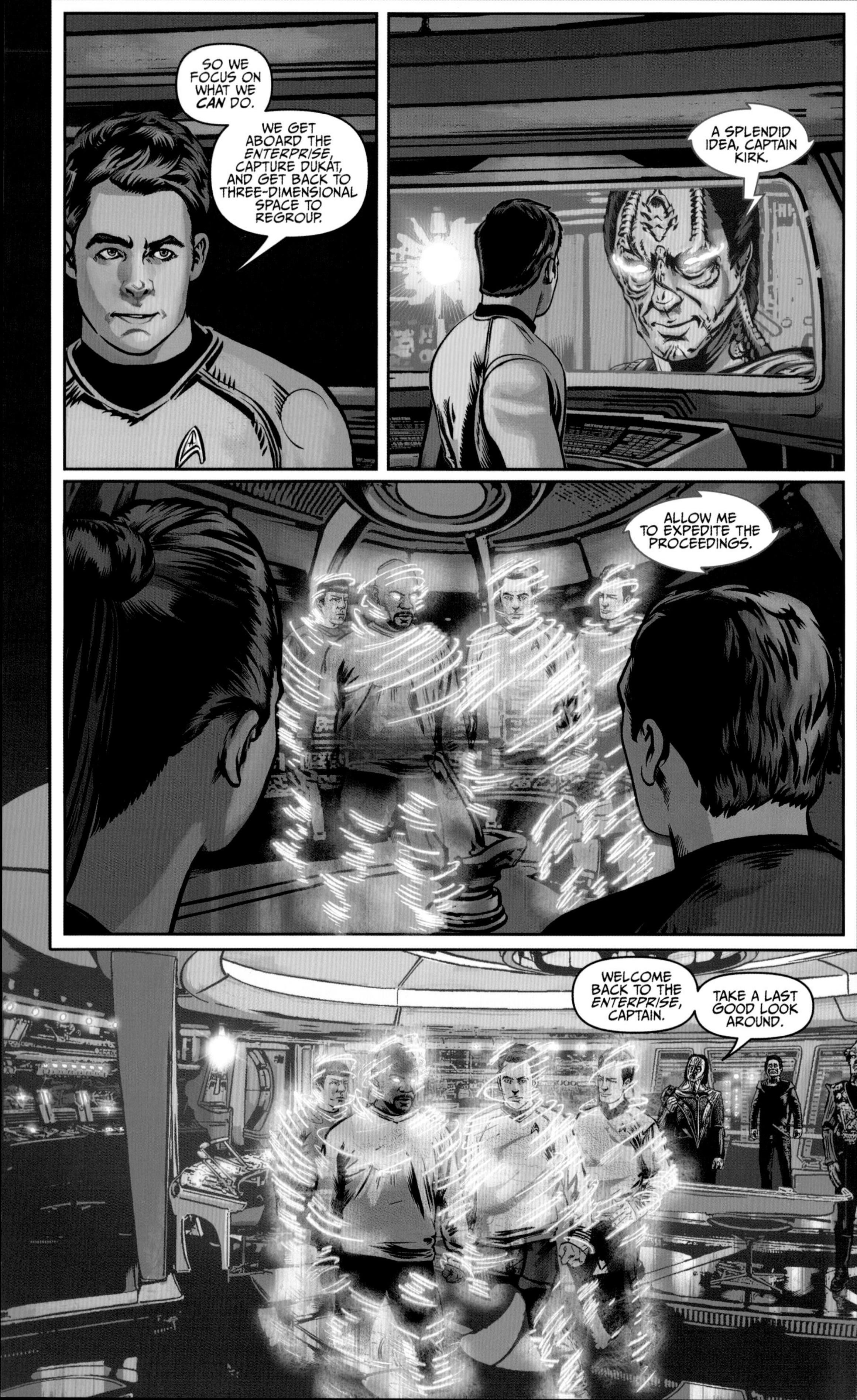
SO WE FOCUS ON WHAT WE CAN DO.
WE GET ABOARD THE ENTERPRISE, CAPTURE DUKAT, AND GET BACK TO THREE-DIMENSIONAL SPACE TO REGROUP.
A SPLENDID IDEA, CAPTAIN KIRK.
ALLOW ME TO EXPEDITE THE PROCEEDINGS.
WELCOME BACK TO THE ENTERPRISE, CAPTAIN.
TAKE A LAST GOOD LOOK AROUND.

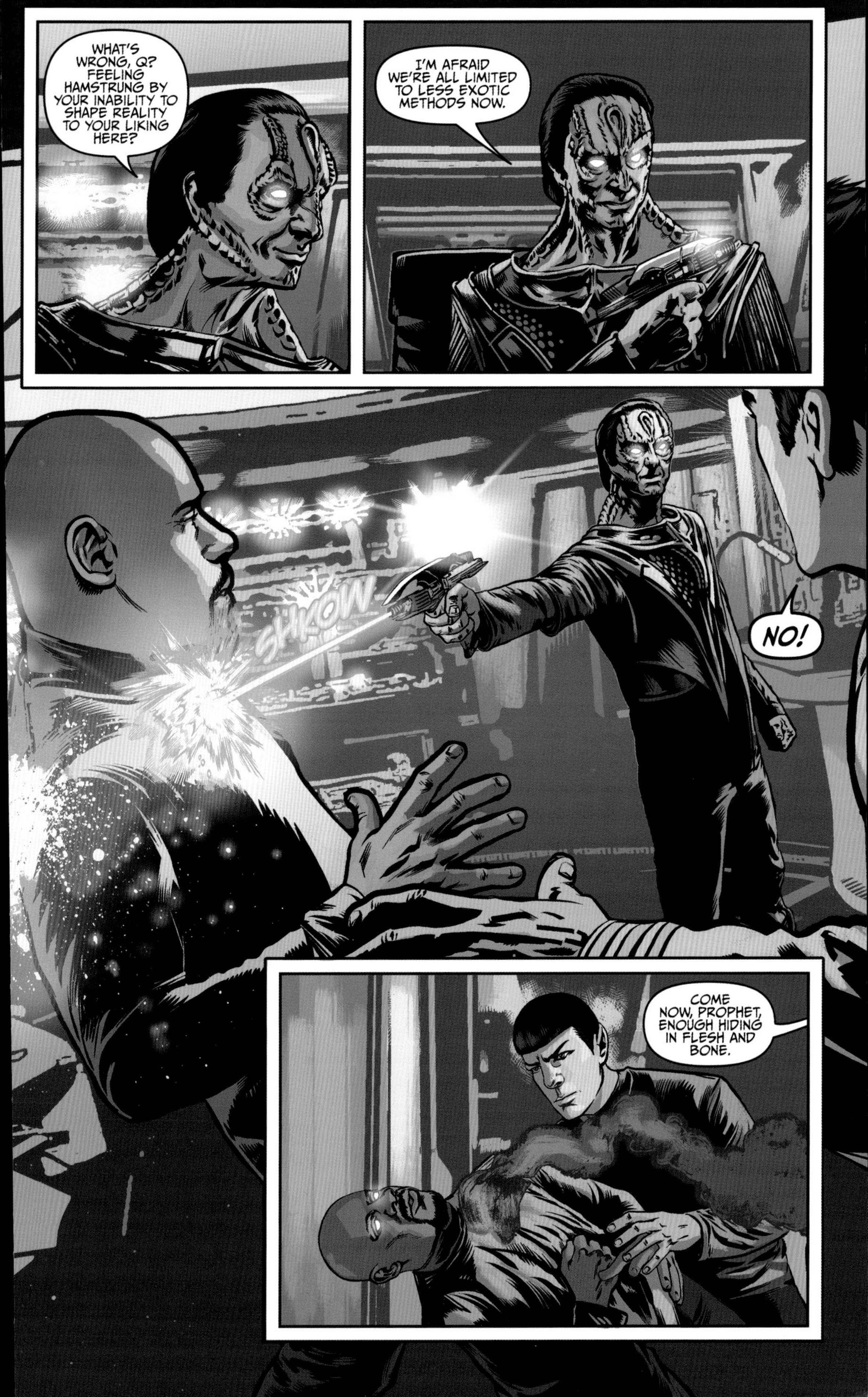
WHAT'S WRONG, Q? FEELING HAMSTRUNG BY YOUR INABILITY TO SHAPE REALITY TO YOUR LIKING HERE?
I'M AFRAID WE'RE ALL LIMITED TO LESS EXOTIC METHODS NOW.
SHKOW
NO!
COME NOW, PROPHET, ENOUGH HIDING IN FLESH AND BONE.

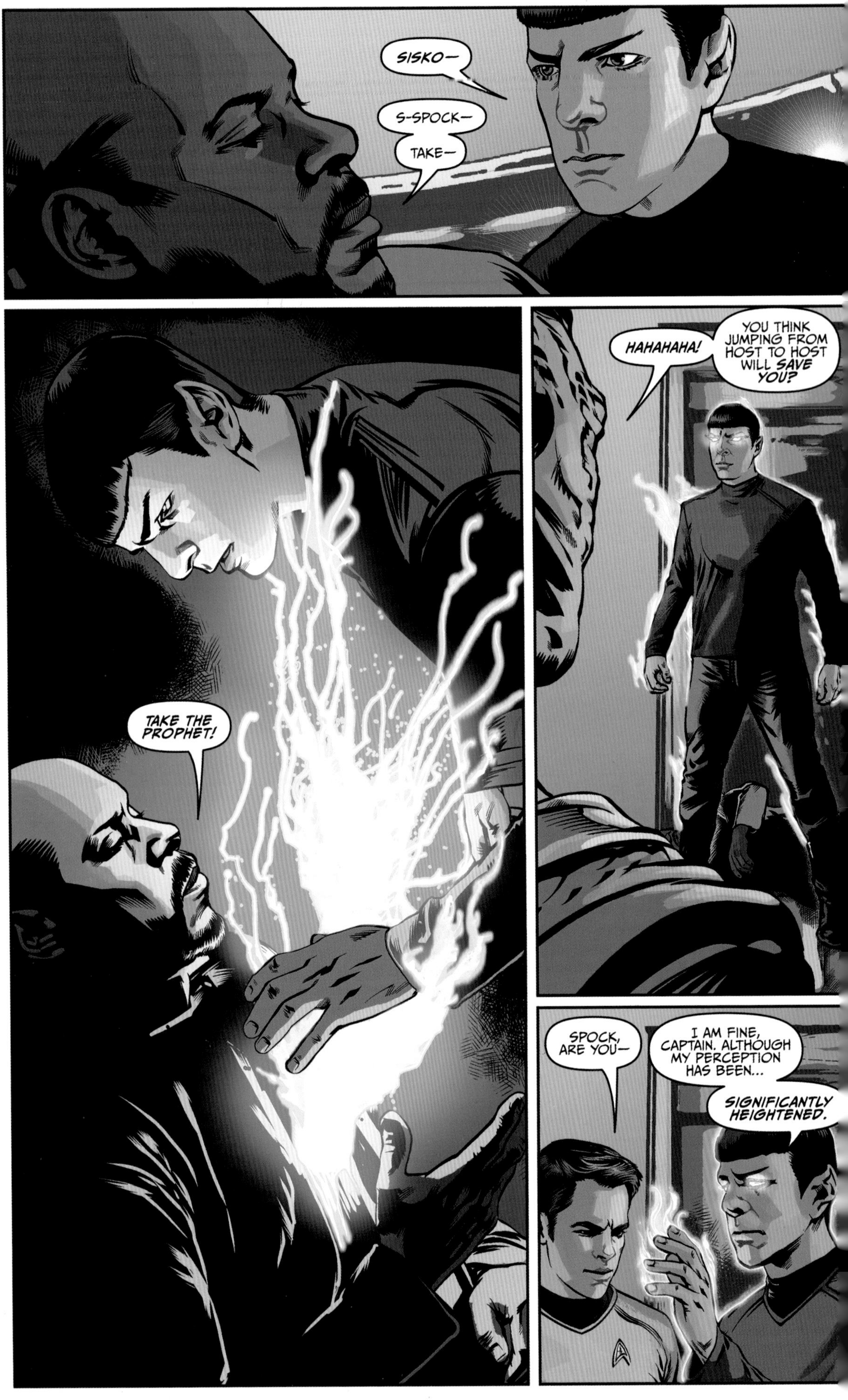
SISKO—
S-SPOCK—
TAKE—
TAKE THE PROPHET!
HAHAHAHA!
YOU THINK JUMPING FROM HOST TO HOST WILL SAVE YOU?
SPOCK, ARE YOU—
I AM FINE, CAPTAIN. ALTHOUGH MY PERCEPTION HAS BEEN...
SIGNIFICANTLY HEIGHTENED.

SPOCK...?

WHY IS THE VULCAN LOOKING AT ME LIKE THAT?

WHY... CAN'T I... MOVE?

IT MUST... BE THE PROPHET'S... DOING...

I KNOW WHAT MUST BE DONE.

WAIT, WHAT ARE YOU—?

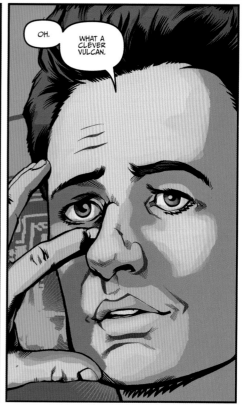
OH.

WHAT A CLEVER VULCAN.

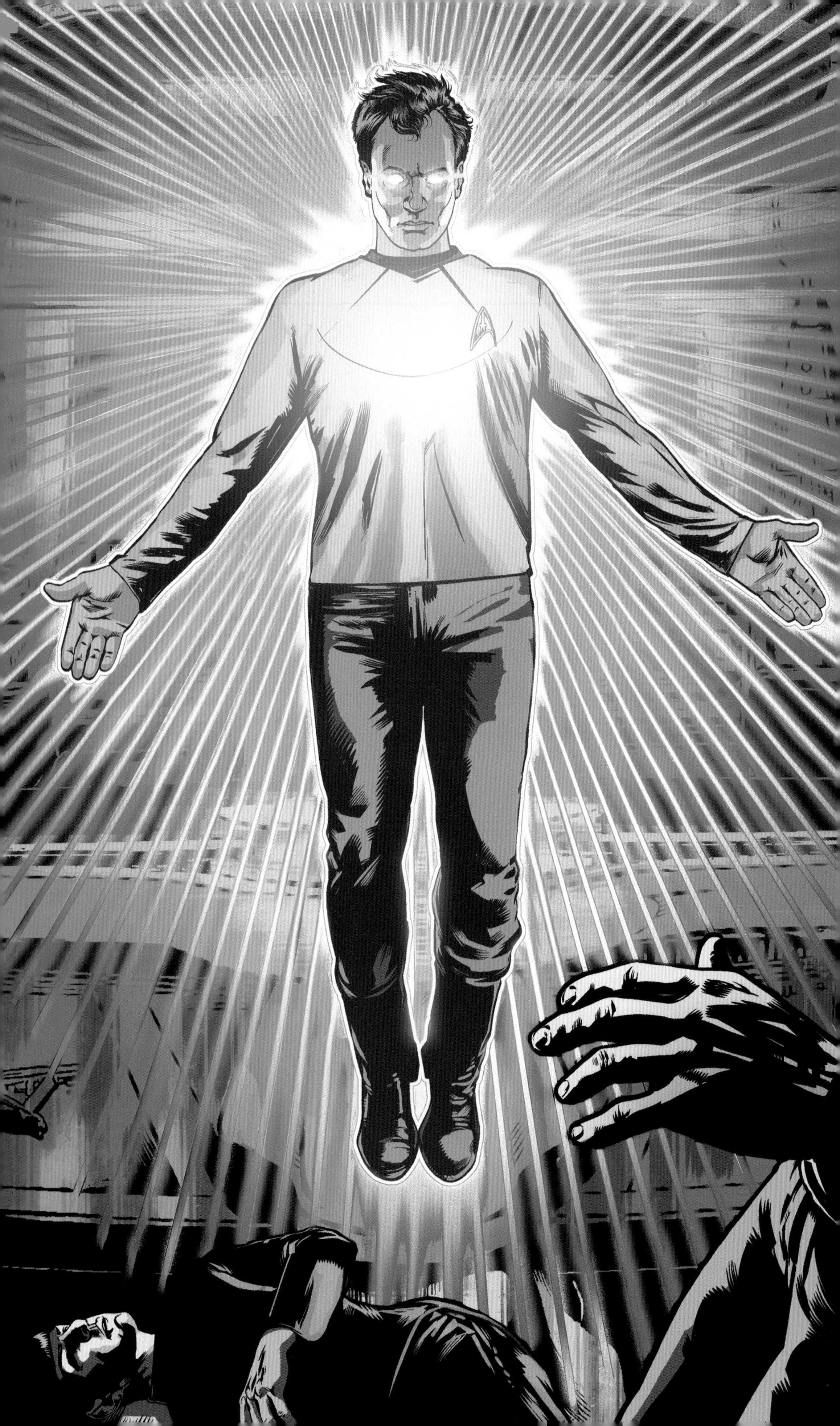

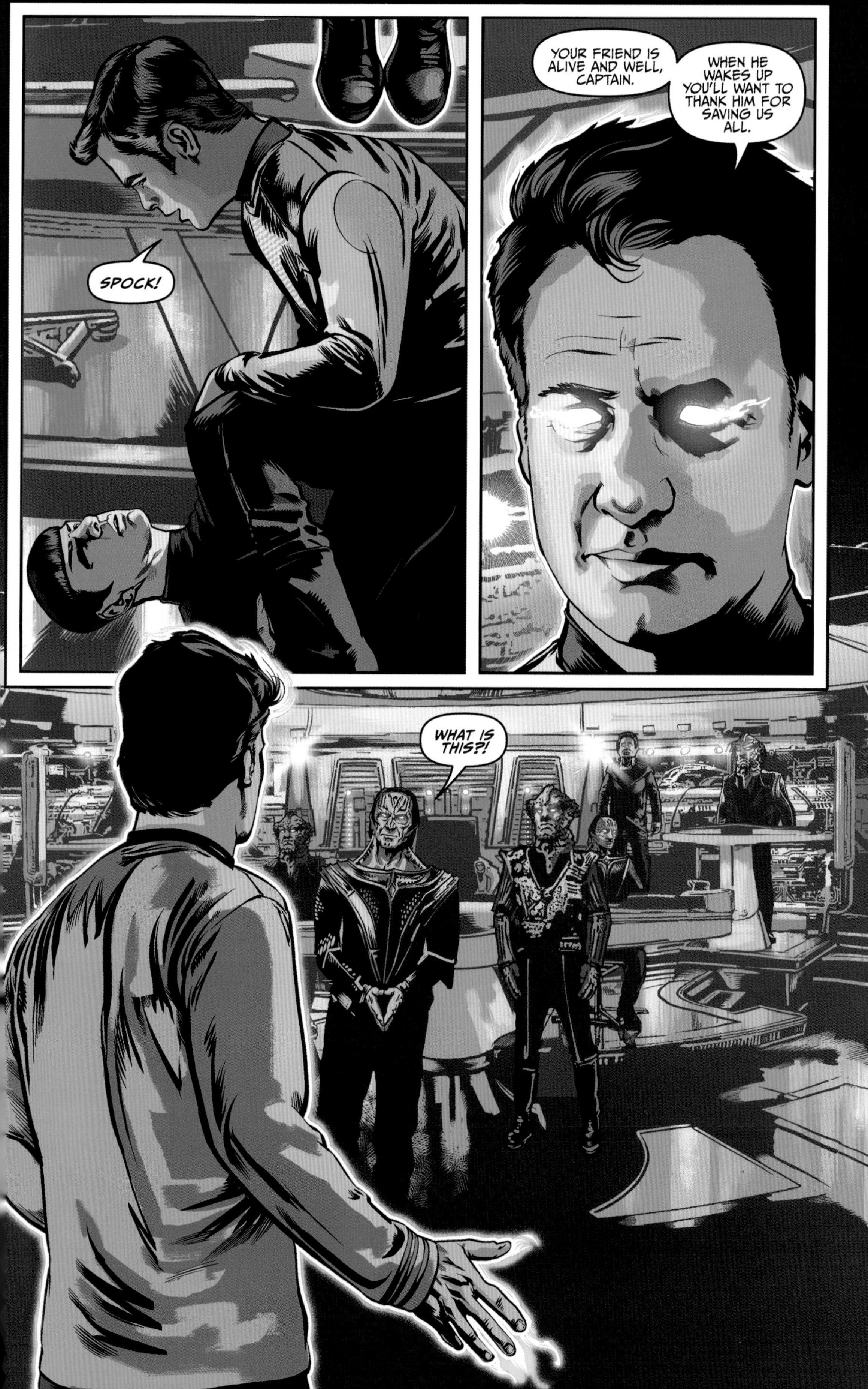
SPOCK!
YOUR FRIEND IS ALIVE AND WELL, CAPTAIN.
WHEN HE WAKES UP YOU'LL WANT TO THANK HIM FOR SAVING US ALL.
WHAT IS THIS?!

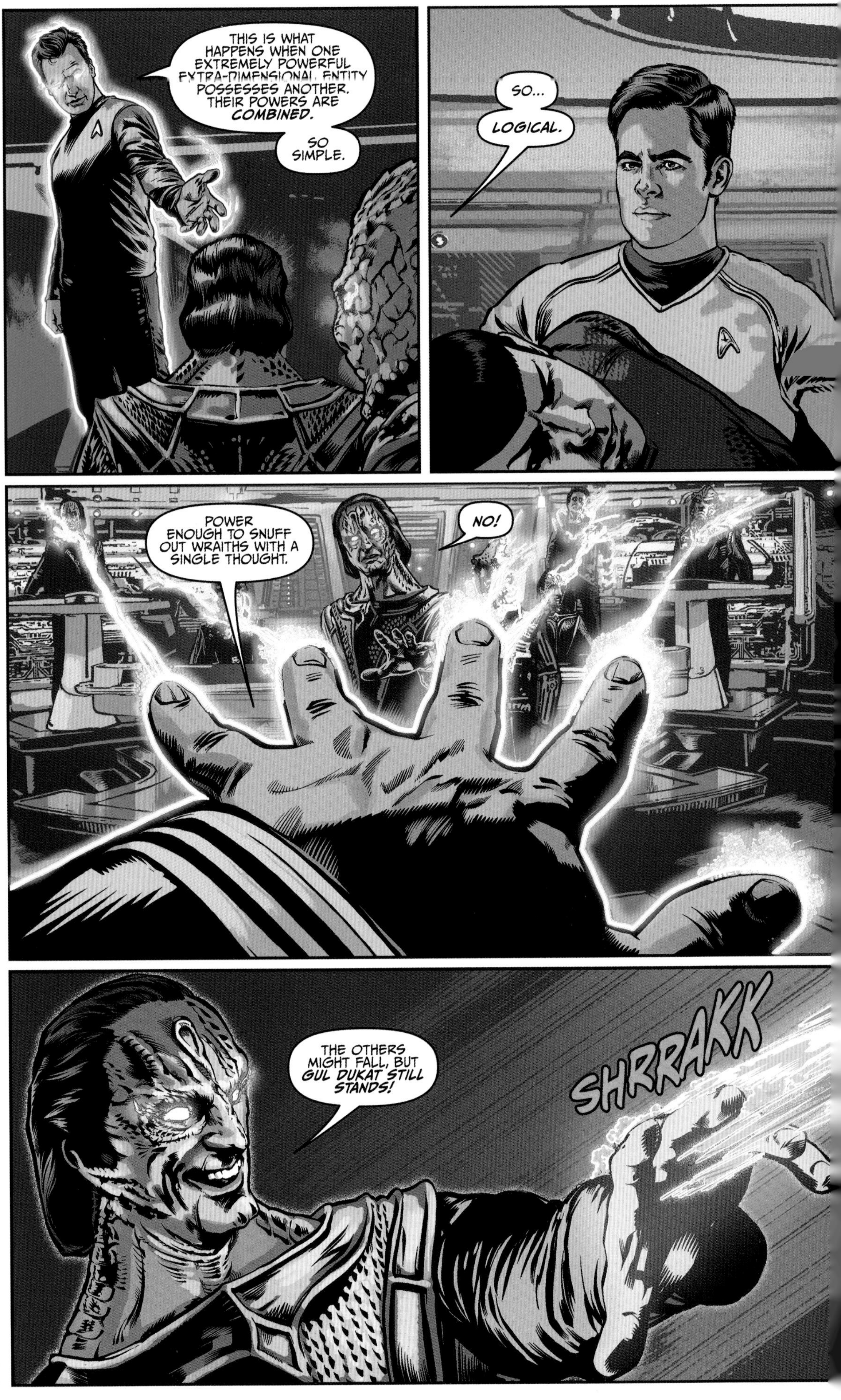
THIS IS WHAT HAPPENS WHEN ONE EXTREMELY POWERFUL EXTRA-DIMENSIONAL ENTITY POSSESSES ANOTHER. THEIR POWERS ARE COMBINED.
SO SIMPLE.
SO...
LOGICAL.
POWER ENOUGH TO SNUFF OUT WRAITHS WITH A SINGLE THOUGHT.
NO!
THE OTHERS MIGHT FALL, BUT GUL DUKAT STILL STANDS!
SHRRAKK

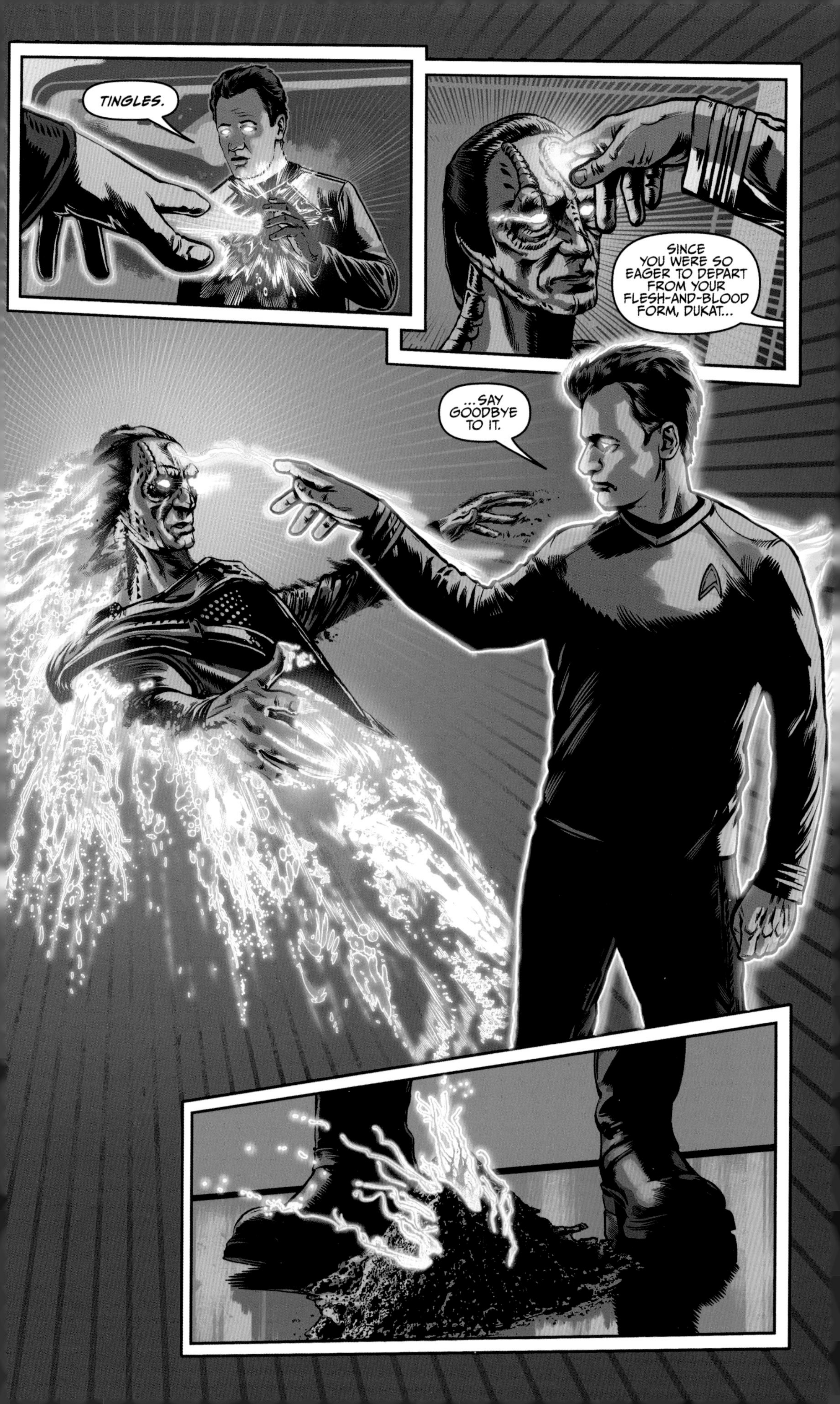
TINGLES.
SINCE YOU WERE SO EAGER TO DEPART FROM YOUR FLESH-AND-BLOOD FORM, DUKAT...
...SAY GOODBYE TO IT.

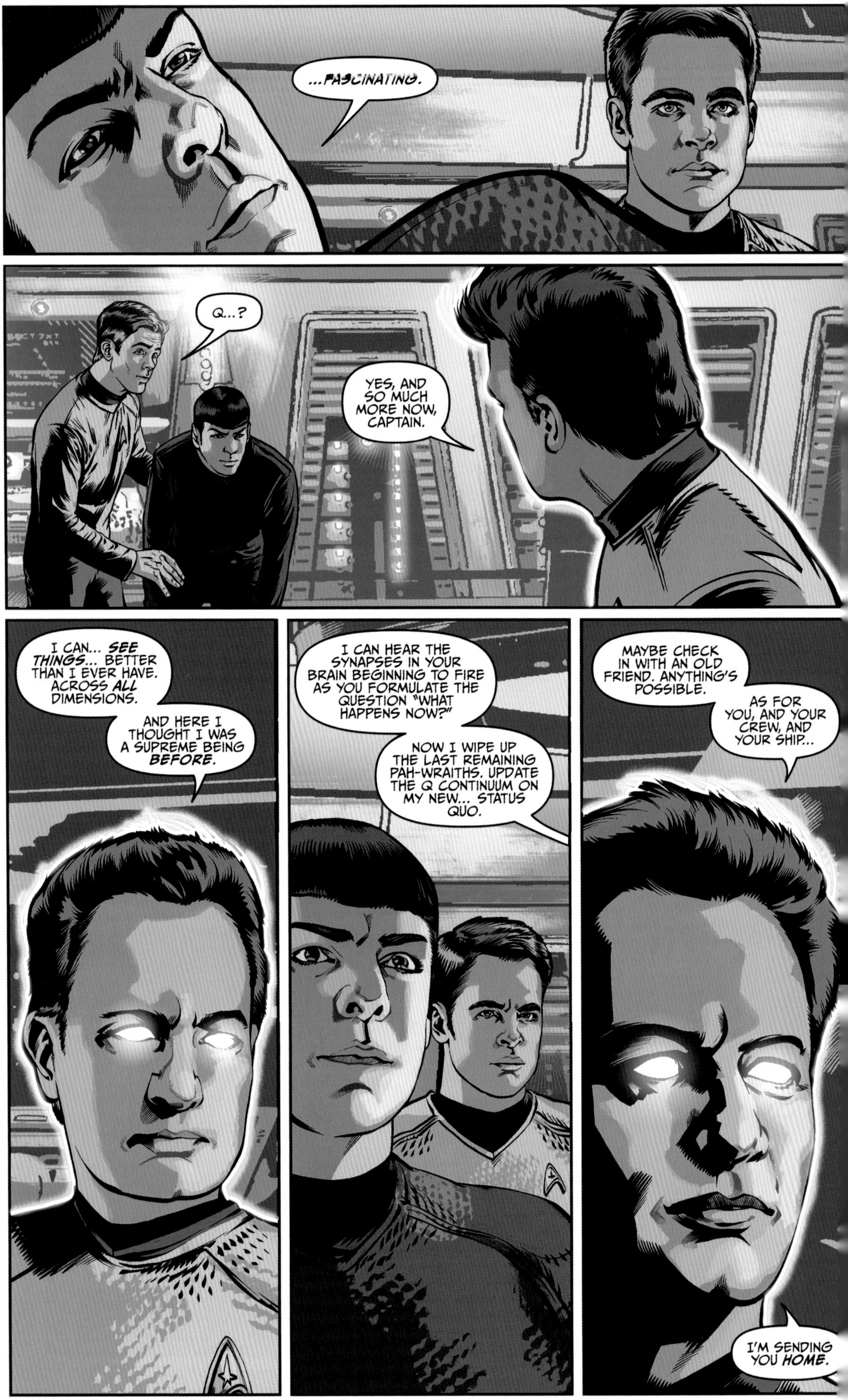
...FASCINATING.
Q...?
YES, AND SO MUCH MORE NOW, CAPTAIN.
I CAN... SEE THINGS... BETTER THAN I EVER HAVE. ACROSS ALL DIMENSIONS.
AND HERE I THOUGHT I WAS A SUPREME BEING BEFORE.
I CAN HEAR THE SYNAPSES IN YOUR BRAIN BEGINNING TO FIRE AS YOU FORMULATE THE QUESTION "WHAT HAPPENS NOW?"
NOW I WIPE UP THE LAST REMAINING PAH-WRAITHS. UPDATE THE Q CONTINUUM ON MY NEW... STATUS QUO.
MAYBE CHECK IN WITH AN OLD FRIEND. ANYTHING'S POSSIBLE.
AS FOR YOU, AND YOUR CREW, AND YOUR SHIP...
I'M SENDING YOU HOME.

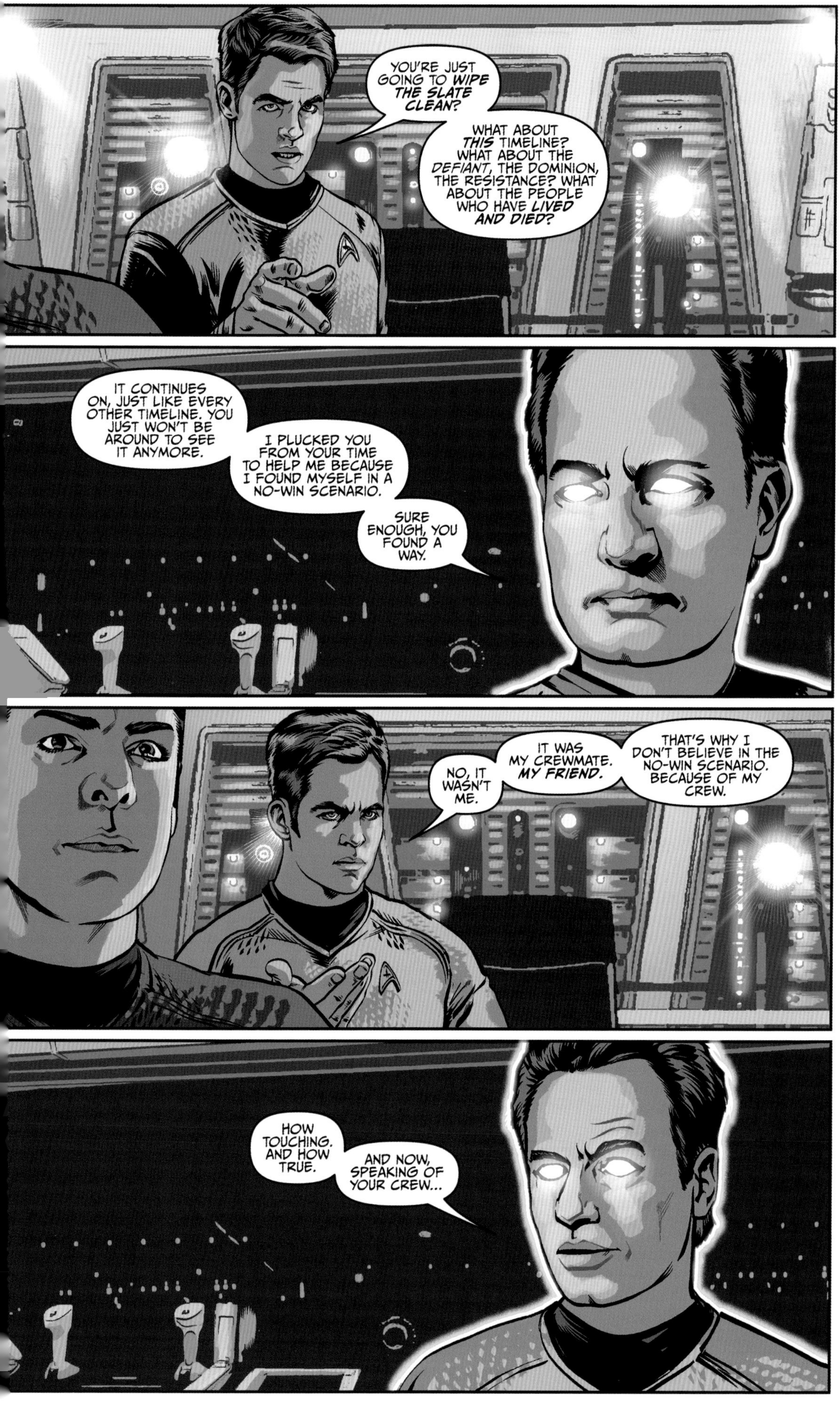

YOU'RE JUST GOING TO WIPE THE SLATE CLEAN?
WHAT ABOUT THIS TIMELINE? WHAT ABOUT THE DEFIANT, THE DOMINION, THE RESISTANCE? WHAT ABOUT THE PEOPLE WHO HAVE LIVED AND DIED?
IT CONTINUES ON, JUST LIKE EVERY OTHER TIMELINE. YOU JUST WON'T BE AROUND TO SEE IT ANYMORE.
I PLUCKED YOU FROM YOUR TIME TO HELP ME BECAUSE I FOUND MYSELF IN A NO-WIN SCENARIO.
SURE ENOUGH, YOU FOUND A WAY.
NO, IT WASN'T ME.
IT WAS MY CREWMATE. MY FRIEND.
THAT'S WHY I DON'T BELIEVE IN THE NO-WIN SCENARIO. BECAUSE OF MY CREW.
HOW TOUCHING. AND HOW TRUE.
AND NOW, SPEAKING OF YOUR CREW...

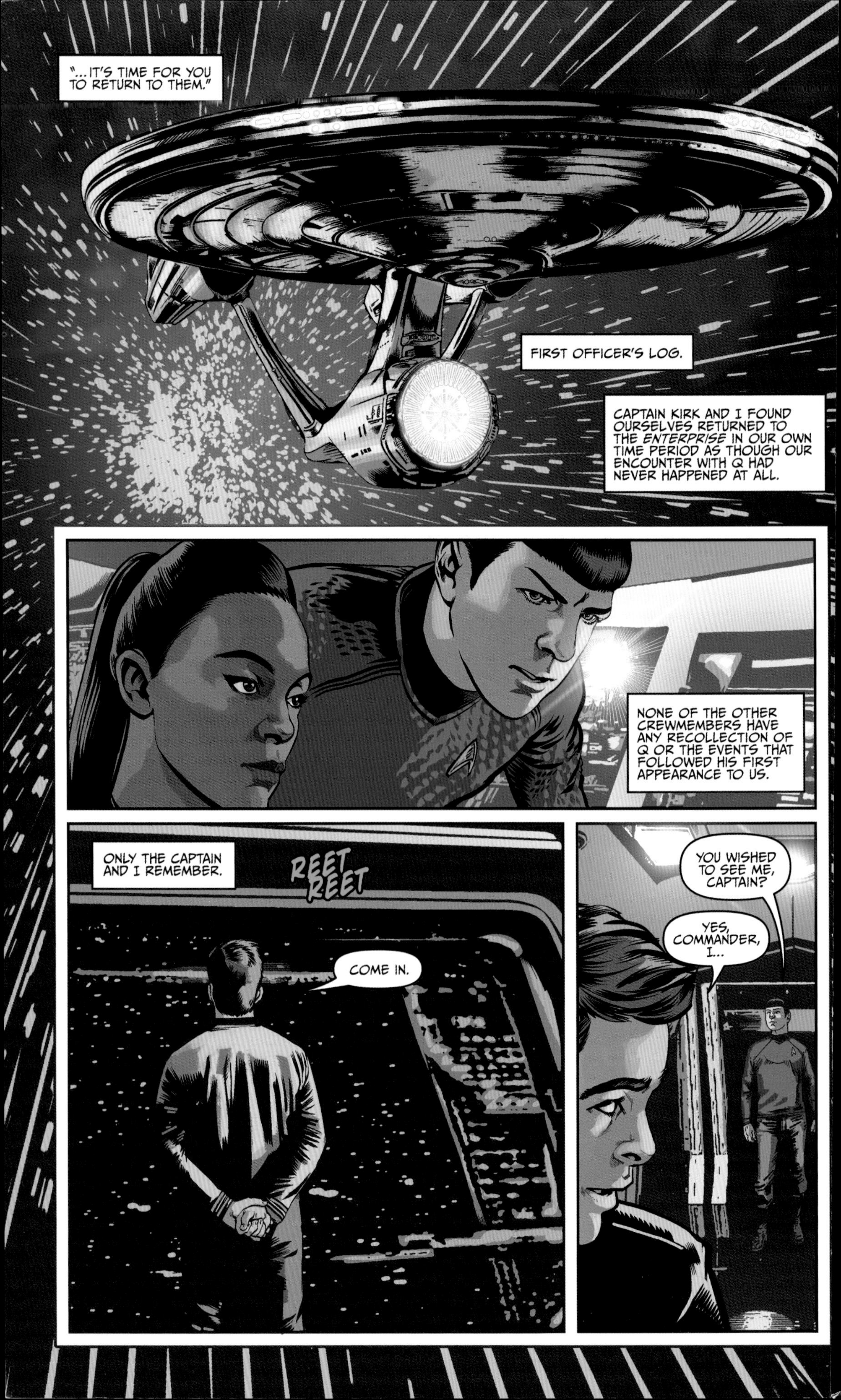
"...IT'S TIME FOR YOU TO RETURN TO THEM."
FIRST OFFICER'S LOG.
CAPTAIN KIRK AND I FOUND OURSELVES RETURNED TO THE *ENTERPRISE* IN OUR OWN TIME PERIOD AS THOUGH OUR ENCOUNTER WITH Q HAD NEVER HAPPENED AT ALL.
NONE OF THE OTHER CREWMEMBERS HAVE ANY RECOLLECTION OF Q OR THE EVENTS THAT FOLLOWED HIS FIRST APPEARANCE TO US.
ONLY THE CAPTAIN AND I REMEMBER.
REET REET
COME IN.
YOU WISHED TO SEE ME, CAPTAIN?
YES, COMMANDER, I...

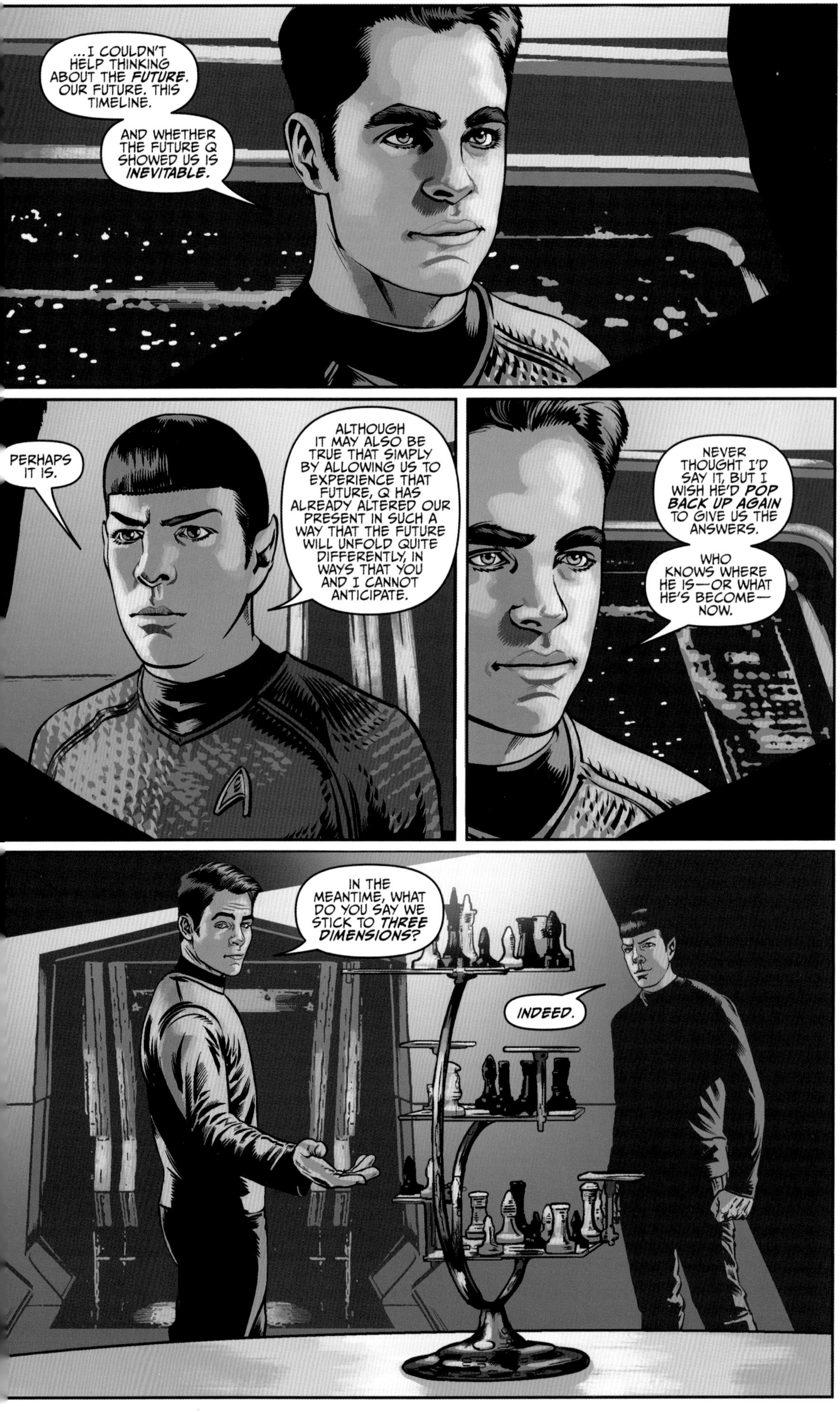

...I COULDN'T HELP THINKING ABOUT THE *FUTURE*. OUR FUTURE. THIS TIMELINE.
AND WHETHER THE FUTURE Q SHOWED US IS *INEVITABLE*.
PERHAPS IT IS.
ALTHOUGH IT MAY ALSO BE TRUE THAT SIMPLY BY ALLOWING US TO EXPERIENCE THAT FUTURE, Q HAS ALREADY ALTERED OUR PRESENT IN SUCH A WAY THAT THE FUTURE WILL UNFOLD QUITE DIFFERENTLY, IN WAYS THAT YOU AND I CANNOT ANTICIPATE.
NEVER THOUGHT I'D SAY IT, BUT I WISH HE'D **POP BACK UP AGAIN** TO GIVE US THE ANSWERS.
WHO KNOWS WHERE HE IS—OR WHAT HE'S BECOME—NOW.
IN THE MEANTIME, WHAT DO YOU SAY WE STICK TO ***THREE DIMENSIONS?***
INDEED.

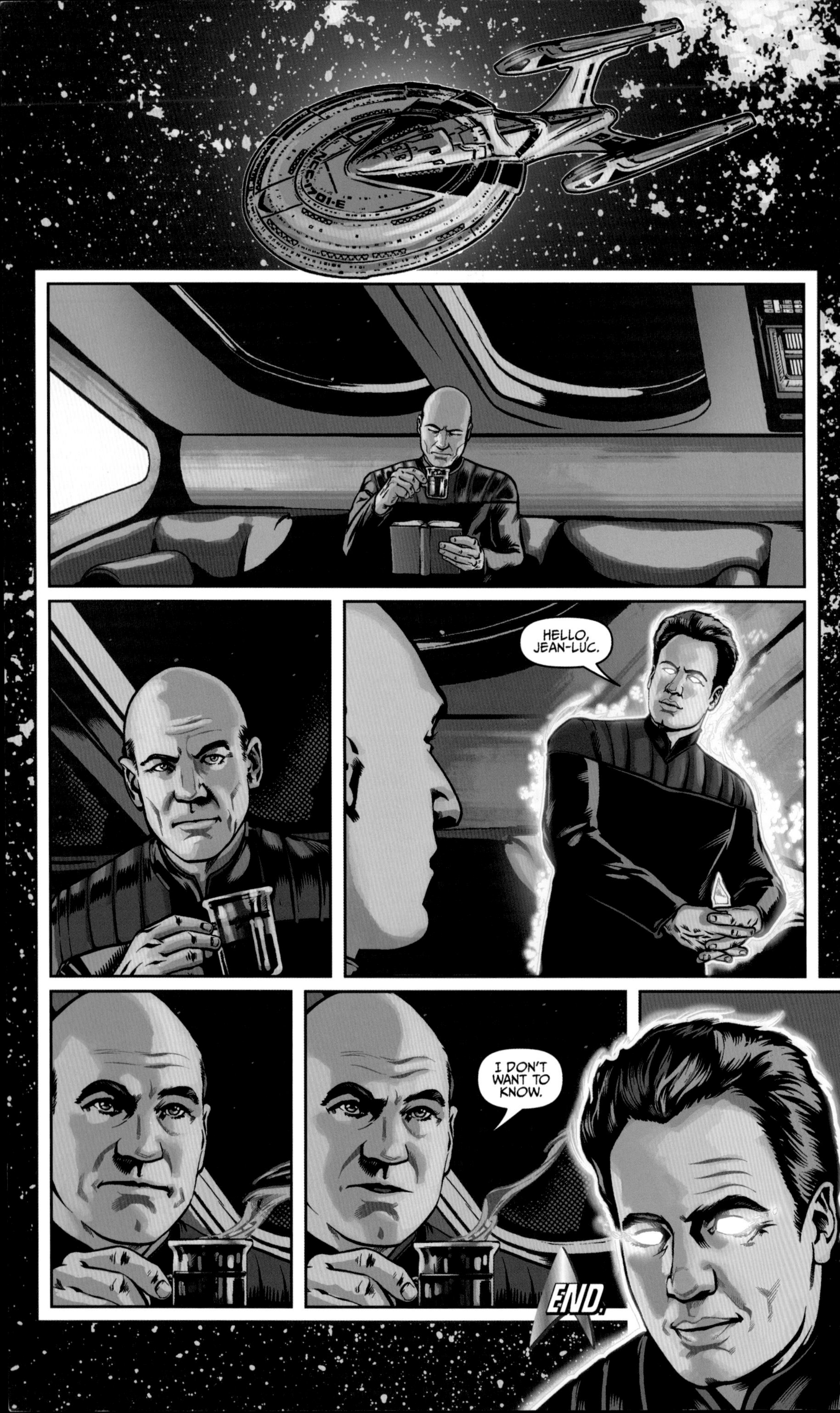
HELLO, JEAN-LUC.
I DON'T WANT TO KNOW.
END.

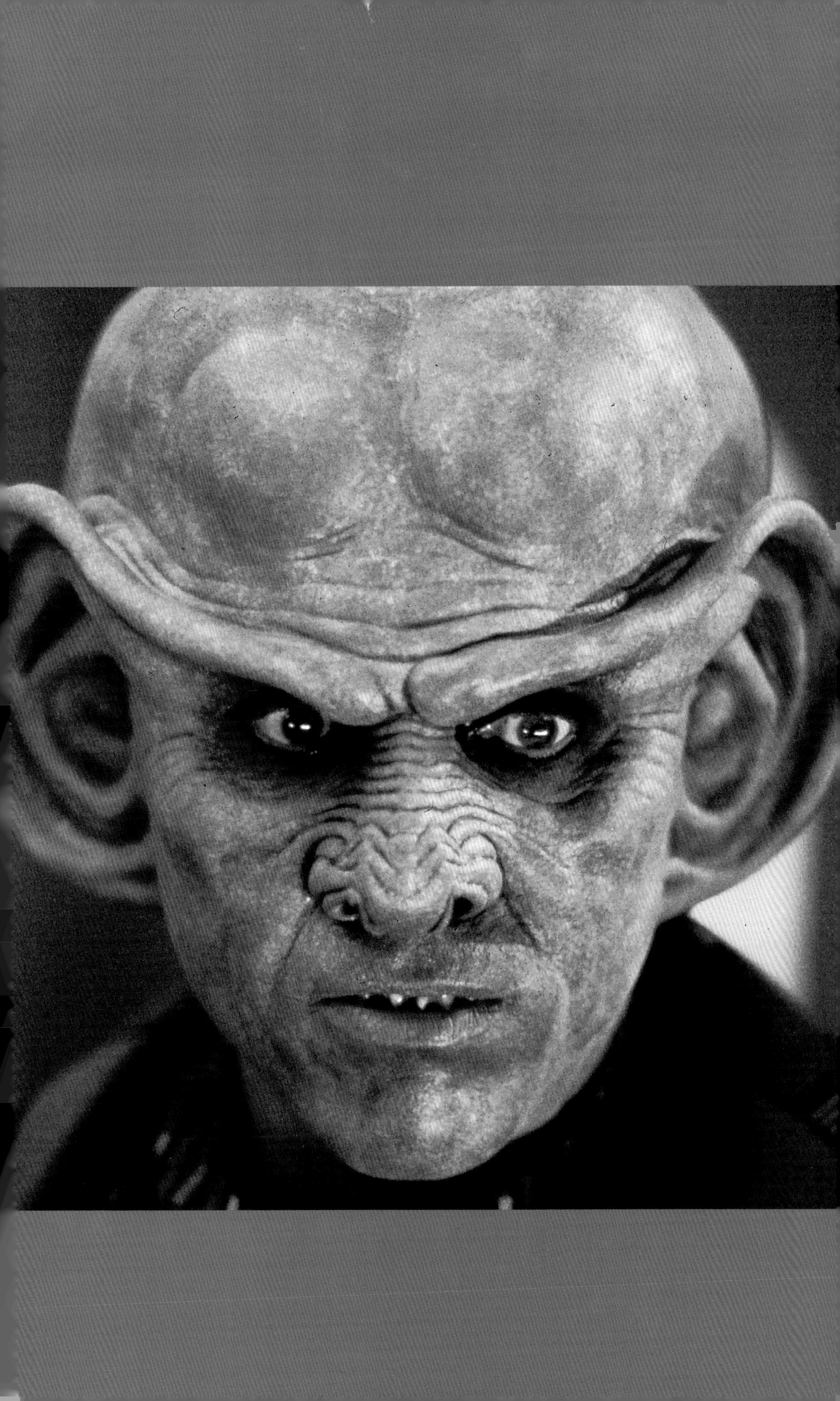

STAR TREK®

THE Q GAMBIT